Thornhill High School Diamond Jubilee
1955 - 2015

By past pupils, for past pupils
(Colour edition)
Preller Geldenhuys

© **Preller Geldenhuys**

Published by old-boy Prop Geldenhuys, trading as Paeroa based Peysoft Publishing.

This Old Boys magazine is available as a free E-pub as well as a minimal cost printed book from Lulu.com. See back page for the Lulu link, to download copies.

PDF/E-pub ISBN: 978-0-9941154-9-2
Printed ISBN: 978-0-9941154-8-5

Hardcover, full colour ISBN: 978-0-9941309-0-7

Fourth Edition

Paeroa
2015

Contents

Thornhill 2015 Magazine 1
Introduction 4
History 11
Musical Productions 66
Reunions 107
    2003 Durban Reunion 109
    2005 Golden Jubilee - Bluff, Durban 109
    Salt Rock Reunion - 2009 111
    Auckland Reunion - 2010 112
2015 Diamond Jubilee Re-unions 116
    London 122
    Brisbane, Australia 127
    Perth, Australia 130
    Harare, Zimbabwe 132
    Paeroa, New Zealand 154
Then and Now Chapter 168
Past Pupils and Staff of Thornhill High School 175
Appreciation for the Thorny Issue 354
In Memoriam 356
Thornhill Roll of Honour 362
Index 366

Introduction

Thornhill High School celebrated its Diamond Jubilee in 2015. Functions were held in the UK, Australia, Zimbabwe, South Africa and New Zealand. This school's magazine commemorates the various celebrations that were held at the various world-wide locations. Special acknowledgement is due to Beverley Nelson who compiles and manages the Thornhill newsletters for the benefit of all past pupils and staff of a great Midlands High School.

Beverley Nelson, with very clever and talented webmaster Tom

The layout of this magazine comprises of three main sections: -

- ➢ Historical events and information
- ➢ Reunions and Diamond Jubilee Celebrations
- ➢ Personalities

Names and events are generally listed in alphabetical order. People are easily located in the Index at the back.

World-Wide Diamond Jubilee Celebrations events took place over several months in England, Australia, New Zealand and Harare. Murray Woodfield got the first event off the ground by arranging a gathering at the Blue Anchor, a lovely old pub on the River Thames in Hammersmith, on Saturday 20th June 2015. The next event was in Brisbane, Australia, where the get-together took place on 25 July. The New Zealand celebrations, held in Paeroa and organized by Prop Geldenhuys, began with sundowners on 16 October and continued until Sunday the 18th. In Zimbabwe, Ray Hewitt, Tracey O'Connor and their committee hosted a series of special events in Harare, beginning with a golf tournament and ending with a braai. The main Harare event was held on Saturday 17 October at Borrowdale Brooke. The final event took place in Perth, where John Wightman arranged a dinner at Zebras Steakhouse on 31 October. Reports and photos can be found in section 3 / middle of the magazine.

Brief History: The first Thornhill High School Magazine was published in December 1958 as Volume 1, Number 1.

Thornhill High School

The Thornhill High School Magazine

| Vol. 1 | DECEMBER, 1958 | No. 1 |

The prophetic words of the Headmaster Philip J Todd read as follows: -

The first time for anything is always an historic occasion and the first issue of a new school's magazine must definitely fall into this category. Of necessity, the early years of our life must comprise chiefly a series of "first times" but the outstanding list is rapidly shortening. The most important aspect of these first times is that standards are being set and it is from standards that tradition grows. We all have a part, an equally important part, to play in the cultivation and growth of this sensitive plant tradition. In an older, longer established institution, the individual contributions do not stand out with the same degree of prominence. A complete edifice is then viewed as a whole, criticised or admired. We carry not only the honour but the much more serious responsibility of foundation members and are still dealing with the bricks, the stones which we are building into our tradition. It is my earnest hope and wishes that in future years, looking back, we can say with pride that we helped to lay the foundation of the Thornhill tradition.

Our first year in our new premises is now coming to a close and already the next extension stage is almost completed. Tennis courts have been constructed and are in use, the cricket squares are showing green, while rugby fields look as if they will be ready for use next year. The School is now definitely taking shape as a School with all its various activities, and for this I would like to express my gratitude to those members of Staff who have co-operated to bring this about with a special word of praise for the enthusiasm and hard work of our grounds man, Mr. John Rowlands.

The next task ahead of us is to complete raising funds to build the stage in the Hall. A splendid start was made with the Fête which brought in £574. The interest and help of parents and the local trading community is deeply appreciated and the School expresses its gratitude.

P.J. Todd
Headmaster.

Mr PJ Todd stood down as Headmaster in 1961 and died in October 1970. He was succeeded by Mr Geoffrey Lambert, followed by Mr John Eadie who lasted for quite a number of years and then came Mr John Drinkwater.

The Arts Class produced the first School magazine cover in 1958

Thornhill High School, as a then and now, is perhaps best illustrated by comparing old photographs with more recent Google Earth screenshots. Then follows the inputs from past pupils, listed in alphabetical order which is hoped will facilitate people finding themselves more easily and be quite a long listing.

Thornhill High School - Then and Now

Thornhill High School late 1990's (Photo credit: Carole Werd))

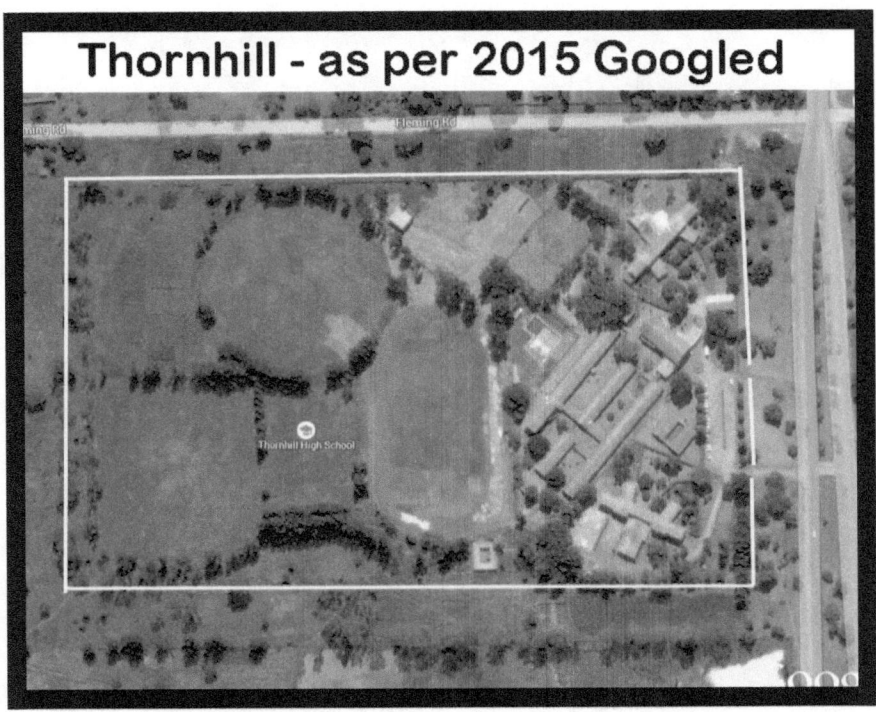

The yellow border is the fence around the school. The buildings are largely the same as those existing in the early 1990's

Note the derelict tennis courts, empty swimming pool, and abandoned cricket pitch.

The Holman Field, named after the Deputy Headmaster who had a huge influence during the formative life of the school.

A Brief History - Very Brief

This following extract is taken from the School's past pupils' website, with thanks to Beverley Nelson, and was supplied by Bev Davidge, Nigel Rowlands and Geoff Day. Minor additional inserts have been made by the author during the editing and layout phases to suit electronic [e-pub] as well as printed publication.

History

The Early Days

Thornhill High School opened on the Royal Rhodesian Air Force base in Gwelo in January 1955. The Headmaster was Mr P.J. Todd (known to the pupils as "Toofy"). The other members of staff were Mr W Doodles Viljoen (Geography, Afrikaans, Woodwork and PT); Mr Frank Taylor (Latin and French); and Miss Christine Roberts. Frank Taylor was responsible for the school motto "Per Spinas ad Culmina" (Through the Thorns to the Summit) - a typically classical pun on the word "Thornhill" and of course, reflecting the schools' connection with the Royal Air Force with its motto "Per Ardua ad Astra" (Through Hardship, or Effort, to the Stars). In the second term, these four teachers were joined by Mr Tommy Burgoyne (History); Mrs Alexander (Domestic Science) and Mrs Oosthuysen. The third term brought Miss Sheila Pett (later Mrs Barbara Coventry) who taught English.

In 1956 numbers rose and more teachers joined the fray. Along came Mrs Myers, Miss Joyce Wilson, and Mr Reginald Cowper (who much later became Rhodesian Minister of Defence) who taught Science. For the second term, Mr Darwin arrived from Plumtree via Guinea Fowl and Mrs Myers left. The third term produced Mrs Niki Antoniadis but Miss Wilson left. A sizeable intake at the start of 1957 produced an impressive crop of teaching staff: Miss Derris Bowyer (who later married Doodles Viljoen), Mrs Muriel Bromley, Miss Carruthers-Smith, Mrs Nell Magness, Mrs Nieuwouldt, Mr Nick Holman (from Chaplin) and Mr Sam McGee from the local builders' Federation (to teach Woodwork). New faces for the second term were: Mr Bates, Mr Geoff Day (from Guinea Fowl), Mr Field and Mr Nel (from Chaplin). At the end of that term, Mr Cowper left. The third term of 1957 additions was: Miss Aylett, Mr Gibbons, and Mr Haines.

Classes were held in corrugated-iron prefabs, assemblies took place in an Operations Room with maps on the walls, gym was in a hangar, and the cricket nets were on the concrete foundations of former barrack rooms. It was the duty of the juniors to sound the siren, which served as the school bell. Hank van de Weg, a founder pupil remarks: "*I will always remember the sound of the training Harvard's droning in the heavy summer sky, lulling me to sleep and preventing me from concentrating on my Latin. And, in the early* days, break time and an illegal excursion to the airplane graveyard, fibre glass rash and breaking open old bombs to get the lead."

School numbers trebled in '56, and by '57 the student numbers topped 250 and the first prefects were appointed.

Judith (Rautenbach) Broodryk comments: *"We really enjoyed the days at the Air Force Base as we had quite a distance to move between classes and so we could waste quite a bit of time and sometimes even bunk a class or two. The girls who were boarders also had the famous tale to tell about the ghost who used to wonder around the dormitory in the middle of the night - the story went that it was a pilot who had fallen off the bed and died of a broken neck. The day scholars would be so envious because we didn't get the opportunity to see him. We were all however very excited to move to the new school buildings and we all worked hard to get the sports fields up and running. The awful part was Tuesday afternoons when we had afternoon school - it was hot and very unpleasant."*

Pioneers Hank van de Weg and Elizabeth Robb - with original school ties - pictured at the 'Barracks' school, Royal Rhodesian Air Force Station Thornhill. Corrugated iron buildings on concrete foundation slabs. (Photo credit: Hank and Sally (Struckel) Callaghan)

The Reminiscing of a THS Pioneer, as told by Hank van de Weg

"I felt quite excited when I heard from my parents that I would be going to a new school situated at the old RAF base at Thornhill Aerodrome up along the Umvuma Road. I had just finished standard 5 at Cecil John Rhodes and had anticipated following my

elder brother, Paul, to Chaplin School. It seemed that a lot of my friends were also going to Thornhill and there was only going to be a Form 1 and 2 to start. The idea of going to an old air force base was cause for much debate and conversation amongst my peers. Eventually the day came, late in January 1955, and off I cycled.

On entering the base, I was told to park my bike in the cycle shed on the right just before the roundabout. I then made my way to the offices where we were all lined up and told which classrooms we had been allocated. More exciting though, was the fact that we were told of certain areas that were out of bounds, the runways, various buildings and the aeroplane graveyard. The latter was a definite destination to set your sights on. We spent many an hour at break climbing all over these old and twisted aircraft. Had a lot of fun taking fibreglass from the wrecks and dropping small bits down the backs of unsuspecting victims. Stuff itched like crazy. I soon discovered that there were stacks of practice bombs. By smashing them open I was able to get to the lead that they were filled with. I took satchel loads back home where I melted them and made small ingots. I was a lead millionaire.

Fun was also had in the old prefab classrooms. We soon discovered that there was a trapdoor at the back of our classroom and I remember one time when most of us boys slowly disappeared down into it leaving the young Afrikaans teacher quite befuddled as to where all her pupils had gone. On another occasion we had made a small hole in the board wall at the back of the classroom. Beyond this wall was the chalkboard of the adjoining classroom and by pushing a stick through the hole we could vibrate the board as the teacher was trying to write. Unfortunately, on one occasion that teacher none other than the feared Bassie Nel. A tyrant who thought nothing of giving you a good klap if he thought you deserved it. Of course we at the back of the class were all innocent so escaped severe punishment but certainly got a good roasting.

There were small rock cairns all around the school area and these were the homes of all sorts of insects and reptiles including snakes and best of all, gogomannetjies and placing them in various girls' desks whilst they were out at break. One particular poor sole was particularly petrified of all creatures great and small and her shrieks could be heard all around the school. I won't mention her name but offer her my apologies.

At the back of the school across a small field was the gym. We did PT there and after school activities such as boxing. To the right of that field were the woodwork workshops where we spent many an hour crafting all sorts of small wooden items. I still have a small casket in which I keep pens etc. Close by was the sports field where we played rugby, cricket and had our athletics events. We had the pleasure of playing our rugby first team from Form 1. Not many people can boast that.

Our science rooms were off to the right of the school where I was taught by Reginald Cowper. He used to call me "Henry" in an ever so upper class accent and gave me excellent marks. He was obviously one of the more astute teachers. He became an MP later on. One of his favourite experiments was to create hydrogen through electrolysis of water and fill a tin with it through a small hole at the bottom. Then, with the lid firmly pressed on, he would take it outside and light a match under it. The explosion would blow the lid sky high and the boom could be heard for miles. Great guy!

We were at the old RAF base for three years before moving to the new school buildings. A wonderful period of my life of which I have fond memories." (Acknowledgement: Hank van de Weg)

Thornhill Air Scouts: Chief of Air Staff Air Vice Marshal Harold Hawkins with Station Commander Group Captain Jock Hilton Barber and No 6 Squadron Commander Squadron Leader Batt Maskill. Last four in the back row are believed to be Brian Authers, Don Lawrence, u/k and Michael Rowe (photo credit: Gill Taylor and scout names - Bev Nelson).

Thornhill High School

Thornhill Pioneers

The following are the names of some of the pupils who attended Thornhill on the old site at the Air Force base (1955 - 1957). This is not taken from any official list, so there are bound to be errors and omissions, given that they come from the collective memory of a group of people who were at the school over 50 years ago.

Alan Rumball, Aletta Bezuidenhout, Alfie Smith, Allan Gordon, Alwyn Strauss, Andrew Norman, Ann von Staden, Anne Panton, Annette Botha, Barry Johnston, Ben Benzies, Ben van der Pol, Bev Davidge, Beverley Mitchell, Brian Buckley, Buddy Nysschen, Bucky Rowlands, Chris ("Broekies") de Jong, Chris Pelly, Chris Skinner, Chris Viljoen, Cliff (Spook) van Rensberg, Colin Green, Colin Smith, Connie Birch, Daphne Cousins, Dave Chalmers, Dave Goddard, Dawn Quincey, Denise Lotter, Denise Wilkinson Donald Gibson, Dorothy Snodgrass, 'Dup' du Plessis, Eleanor Baier, Ena Nysschen, Enid Bott, Enid Lee, Ernest Botha, Evans, Grant Hundermark, Felicity Barry, Fred Munger, Fred Strauss, Gail van Niekerk, Gayle Robertson, Gerry Dippenaar, Hank van de Weg, Heather Hatt, Ian Gordon, Jacobus Hoffman, Janet Lancaster, Jannie Olivier, Jannie Nell, Jennifer Blankenberg, Scheitel, Johan Kriek, John Alexander, John Cunliffe, John Davies, John Gordon, John Moren, Judith Gatiss, Judy Rautenbach, June Bennett, Karlynn County, Lawrence Boddington, Leslie van de Poll, Llanis Pringle, Lynette Palmer, Margaret Nish, Marie Dippenaar, Matthys van Schalkwyk, Megan Winter, Michael Columbine, Mike Dubell, Michael Eckhardt, Mike Mellody, Mike Stewart, Molly McGowan, Nan Winter, Neil Willemsen, Nick Carter, Nigel Rowlands, Noeline Russell-Smith, Nora Archer, Norma Rowlands, Patricia Barlow, Peter Cowan, Pieter van Niekerk, Pinkie Pieters, Ray Kaschula, Ray Parker, Ray Wyatt, Reg Kaschula, Reg Wickens, Reggie Cousins, Rob McGowan, Robbie Bester, Robert Redman, Rodney Giles, Ronald Cousins, Ronnie Benzies, Rosalie Hughes, Roy Davis, Roy Kalil, Ruth Sercombe, Sally Scott, Sally Struckel, Sarah Dippenaar, Sheila Murch, Sheila Plenderleith, Sophia Nysschen, Stan Price, Steve Theron, Susan Daynes, Susan Priest, Thomas van Blerk, Victor Reece, Veronica Steffen, Virginia Pringle, Wendy Sparg, William McFarlane, Winifred Callow, Yvonne Emslie.

(Extracted from the Old Pupils and Staff website)

The New School

In January 1958, the school packed its bags and moved to its present site leaving the airfield without regret to the fledgling Federal Air Force which promptly brought in a howling squadron of Vampire jets believed to have been too much for the tender ears of the citizens of Salisbury. Gwelo Town Council was pleased, because an empty airfield was bad news for local trade.

John Rowlands was the grounds man and it was he who lay out and established the grounds and playing fields at the school's present location. Mike Stewart, a past pupil, remembers having to crawl painstakingly, on hands and knees, around the playing fields for hours picking up every stone and hard clump of dirt, under the ever-watchful eyes of Meneers Nel, Viljoen and Johan Steenkamp, so that the games fields would be the best in town.

The Gilbert and Sullivan operetta "HMS Pinafore" was produced in 1958 by Mrs Niki Antoniadis and performed by the pupils though Mr Frank Taylor, who had a lovely tenor voice, took the lead male role. For many of the pupils who took part, it is one of their fondest memories of their schooldays. But not all the pupils were musically talented.

Sally (Struckel) Callaghan's memories of "HMS Pinafore":

"There were a few of us boarders (who sang like frogs in a tin pot) who were not even picked for the chorus. They debated whether we should be included and just keep our mouths shut or be left out altogether. The latter was decided because of the expense of the costumes.

The hall was not on the premises, so instead of sacrificing one of the staff to look after us, we went in with the rest and because of all the excitement were forgotten about. This led us to discover that if we climbed up the outside of the building and pulled ourselves onto a ledge where there was a clear pane just under the roof, we had a bird's eye view of everything below us. This was our viewing post every night, and when Mr Taylor (our Latin teacher) and Gayle Robertson (a pupil) who both had lovely voices, had to hold hands and sing their song, we used to erupt cheering, wolf whistling, chanting in Latin and behaving like "idiots" but it was great fun and we were never caught!

The line-up of staff for the 1958 photo-call was: Mr. Todd (Head and Supt Cranwell House), Mr. Holman (Deputy Head), Mrs. Alexander, Mrs. Bartlett (Secretary), Mrs. Muriel Bromley, Mrs. S Coventry, Mr. Day, Mr. Gibbons, Miss Audrey Gudath (later Mrs Reginald Cowper), Miss Heath, Miss Lamport (Supt Halton house) Mr. Sam McGee, Mr. Nel, Mrs Orsmond (Music), Mr. Ould, Mrs Porter, Mrs Rochester, Mr. Johan Steenkamp, Mr. Frank Taylor and Mr and Mrs. Viljoen. Mrs. Niki Antoniadis was away on leave.

THE STAFF, THORNHILL HIGH SCHOOL
Back row, left to right: Mr. Steenekamp, Mr. Viljoen, Mr. Gibbons, Mr. Ould, Mr. McGee, Mr. Burgoyne, Mr. Taylor, Mr. Nel.
Middle row: Mr. Day, Mrs. Porter, Mrs Viljoen, Mrs. Coventry, Miss Gudath, Mrs. Bromley, Mrs. Bartlett.
Front row: Mrs. Orsmond, Miss Lamport, Mr. Holman, Mr. Todd, Mrs. Rochester, Mrs. Alexander, Miss Heath.

In 1959 Nan Winter and Nigel Rowlands were appointed head girl and head boy respectively for the school's inaugural Lower Sixth and Upper Sixth years ('59 and '60). By '60 Upper Sixth pupils from Chaplin were coming to Thornhill for shared science classes and Upper Sixth from Thornhill were going to Chaplin for shared arts subjects.

Mr Geoff Day (member of staff from 1957 to 1964) remembers: *We started out in 1958 in a school designed to look like a chicken farm amidst a sea of mud and builders' katunda, but with a dizzy selection of educational toys. Labs, workshops and classrooms furnished and equipped to a high level. Alas, we had no library, gymnasium, playing fields, swimming pool, and hall with stage, offices or staffroom. There were pupil's toilets, but the staff was expected to grin and bear it. Such refinements all came later. Slowly.*

Sketch by Arts Teacher Mr Geoff Day - 1959

Library sketched by Art Teacher Mr Geoff Day 1959, and photo taken 1975

(Photo Credit: Carole Ward)

For some reason I never fathomed, the Art room was easily the darkest of all on the campus. But I recall it as a busy, productive place. We did pottery, weaving, scenery painting, 16mm film shows, and poster production for many events. We even found time for some drawing and painting and from the start there were entrants to Cambridge School Certificate and later 'O' levels every year. I cannot recall one single failure. One form, the Remove, helped me screen print the cover of the first issue of the School Magazine - around two hundred of them, all spread out to dry on the floor (covers, not pupils). I told them I would kill anyone who trod on one - and I meant it; for we did it on one of those dreadful Tuesday afternoon school sessions in hot October when murder came easy. Many other willing (?) hands painted scenery with me from dizzy dangling trestles. One form had the enormous pleasure of seeing me walk off the end of a plank and tip a whole large tin of paint over myself.

I took over the General side in 1960 - a part of the school that I always felt had been neglected. Except, of course when it came to teams and other physical activities. COP Certificate was introduced and those of us concerned buckled down to getting a qualification for our charges. It was not a highly regarded examination, but it was a public one and UK-based. I was critical of it but it was the best we could muster at the time, and many steps ahead of the nothing there had been before.

I was in charge of the Audio- Visual equipment for the school - projectors, recorders and even the grand piano (!). Those who were boarders during my years will recall the Saturday evening film shows in the Hall where the acoustics were so diabolical you couldn't tell the difference between Frank Sinatra and Doris Day.

(Acknowledgements to Nigel Rowlands and Geoff Day)

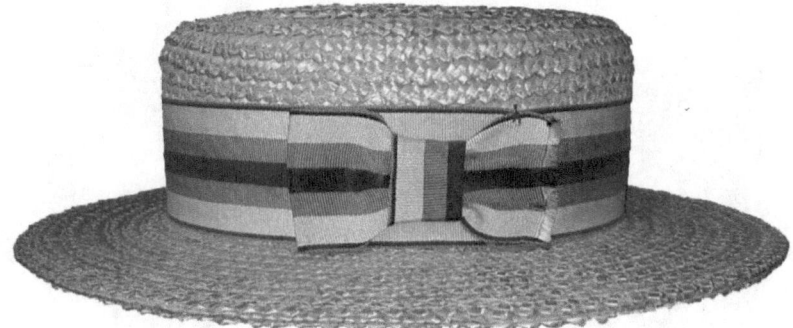

Bashers were introduced in the late 1950's - with much damage incurred with tossing them in the air when celebrating First Team wins at Rugby

U15 Rugby Team - 1958

Most Under-15 Team players were promoted to the 1st 15 Rugby Team which included the writer, Preller Geldenhuys, Rodney McNeill, Bucky Rowlands, Roy Kalil, Karel Coetzee, Hendrik Malan, and Alwyn Strauss

1958 Hockey Team

Standing: Anne van Niekerk, Miriam Jack, Cheryl Westgate, Betty van der Merwe, June Bennett (vice Capt.) Sitting: Molly McGowan, Eve Bennet, Sally Callaghan (Struckel) (Capt), Jennifer, Maria and Veronica Steffen the Goalie. (Photo credit: Sally Callaghan)

Thornhill High School

1959 Sports Meeting

The Fifth Annual sports meeting was held on Saturday 18th April 1959. Grounds preparation by Mr John Rowlands contributed to old records broken and many new ones established.

3. 100 yds. Boys Open

1. L. De Haas (G) 2. R. Tunnard (H) 3. C. Ferguson (G)

Time 10 sec.

(Standard 11.5 secs. Record 11 secs.—R. Townsend, 1958)

5. 100 yds. Middle Girls

1. R. Rish (G) 2. R. Malan (G) 3. S. Norse (H)

Time 12.9 sec

(Standard 13.5 secs. Record 12.2 secs.—J. Lancaster, 1958)

6. 100 yds. Junior Boys

1. Malan (G) 2. De Haas (G) 3. Van Loo (H)

12. 220 yds. Middle Girls

1. R. Rish (G) 2. S. Norse (H) 3. R. Malan (G)

Time 30.5 sec

(Standard 34.5 secs. Record 29.6 secs.—J. Cloete, 1958)

23. Hop, Step and Jump. Middle Girls

1. S. Norse (H) 2. Malan (G) 3. Nish (G)

Distance 17ft 9¾ ins

(Standard 24 ft. Record 29 ft. 6¼ in.—M. Smith, 1958)

Louis de Haas shattered Roy Townsend's 100 yards' record by a full second. Courtney Ferguson came third. Rina Geldenhuys (Malan) beat her rival Shirley Kuttner (Nourse) in the 100 yds Middle Girls. Rina's brother Phil Malan won the 100 yards junior boys, just beating Louis de Haas's brother Karel. Shirley turned the tables on Rina in the 220 yards Middle Girls and also in the Hop, Step and Jump events.

16. Long Jump. Junior Boys

1. P. Malan (G)   2. Davidge (G)   3. B-van as (G)

Distance 15' 2½"

(Standard 12 ft. 6 in. Record 14 ft. 7¼ in.—
I. Gordon, 1958; B. Davidge, 1957)

19. 220 yds. Junior Boys

1. P. Malan (G)   2. De Haas (G)   3. B van eo (H)

Time —

(Standard 31 secs. Record 29.4 secs.—I. Gordon, 1958)

28. Long Jump. Middle Girls

1. Pat Malan   2. Nourse   3. —

Distance 15 ft 5 ins

(Standard 12 ft. Record 13 ft. 11¼ in.—J. Lancaster, 1958)

33. 440 yds. Junior Boys

1. P. MALAN (G)   2. K. DE HAAS (G)   3. LANCASTER (G)

Phil Malan did particularly well in the Long Jump, 220 Yards and 440 yards for junior boys. In the Long Jump for girls Rina Geldenhuys (Malan) turned the tables on her arch rival Shirley Kuttner (Nourse), by setting a new record of 15 feet 5 inches, beating Janet Marchussen (Lancaster)'s record of 13 feet 11¼ inches.

New records were also set by Karel Coetzee Throwing the cricket ball 102 yds 2 ft 2 in beating Glen Kalil's records of 88 yds, 1 ft 6 ins; E Swanepoel clocking 12.5 secs for the 100 yds Junior girls, versus M. Nish's two-year record of 13 secs; Courtney Ferguson shattering the Shot Putt record of 34 odd feet to 42 ft 6¾ ins; and quite a few other records too numerous to mention in detail.

Captains of Houses:

GRAHAM (Green).—Boys: C. Ferguson. Girls: J. Lancaster
HOWIE (Blue).—Boys: C. Viljoen. Girls: J. Cloete

Courtney Ferguson and Janet Marchussen (Lancaster) were the winners for Graham.

The writer captained the 1st 15 Rugby Team during his final year in 1961

The Sixties

1960 saw the introduction of a special 'colours' blazer. The musical "Goodnight Vienna" was directed by Mrs Niki Antoniadis and Mr Tommy Burgoyne.

Building began on the new commerce block. The first Rugby XV had a wonderful season, winning 12 out of 14 matches played. Mary Botha from the First Hockey Team was selected to join the Rhodesian Schools hockey team on their tour of South Africa.

The Hockey team players in 1960 were Jennifer Bushell, Betty van der Merwe, Myfanwy Rowlands, Rina Malan, Anne Rawstone, Judy Rautenbach, Janet Lancaster (Capt - wearing the Colours Blazer for Hockey), coach Mr Andy Evans (passed away 2002), Noelene Russell-Smith, Shirley Nourse (absent from the team photograph are Lynette Palmer) passed away 2003, and Susanna Snyders).

Producing musicals proved a hit. Goodnight Vienna followed in 1960; The Mikado in 1961; Iolanthe in 1962.

1st Hockey 1960
Back Row - Jennifer Bushel - Betty v d Merwe - Myfanwy Rowlands - Rina Malan - Ann Rawstorne -
- Judy Rautenbach - Janet Lancaster - Andy Evans - N Russel-Smith - Shirley Nourse Lynette Palmer - Susanna Sn

(Photo: Past pupils and staff website)

Louis de Haas succeeded Preller Geldenhuys as Head of Cranwell House in 1962. Louis was also appointed Head Boy.

Thornhill High School

THS - CRANWELL HOUSE PREFECTS - 1961

Louis de Haas, Preller Geldenhuys, Rodney McNeill, Karel Coetzee and John Perie

FIRST XV. *Back row (left to right):* Nell, McFarlane, Cupido, de Haas, McNeill, Kennedy, Davidge, Malan, Giles, Reece.
Middle row (left to right): Coetzee, Kalil, Mr A. Frost, Geldenhuys (Capt.) Mr W. J. Viljoen, de Haas, Rowlands.

1961 1st XV Rugby Team

Frik Nel, Nigel McFarlane, Jan Cupido, Karel de Haas, Rodney McNeill, John Kennedy, Bev Davidge, Phil Malan, Rod Giles, Vic Reece; Karel Coetzee, Roy Kalil, Mr A Frost, Preller Geldenhuys (Capt), Mr Doodles Viljoen, Louis de Haas, Bucky Rowlands, Alwyn Strauss, AN Other and Alec Blackadder

Rina Malan is seated on the right. Her good friend Shirley Nourse is on the other side, next to Andy Evans. The full team are, standing: M. Connor, S. Paterson, Wendy Rademeyer, S. Bloem, M. Taylor, J. Wilkinson and A. Smith. Sitting: Miriam Jack, Shirley Nourse (Captain), Mr Andy Evans, Mfanwy Rowlands and Rina Malan.

Mary Botha, Shirley (Nourse) Kuttner, Janet (Lancaster) Marchussen and Judith (Rautenbach) Broodryk - great sportswomen in 1961 and still in 2015

Thornhill High School

SCHOOL PREFECTS, 1961. *1st Row Standing:* R.McNeill, R. Fletcher, L. de Haas, M. Winter, J. Perry
2nd Row Seated: P. Geldenhuys, J. Lancaster (Head Girl), Mr Todd, B. Davidge (Head Boy), J. Doyle
M. McGowan, K. Coetzee, R. Hughes

1961 School Prefects: Rodney McNeill, R Fletcher, Louis de Haas, Megan Winter, John Perry, Preller Geldenhuys, Janet Marchussen (Lancaster)(Head Girl), Mr PJ Todd, Bev Davidge (Head Boy), Jenny Doyle, Molly McGowan, Karel Coetzee and Rosalie Hughes

Head boy Louis de Haas bidding farewell to Headmaster Mr Todd

Phil Todd retired as Headmaster at the end of 1961 but then taught Science for a short time at one of the African high schools. The photo shows head boy Louis de Haas and head girl Megan Winter bidding the headmaster farewell.

The following tribute to the founding headmaster as documented in the December 1962 School Magazine.

Thornhill High School Magazine

OUR FORMER HEADMASTER
MR. P. J. TODD

MR. P. J. TODD, who was born in Edinburgh in 1902 and educated at George Heriot's School in that city and graduated from Edinburgh University (B.Sc.) in 1922, spent his early manhood on rubber estates in the Dutch East Indies and Malaya.

of Dr. Kennedy Grant, were married in returned to the United Kingdom and took coming out to Rhodesia in 1934.

ern Rhodesian teaching service for a couple ver the acting headship at Que Que School for two terms.

In the following year he joined the staff of Chaplin, and with the exception of a term at Enkeldoorn and two as headmaster at Beatrice, he remained with Chaplin for the next 20 years. During that period he was Superintendent of Maitland, House-master of Duthie, Deputy-Headmaster and, for the first term of 1954, Acting Headmaster.

In January, 1955, he was given the pioneer task of founding the town's second co-educational secondary school which began its history in the buildings vacated by the Royal Air Force at Thornhill Air Station.

Mr. and Mrs. Todd have four sons. Three of them (all married) are graduates of Rhodes University and have followed their father's footsteps into teaching careers. The fourth is in his third year at Rhodes.

Mr. Todd was for two separate years Chieftain of the Southern Rhodesian Caledonian Society.

In 1955 he retired with the rank of Major from the Territorial Active Force and holds the ED and the Coronation Medal.

Extract from the Gwelo Times issue 13th April, 1962

It reads as follows - "Mr P.J. Todd, who was born in Edinburgh in 1902 and educated at George Herriot's School in that city and graduated from Edinburgh University (B.Sc.) in 1922, spent his early manhood on rubber estates in the Dutch East Indies and Malaya.

'He and Mrs Todd, who is a sister of Dr. Kennedy Grant, were married in Singapore in 1930. In 1933, Mr Todd returned to the United Kingdom and took a teaching diploma at Edinburgh before coming out to Rhodesia in 1934.

Mr. Todd had only been in the Southern Rhodesia teaching service for a couple of days when he was called on to take over the acting headship at Que Que School for two terms.

In the following year he joined the staff of Chaplin, and with the exception of a term at Enkeldoorn, he remained with Chaplin for the next 20 years. During that period, he was Superintendent of Maitland, Housemaster of Duthie, and Deputy-Headmaster and, for the first term of 1954, Acting Headmaster.

In January, 1955, he was given the pioneer task of founding the town's second co-educational secondary school which began its history in the buildings vacated by the Royal Air Force at Thornhill Air Station.

Mr and Mrs. Todd have four sons. Three of them (all married) are graduates of Rhodes University and have followed their father's footsteps into teaching careers. The fourth is in his third year at Rhodes.

Mr Todd was for two separate years Chieftain of the Southern Rhodesian Caledonian Society.

In 1955 he retired with the rank of Major from the Territorial Active Force and holds the ED and the Coronation Medal.

(Extract from the Gwelo Times issue 13th April, 1962)

The new Headmaster was Geoffrey Lambert, who arrived from Hamilton in Bulawayo and remained until the end of 1967 when John Eadie from Cranborne in Salisbury took up the headship.

The visit to Thornhill High School by World War II fighter pilot Douglas Bader was a highlight in 1965. Both Liz English and Valerie Malcolm made special mention of the visit. Douglas Bader's Reach for the Sky had an impact to the writer becoming a pilot. He was a hero and inspiration to many. He overcame the loss of both legs, continued flying as a Battle of Britain pilot, was taken prisoner after crashing again in Germany, and after the war was over, even managed to play golf on his artificial pins. The epitome of not thinking of himself as disabled. He came to Thornhill School because of its relationship to aviation.

Douglas Bader with Dianne Palmer, Lynette Bugler, Cathy Bromley and Sylvia Palmer. Photo credit is from Liz English

Merle and Marilyn Atkinson twins, class of 1969.
Both live in Durban, Merle is married to Smith and Marilyn married Marco Darné in 1974.

Thornhill High School

1968 1st Team Hockey
<u>Back Row</u>: Dianne Palmer, Lynette van Heerden, Brenda Martin, Carolyn Fox, Liz English, Kathy Ballantyne. <u>Seated</u>: Lorraine Godsmark, Heather Roselt, Mr Nick Holman, Penny Doyle, Brenda Waring and Goalie Lynda Fagan

1969 1st Team Hockey
Photo credits by Beverley Nelson, Dianne (Palmer) Baldwin and Liz English. Dianne was noted for earning her Colours Blazer, as did goalie Lynda Fagan

Thornhill High School

1969 1st XV Rugby Team

Back Row: Ray Stout, Dave Krause, Howard Crookes, Rob Hendry, G Smith, Peter Milner, Rob Burkett, Mark Pemberthy, *Middle Row*: Ben Pretorious, Bill Malkin, P Bakkes, Mr Peter Kolbe, Alan Stals (Capt), Mr Pluke, Dave Marshall, William Robb. *Front Row*: H Marillier, Spud Murphy, Rob Matthews, J van Vuuren

1969 1st XI Cricket Team (Photo credits: Bill Malkin)

Back Row: Rob Matthews, Gordon Fraser, P Bakkes, Bill Malkin, Hilton Marillier, Paul Newman and G Wall. *Front Row*: Malcolm Woodfield, Spud Murphy, Alan Stals, Mr Peter Kolbe, Dave Marshall, Tom Benade and Eddie Meth.

Thornhill High School

1969 Athletics Team

The Early Seventies

The great event of 1970 was the opening of the long-awaited swimming pool.

Several developments happened in the school from 1971 to 1974. One of these was the revival of the (almost) annual musical production, with "South Pacific" directed by Mr Gordon Dykstra being staged in 1971, "Oliver!" in 1973 and "Annie Get Your Gun" in 1974. In 1972, the hall finally got a stage, and the inaugural production was "Wait until Dark" in the second term.

(Photo Daniel)

The swimming pool - put to good use

On the academic front, the announcement in 1972 that Thornhill was to become the country's first Agricultural High School caused consternation in some circles and excitement in others. The Headmaster and Staff were convinced that it would be a good thing for the school, and assured concerned parents that it did not mean that academic standards would fall. Other developments were the introduction of Objective Testing in 1971, and the restructuring of Rhodesia's examination system. The old C.O.P. exams were discontinued and were replaced by the Rhodesia School Certificate Higher Level.

Thornhill High School

PREFECTS – 1970

Back Row, Left to Right: R. BERRY, J. WELSH, R. HENDRY, R. BURKETT, S. MURPHY, R. DIXON.
Centre Row: E. ENGLISH, H. SPENCER, C. FRIEDRICKS, C.d'HOTMAN, A. ASHFORD, S. MARSHALL, P. FORD.
Front Row, Left to Right: D. MARSHALL, D. PALMER, W. ROBB (Head Boy), Mr. J.E. EADIE (Headmaster), H. SQUAIR (Head Girl), R. STOUT, P. POLLARD.

1970 Prefect's names corrected – Dave Berry, James Welsh, Robert Hendry, Robert Burnett, Robert Burkett, Steven Murray and Roderick Dixon. Middle Row: Elizabet English, Hilary Spencer, Carol Friedrichs, Sheryl d'Hotman, Ann Ashford, Susan Marshall and Penelope Ford. Front Row: David Marshall, Dianne Palmer, William Robb, Mr John Eadie, Marilyn Squair, Raymond Stout and Pauline Pollard Photo credit: Beverley Nelson

In 1972 the school said farewell to an old and tried (or trying!) friend. The old school bus (the only "runner" of its class left on the African continent, according to an 'expert' in Cape Town) finally retired and the purchase of a new one meant that sports teams were able to arrive on time for fixtures for the first time in ages.

Thornhill High School

Photo credit: Yolanda MacIntyre

The New Busses

The Old and the New

The staff list in the 3rd term of 1971 was:

Mr John Eadie (Headmaster), Mr Peter Siebert (Deputy), Mrs Dot Cairns (Senior Mistress and Halton House Superintendent), Mrs O. Alexander (Domestic Science), Mrs R. Browne (Art), Mrs E.M. Chamberlain (History), Miss C. Chalmers (P.E.) Mrs Margie Cunliffe (Science), Mr Gordon Dykstra (Geography), Mrs Jane Few (Geography), Mr Terry Hart (French and Cranwell House Superintendent), Mrs Yvonne Hart (Afrikaans), Mr D. Larkworthy (Woodwork), Mr C. Leaman (English), Mr B. McDowell (Maths), Mr D. McGaw (P.E.), Mrs J. McGaw (Maths), Mr R. Moore (Commerce), Mr M. Morrel (English and French), Mr Chris Pluke (Science), Miss J. Pyatt (English), Mrs G. Smith (Music and Afrikaans), Mr A. Smith (Maths and Science), Mr G. Wilkes

(Technical Drawing), Mr W. Young (Maths), Mrs E. Viljoen (part-time), Mrs Kay Pluke (Librarian), Mrs M. Segal (Bursar), Mrs M. Wilkes (Secretary). The grounds man, Mr John Rowlands, retired at the end of the year, having served the school since its founding.

1971 Team: Marcelle Bischoff (now Simmonds), Judy Marshall, Jenny Holmes, Mae Swart, Janet Evans: Front Row; Debbie Knott, Linda Rademeyer, Elaine Radloff and Elaine Knott. (Photo enhancement credit: Will Flanagan)

1972 was a productive year, with 3 members of staff welcoming additions to their families: a daughter for the McGraw's and sons for the Few's and the Plukes. Mr Baker took over Mrs McGaw's Maths classes, Mr Case (an old boy of the school) took over from Mrs Jane Few, and the post of librarian was filled by Mrs Larkworthy. At the end of the year, several long-serving members of staff left the school: Mr Peter Siebert, Mr B. McDowell and Mr Pluke left on promotion, Mr Baker went to St Stephen's, Balla Balla, and Mrs Margie Cunliffe was transferred.

In 1972, the chairman of the Old Thornhill Association, Louis de Haas, reported that there were 19 fully paid members.

Thornhill High School

Class of 1972

Class of 1972

Louis McHugh, Linda Eekhout, Joyce Veldhuizen, Danie Schoeman, Allan Ramsey, Nev Fromburg, Petronella Jordaan, Kevin Burgess, Annette Robb, Colin Chase, Billy Hand, Kim Kendall, Wyndom Dallas, Gordon Carmel, Mike Stobart Vallaro, Patrick Ford, Lauren McLean, Brian van Rooyen, Daphne Vermaak, Patty Lamb, DJ Voyce, Cynthia Frew, Oscar Bekker and Andre Scheepers.   (Kevin Law photo)

Thornhill High School

A long way back - a life time ago

1973 with Lu le Quesne Dormer, Joan Gihhard, Fanie Liz Steyn, Helga Toland (sitting), Zelda Arnott, Noreen Daniel, Elaine Evans

Cranwell House prefects were well documented. 1973 was no exception. Head of House was Mr Reeve-Johnson and Head Prefect of Cranwell House was Steve Cloete.

Thornhill High School

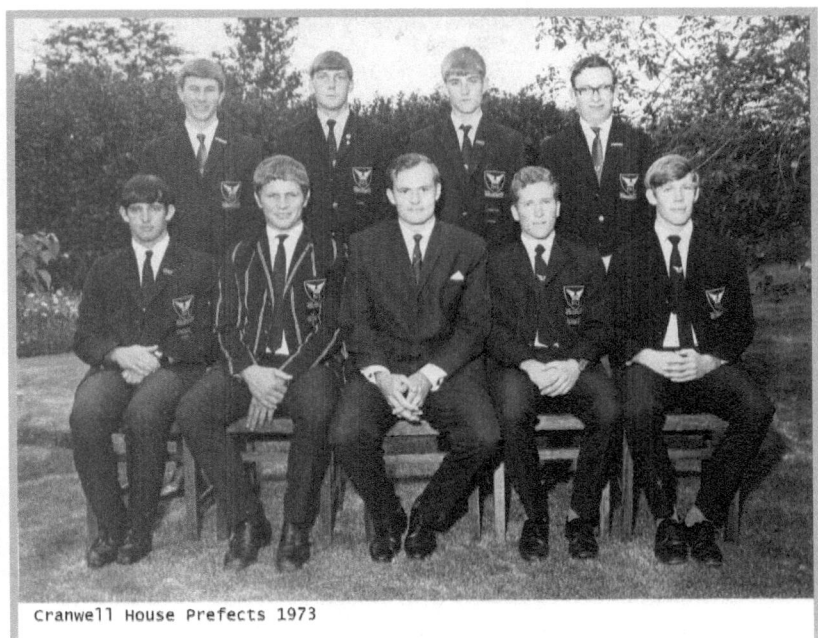

Cranwell House Prefects 1973
Back row left to right:
M. Taylor D. Steele D. Ward B. Patterson
Front row left to right
B. Waring S. Cloete Mr. Reeve-Johnson R. Wermuth G. Collett

Cranwell House Prefects

M. Taylor, Duncan Steel, Dave Ward, B Patterson
Bruce Waring, Steve Cloete, Mr Reeve-Johnson, R. Wermuth, Jeff Collett

In his report in the 1974 school magazine, the Deputy Head, Mr Andersen, remarked that Thornhill possessed a number of advantages: a happy and reasonably stable staff, above-average academic results, a good sporting image, a keen and hard-working PTA committee, a School Council devoted to the interests of the school, facilities second-to-none (such as the swimming pool, playing fields, tennis courts, hall, and language laboratory) and last, but not least, a solid core of good pupils.

One of the enduring memories of that year was the rain, which kept the playing fields virtually under water for the whole of the first term. Also, a little spring that appeared beside the First XI cricket wicket. However, the pupils were not inactive, as they embarked on a sponsored cycle ride which raised enough money to buy an electronic organ.

Thornhill High School

(Acknowledgements to DJ and Sharon Voyce for supplying this information)

The Rugby results for 1974 kindly supplied by Gerry van Tonder:-

```
Results
        vs Northlea        won       16 - 15
           Que Que         drew      16 - 16
           Sinoia          lost      12 - 6
           Lord Malvern    lost       4 - 28
           Oriel           lost       8 - 33
           St. Stephens    lost       8 - 31
           Guinea Fowl     lost       3 - 33
           Chaplin         lost      10 - 31
           Ft. Victoria    lost       6 - 32
           Jameson         cancelled
           Que Que         lost       6 - 32
           Ft. Victoria    lost      12 - 32
```

Only won the first match against Northlea. Thornhill lost badly against Guinea Fowl and Chaplin. Results were taken from the 1974 school Mag.

Music, Choirs, Bands and musical productions played a huge part of the school's life. Memories and traditions have lasted a life time.

1968 Band
Roger (Spider) Atkinson, Eric Bradnick, Ian Dunbar and Bill Malkin
(Photo credit: Bill Malkin)

Bill Malkin formed the Thornhill High School Thyme-Agin in 1978 with the above band members. The following year, Eric Bradnick was replaced by Gordon Fraser. Thyme-Agin played at the Que Que High School dance, as per photo sent to the writer by Bill Malkin.

Que Que High School dance

Band members Craig Hepburn, Colin Till, Brandon van Niekerk, Gavin Hensberg, Garry Perryman, Craig Byrne, Neil Calder, Michael Nesbit, Alun Hart, Debbie Finlay, Alison Yates, Karen Johnson, Denise Beuke-Norval, Elsa Taylor, Simone Joss, Sharon Cochrane Arlene Hepburn, Paul Davidson, Eric Budd and Bob Johnson

Form 2A in 1975 was kindly supplied by Mark Templemore-Walters (standing next to Class Teacher Mrs Becky Short).

Thornhill High School

Back row: Flo Manning, Julie Waters, Ingrid Marais, Barbara Bassi, Colleen ?, Kathy Swanepoel. Middle Row: Clive Fletcher, Rhodes Bezuidenhout, Mark Templemore-Walters, Teacher Mrs Becky Short, Johannes Grobbelaar, Lorraine Weideman and Eileen McGarvie. Front row: Phil de Wet, Maria Nicolaou Lapsley, Maria Campbell, Caroline Cheneau Respond, Julie Churney (with dog) and Sharon Hepburn.

Thornhill School Choir - 1976

Thornhill High School

Alan Hagemann, Graham Juby, Greg Mountjoy, Gary Fowlie, Martin Terence Byrne, Eric Budd. <u>2nd Row</u>: Nadine Budd, Denise Shillinglaw, Steve Prophet, Mark Jefferies, Rob Hardy,??, Bronwyn Smith, ?. <u>3rd Row</u>: Terri Murdoch, Anne Millward, Richmal Nordin Karthy Swanepoel, ?, ?, Annette Hahn, Piet Buys, ?. <u>4th Front Row</u>: Sue Armstrong, Bentley, Ona Steyn, Kathy Sullivan, Karen Johnson, Heather Robertsonvan der Riet, Avril Drew, Judy Brooke-Mee, ? Kendal Nordin.

(Acknowledgement to Karen Johnson for her photographs and supplying loads of information).

1976 Thornhill School Choir: Terri Murdoch-Coyle, Ann Milward, Richmel Nordin, Kathy Sullivan; Sue Armstrong Bentley, Ona Steyn, Kathy Sullivan and Karen Johnson

Several names from the 1976 School Choir remain unknown. It is hoped that with the publication of this commemorative magazine, memories may be jogged so that the gaps can be filled in before the year end when a revised edition will be published. More photographs will then be added.

Thornhill Gymnasts performed particularly well at the inter-schools competition. A news clipping "Thornhill Gymnastic Team A Winner" is of too low a resolution to be readable. In essence it mentions that the school gymnasts travelled to Salisbury to compete in the second Rhodesian Inter-Schools Gymnastics Competition. There was an 'A' and 'B' section in both the boys' and girls' events. Eight boys' schools and nine girls' schools took part.

The 'A' team boys had an outstanding day and won the 'A' team event convincingly beating their nearest rivals Umtali by more than 10 points.

The Headline in the Times, August 18, 1977

(Photo credit: Rupert van Heerden)

Alan Hagemann came first on the horizontal bar, parallel bars, pummel horse and still rings and came second on floor work and vaulting. Mr Hennie Lowe, the director of gymnastics from the Sports Foundation of South Africa and chief judge said Hagemann was approaching international standard. Peter Sanders came 5th overall and Mike Collins sixth and Craig Jones seventh.

The girls did fairly well with Debbie Coetzee taking 6th place. Sharon O'Bree came first on the asymmetric bars.

The full article:

Thornhill High School

The 1977 School Leavers' photo popped out of the woodwork when the writer was trying to find the names of past pupils.

Thornhill High School

Top to bottom: Ian Ferguson, Joe Ward, Yolanda Coetzee, xx, Wendy Whewell, Rob Collins, Sheldon Dudley, Michael or Mike Collins, Leigh Cranswick, Judy Brooke-Mee, Alan Hagemann, Chalky White, Gary du Bernard, Paul Rigby and Leigh Bristow

Fund raising for touring sides - sketch submitted by Rupert van Heerden

Thornhill High School

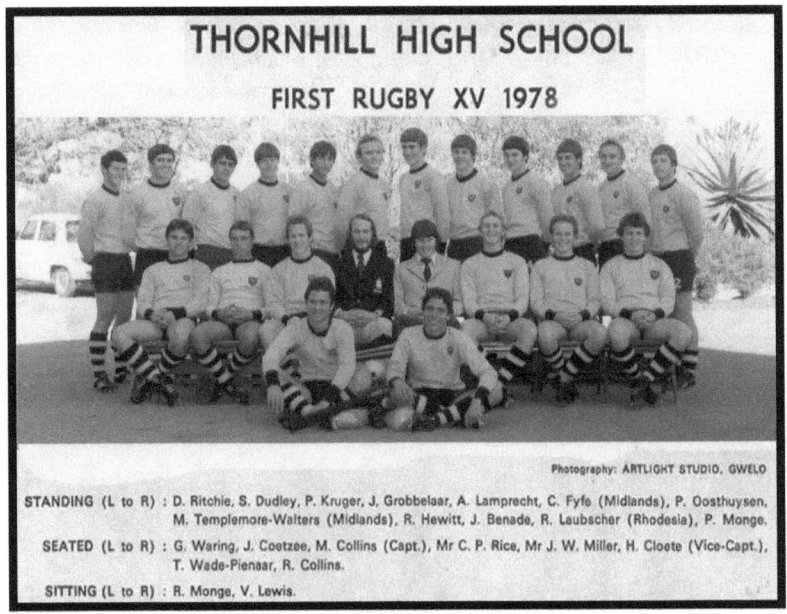

The team members are: <u>Back row</u> - D. Richie, S. Dudley, Johannes Grobbelaar, Andries Lambrecht, Chris Fyfe (Midlands), Phillip Oosthuysen, M. Templemore-Walters (Midlands), Ray Hewitt, J. Benade, Roger Laubscher (Rhodesia), P Munge. <u>Seated</u> - George Waring, J. Coetzee, Mike Collins (Capt), Mr C.P. Rice, Mr J.W. Miller, Hendrik Cloete (Vice-Capt), Tim Wade-Pienaar; <u>Sitting</u> - R. Monge, Rob Collins (Acknowledgement: Paddy Kruger)

<u>Standing</u>: Willie Swartz, Steve Brown,?, Shaun de Bernard,?, Andrew Niewoudt, Stewart Papadopoulos, ? and Nittin Patel.

Sitting: ?, Joe Keith, Roger Jervois, Brian Tooze, Steve Hewitt (RIP), Ralph Sutherland, Craig Stotter and Dean Burns.

(Acknowledgement Carole Ward)

Standing: x,x, Gavin Ellis, Ralph Sutherland, Kevin Law, Martinus Johnstone, x, Rob Cornwell, Don Ward and Brian Tooze. Sitting: ? Strydom, Hannes Blignaut, Mark Denton, Tim Wade-Pienaar Phillip Oosthuysen,?, Neels Blignaut and Gavin Ball. (Acknowledgement: Kevin Law)

BANDIT - by Garry Poole

Thornhill High School

1978 Water Polo Team

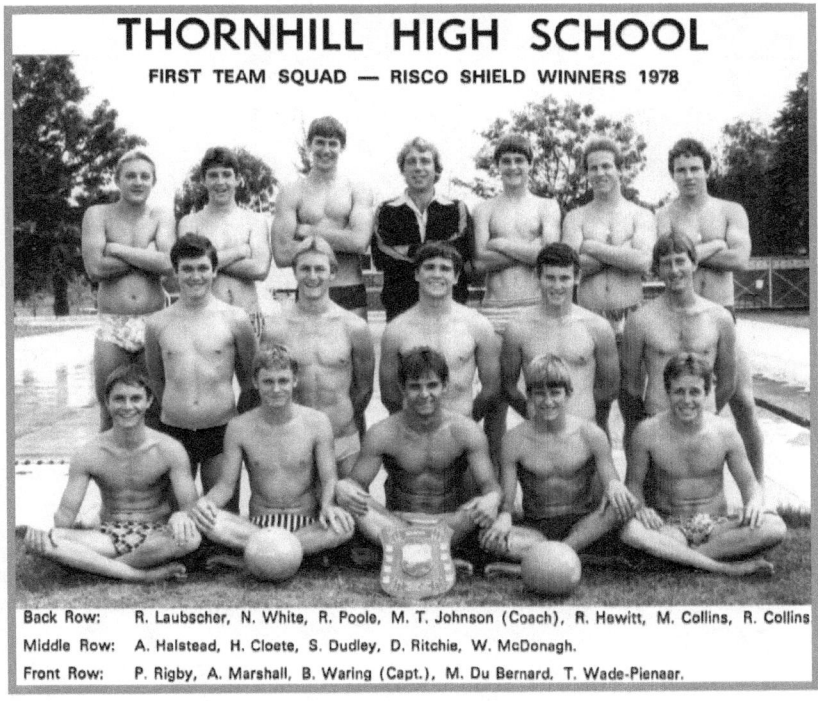

Winners of the Risco (Rhodesian Iron and Steel Company) Shield

Roger Laubscher, Neil White, Russell Poole, Mr M. Tom Johnson (Coach), Ray Hewitt, Mike Collins, Rob Collins, *Middle Row*: Arthur Halstead, Hendrik Cloete, Sheldon Dudley, Derek Richie, William McDonagh. *Front Row*: Paul Rigby, Alan Marshall, Brian or Bruce Waring (Capt) Mark du Bernard and Tim Wade-Pienaar.

The 'Stanard' House badge

Thornhill High School

Halton Girls – 1978

Delise Swift, Jean Millward, Maria Nicola Timveos, Tanya van Eeden (out of unifiorm), Stella Friedrich, Flo Manning, F. Funck, Lyndsay Johnstone, Fiona Stoddart, Viv Simpson, Vivienne Verdelli, Charmaine Green, Annette Hahn, Cheryl O'Connor, Heather Robertson, Kathy Swanepoel, Charmane Proctor and Anna Bakkes van Druten.

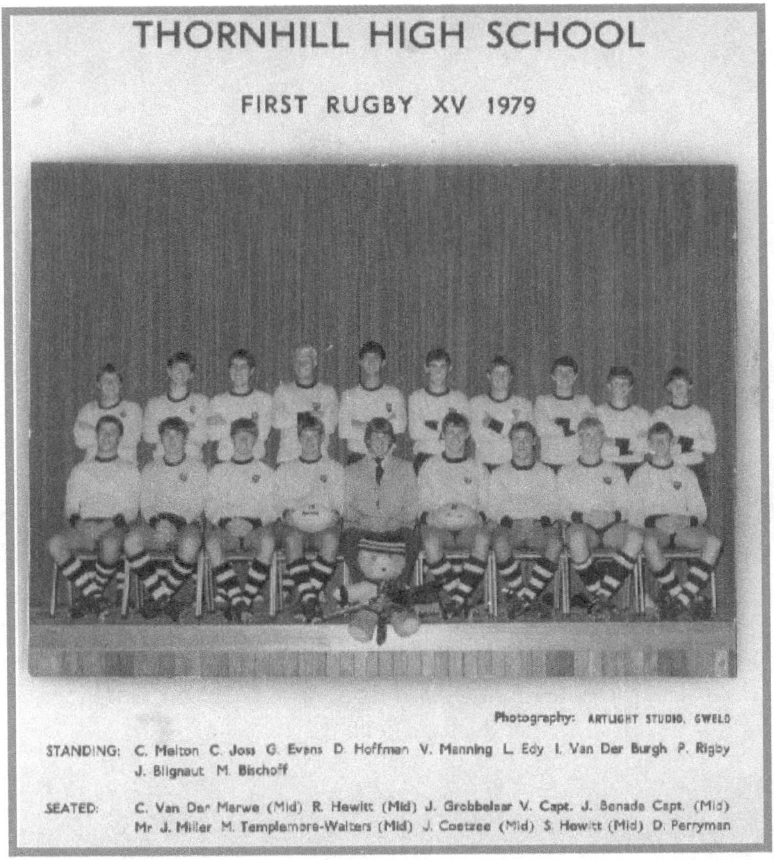

THORNHILL HIGH SCHOOL

FIRST RUGBY XV 1979

STANDING: C. Melton C. Joss G. Evans D. Hoffman V. Manning L. Edy I. Van Der Burgh P. Rigby J. Blignaut M. Bischoff

SEATED: C. Van Der Merwe (Mid) R. Hewitt (Mid) J. Grobbelaar V. Capt. J. Benade Capt. (Mid) Mr J. Miller M. Templemore-Walters (Mid) J. Coetzee (Mid) S. Hewitt (Mid) D. Perryman

Standing: Clive Melton, Craig Joss, Grant Evans, D Hoffman, Vince Manning, Lex Edy, I van der Burgh, Paul Rigby, Johannes or Hannes Blignaut and Mike Bischoff. *Seated*: C van der Merwe (Mid) Ray Hewitt (Mid), Johannes Grobbelaar V Capt, J Benade (Capt) (Mid), Mr JW Miller, Mark Templemore-Walters (Mid), BJ Coetzee (Mid), Stephen Hewitt (Mid), Derek Perryman

Cranwell -fenced and gated (to keep boys in at night): Halton House - very well fenced and gated (to keep boys out at night)

Thornhill High School

St Johns: x, Gail McGowan, Linda Flanders, Joanne Naude, Sharon Kilpatrick, Karen de Reuk, <u>Sitting</u>: Karen Johnson, Debbie Hahn-Dyer, Debbie Finlay (Johnson), Maura Etherman, Fiona Nuttal-Smith &?

<u>Back 2 Rows</u>: Don Ward, Chris Fyfe, Neels Blignaut, Roger Laubscher, Johannes Grobbelaar, George Bruce Waring, Ray Hewitt, Mark Templemore-Walters, Hendrik Cloete, Ben Kota Benade, Robert Cornwell, xx, Craig Joss. <u>Middle row</u>; xx, Craig Holmes, Shaun du Bernard, BJ Coetzee, Mr X, Mark 'Wire' du

Bernard, Lex Edy and Tod Burns. <u>Front</u>: *Bernard Kung, xx, xx, Michael Bares, Lee Child, and Craig Hattle (Photo credit: Karen Johnson and Lex Edy)*

The Eighties

Thornhill High School 1977 – 1981, recollections by Rupert van Heerden: "It was a nervous first day walking up to the entrance gates at Thornhill, I guess it was the anticipation of what was to come after being a big fish in a little pond now a very tiny Kapenta in a huge sea. All the present pupils looked so big and as they do all waiting at the gates watching all the fresh, new kids arriving. Once through the gauntlet of the gate so many people milling around so all you do is look for a familiar face and wait for instruction.

"Then the siren goes and the Prefects direct us into the Great Hall for assembly, I had never seen so many people and the nerves are now on high alert, the Choir file in and then the Staff come in all with their University regalia, they all sit up on stage. All of a sudden they all stand up, now I'm wondering is assembly over already, wrong! The Deputy Headmaster and Headmaster, Mr Eadie, walk down the centre of the hall and take their place on stage and with that assembly begins.

"After assembly we are sent off to the Boys Hostel for aptitude tests to put us in the various classes. When we get to those classes we all stand there sizing each other up as there are a lot of new faces and also it's Day Scholars versus Boarders, I'm sure it is a guy thing.

"When the siren goes for break we are told to go to the Hall and see the Head boy and his team of Prefects, we are told to learn about Thornhill High School, names of Head boy and Head girl, Sports Houses (the only important one was Stannard), Hostel Names, Field Names, in particular the 1st Team rugby and hockey fields, the Thornhill War Cry, names of all the teachers, where we could walk and go and where we could not, also where the Prefects Common Rooms were and how to address the Prefects. We would be tested the next day, safe to say I passed. Upon leaving the Hall a few Seniors were picking off which Skivvies had not been selected by Prefects, and told where to find their books and timetable and to make sure their books were at the next class before they were, those were the days and so that was my 1st day of High School.

"Over the following years I became somewhat of a Special Report specialist also the occasional bending over the Deputy Headmasters desk looking at mates watching you at a vantage point from C-Block Domestic Science room.

"I loved the after school sport - Go Stannard; I couldn't wait to get back to school in the afternoons for whatever sport was being played and the Saturday Rugby especially against Chaplin was a definite highlight we also used to play Chaplin midweek and just about the whole of Gweru would shut down for the derby.

"In 1978 Thornhill U-14 rugby team was unbeaten and the 1st XV had also beaten Chaplin but lost to Guinea Fowl in a game that was one of the best games played, a bit of a dodgy ref, I'm sure the Guinea Fowlers would argue that point. In 1981 we beat Chaplin again."

Rupert left Thornhill at the end of 1981

3 P.M.		4 P.M.		
CHAPLIN 3RD XV	THORNHILL 2ND XV	CHAPLIN 1ST XV		THORNHILL 1ST XV
I. BARNARD	S. NCUBE	M. COUGHLAN	15	G. PARKIN
F. CLAASENS	C. HOLMES	A. WATSON	14	B. BLIGNAUT
K. SWANEPOEL	W. CLOETE	C. FREELAND	13	J. MOORE (V.CAPT)
C. WHEELER	D. BURNS	J. JORDAAN	12	A. HART
V. MAJOR	S. BROWN	L. MELLET	11	L. CHILD
C. FREEMAN	T. BURNS (CAPT)	G. VILJOEN	10	S. DU BERNARD
G. BARRY	M. BATES	J. DOLLAR	9	C. DU BERNARD
D. VERMAAK	E. COELHO	C. POHL	1	E. PAPADOPOULOS
J. FIELDING	B. WILDE	L. VAN STADEN (V.CAPT)	2	C. BYNE
D. SHAW	R. VAN HEERDEN	M. ROBERTSON	3	S. DREW (CAPT)
H. TRAKOSHIS	T. BOWMAN	T. RENSBURG	4	M. MARAIS
D. HONIB	G. POOLE	L. WESSELS	5	I. CHAMBERLAIN
B. NELL (CAPT)	A. BOYSENS	I. BUITENDAG	6	C. HATTLE
I. OGILVIE	B. VAN NIEKERK	T. BRONKHORST	7	A. JAMES
P. HENNING	R. SHENTALL	M. JORDAAN (CAPT)	8	V. MARKRAM

REF. F. GOODES   REF. D. DEYSEL

The 1st XV team players were Iain Chamberlain, Lee Child, Shaun du Bernard, Gary du Bernard, S Drew (Captain), Alun Hart, Craig Hattle, A James, Mark Marais, J Moore (Vice Captain), Victor Markram, E Papadopoulos, G Parkin and with Dux Deysel as the Referee.

2nd XV team players were Michael Bates, Dean Burns, Tod Burns, Steven Brown, T Bowman, A Boysens, Eduardo Coelho, Craig Holmes, S Ncube, Garry Poole, R Shentall, Rupert van Heerden, Brandon van Niekerk and N Wilde. (Acknowledgement: Rupert van Heerden)

(Acknowledgement: Rupert van Heerden)

Staff 1980 - with John Eadie, Jane Few, Gordon Dykstra and EM Chamberlain

In 1981 John Eadie retired, and was succeeded as Headmaster by John Drinkwater, who had previously taught at Chaplin, Guinea Fowl and Fort Victoria. The next few years saw great changes at the school, as newly independent Zimbabwe opened formerly white schools to pupils of all races. Owing to the fact that all junior school leavers took the same Leaving Certificate and schools could pick and choose to some extent, the calibre of entrants remained high and standards were maintained. Much of the credit must go to the staff, including many "old stalwarts" like Barbara Coventry, Derris

Viljoen, EM Chamberlain, Gordon Dykstra, and Terry and Yvonne Hart. Many other staff posts were filled by 'imported' teachers from UK, Australia and Mauritius, on short-term contracts. Exam results (still the old Associated Examining Board GCE) were pleasing, and certainly up to the level of previous years.

Thornhill win rugby derby in 1981

Thornhill defeated Chaplin 7 - 4 with a try by Craig Byrne and the winning penalty kicked by Shaun du Bernard fifteen minutes before full time. The referee for the match was Mr A. Kraan.

Thornhill win rugby 'derby'

ON WEDNESDAY last week, Thornhill 1st XV Rugby side succeeded in narrowly defeating Chaplin by a try and a penalty to a try. Neither side dominated the forward play which was fiercely contested in the first half.

Thornhill opened the scoring with a try by Craig Byrne who followed up extremely well throughout the game. Chaplin replied later in the first half with a try by A. Kraan. The referee maintained firm control of two determined packs with the hard play continued throughout the second half, Chaplin forwards gaining more possession of the ball.

Shaun du Bernard converted a penalty, 15 minutes from time, to bring the score to 7-4 in favour of Thornhill. Chaplin pressurised the Thornhill line, but solid defence by the home side gave the Thornhill team their first victory over Chaplin for three years.

(Acknowledgement: Rupert van Heerden)

1982 Domestic Science

Teacher Mrs Jane Few toasting her last 'O' Level Cookery class pupils Sandy, Karen de Reuck, Nicky Roux, Caroline Ehlers and Merlene. The champagne flutes engraved with their names. (Photo: Thornhill website)

1982 was Jane Few's final year at Thornhill – having taught Geography and Domestic Science for some 15 years at the school.

Thornhill High School

1982 First Team Hockey

Standing: Bridget Hepburn, Tracey O'Connor, Audrey Folkertsen Nieuwenhuizen, Janet Medland Udi, Lorraine Hewitt Triggs and Pam Moore. *Sitting*: Nicky Chamberlain, Cindy McCabe, ?, Sonya Martell Vanessa Pfaff & goalie Jenny Poole.   (Photo: Janet Medland Udi)

1983 First Team Hockey

Standing: Eulalie Barry, Claire Forder, V. Manning, Rene Jordan and Leslie-Ann Hector: *Seated*; LH, Janet Medland Udy, Jenny Poole, Lorraine Hewitt Triggs and Elsa Taylor.   (Photo credit: Janet Medland Udy)

Thornhill High School

Gary Drew with Mr Hart

In 1984, the first black head boy and head girl were appointed, and did a very good job. Noel Gocha became the first black deputy head (and later the first black headmaster).

Delise Swift-Joubert with Sharon O'Bree – in their green prefect dresses, with the Holman Field in the background

The School, in its heyday, cultivated and well maintained

The PWD provided the school with a brand new bus because the old bus broke down on some sporting trips, causing concern among the parents. Sport, however, began to decline as the number of staff able to coach to first team level decreased. The high cost and scarcity of sporting equipment didn't help either. The last first XI cricket fixture was in 1983, when the Thornhill team, coached by John Drinkwater, had a comfortable win over their Chaplin rivals, coached by Doodles Viljoen. In 1984, the rivals became partners in joint fixtures as a combined team. In the same year, the Thornhill Athletics team won at the Midlands Inter-Schools meeting.

(Acknowledgement to John Drinkwater)

The post Two Thousands

The Thornhill High School Alumni Association (Gweru, Zimbabwe) web-site was created with the object of bringing together former students and teachers and provides an update on the progress and success of the Thornhill High School Alumni. It was hoped that this site would enable alumni members to contribute to the success of this group to meet its objectives.

In June 2011 a group called THS Reunion was created on Facebook to organize a reunion for students, set to take place on December 2011.

In August 2011 recent pictures from the school were posted. The posting of the pictures changed the whole landscape of the group and its initial intentions, reflecting the relevance of the group's vision and dire challenges currently facing the school. This resulted in a significant expansion of the group, from below 60 members to over hundred in a short period of time.

The idea to establish an Alumni Trust was raised to enable fund raising initiatives to be carried out in a transparent and legally structured framework. Following on from the establishment of a steering committee (SC), the SC started to work on this project, putting in place structures and a strategy to achieve the aims of the Thornhill High School Alumni Trust- to bring back our school to its former glory - *Through the thorns to the hilltop- Per Spinas Ad Culmina.*

To ensure success of the project, we realised the importance of getting buy-in from the existing school administration, the Thornhill High School School Development Association {SDA}, the Parent Teacher Association {PTA} and the School Staff. It was then decided by the group that a team would meet with the headmaster, SDA and PTA and share our objectives.

As of October 2011, the Thornhill Alumni Trust had over 900 members.

The Trust has a set up a bank account with the trust administrators. The aim is to raise the first $100,000 within a year. The money will be used to finance identified projects ranging from school renovation work, purchasing new furniture, developing the library and sports facilities etc.

The Alumni Association is relatively quiet. The Facebook group is livelier.

Cranwell House in 2007 - a sorry state indeed as can be seen by the poor state of repair and maintenance (Writers Note: See the significant improvements captured by Karen Johnsons lens immediately after celebrating the School's Diamond Jubilee in October 2015)

Thornhill in 2011 - the School's cheerleaders leading the headmistress and staff into the hall.

Internet photo circa 2011

Musical Productions

Gilbert and Sullivan, and Rogers and Hammerstein musical productions played a big part of the tradition developed over time at Thornhill. Unbeknown to most of us at that time, it was a brilliant character building and life-skills development for every person involved with these grand productions. From their small beginnings they soon developed into the grand affairs upon which reputations are made. The musicals are deliberately showcased as a stand-a-lone chapter to emphasise a proud heritage and tradition established in the school's heyday.

HMS Pinafore

Thanks to Yvonne (Emslie) Twilley for supplying the programme.

Musical Productions

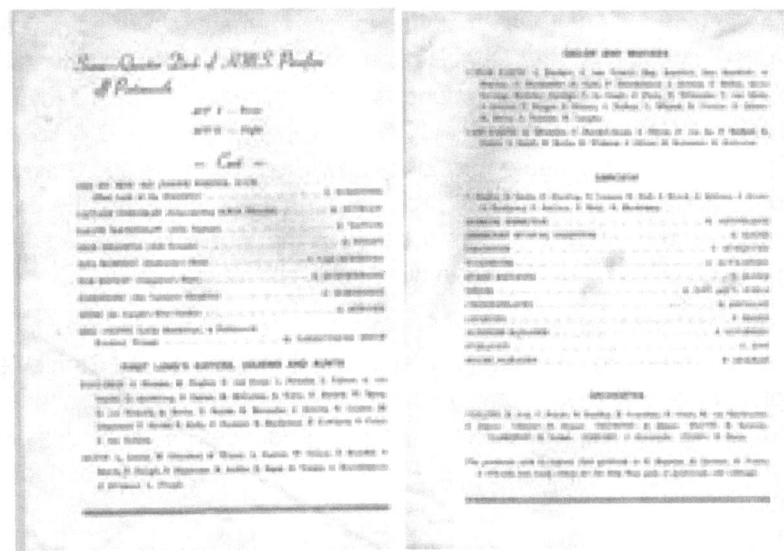

The next few years saw further musical productions directed by Mrs Niki Antoniadis:

Pirates of Penzance - June 1959

Produced by Tommy Burgoyne and with much credit to musical director Mrs Niki Antoniadis who knew just what was needed to make this Gilbert and Sullivan musical the success it was.

Musical Productions

The setting for Act 1 was rocky seashore on the coast of Cornwall. In the opening scene, the Pirates of Penzance are discovered celebrating the end of Frederick's apprenticeship - played by B Tasker. Ruth, the Pirate Maid of All work, played by D Viljoen, Frederick's former nurse, discloses how Frederick was apprenticed to a pirate instead of to a pilot, through her confusing the two words, and Frederick informs the pirates that not only is he leaving them, he is also determined to wipe them out.

Ruth, determined to marry Frederick, who has seen no other women, tells him how attractive she is, but Major-General Stanley's -played by teacher Tommy Burgoyne, appears on the scene. Frederick, realising he's been tricked, renounces Ruth, and asks one of the girls to accept him. Mabel, played by Gayle Robertson, obliges.

At this point, the pirates return, seize the girls, whom they are about to marry on the spot, when the Major-General arrives. To save his daughter she tells the pirates he's an orphan, for pirates don't molest orphans. The lie saves both the General and his daughters, though the latter are horrified at the deception.

Act 2 - A ruined chapel by Moonlight.

General Stanley is in the ruined chapel with his daughters. His conscience is troubled by the lie he has told the pirates. Frederick enters to announce that the expedition against the pirates is ready and summons the police, who are in great fear of the pirates.

When the police have departed, Frederick is surprised by the arrival of Ruth and the Pirate King - played by bearded schoolboy Neville Harcombe - who reveals that, owing to his being born on the 29th February; his indentures haven't expired, as he is bound to serve the pirates till his 21st birthday. Frederick, a slave of duty, re-joins the pirates, to whom he discloses General Stanley's lie.

The pirates, intent on revenge, overcome the police and the General, but they themselves surrender to the police "In Queen Victoria's name." When Ruth reveals that the pirates are "Noblemen who have gone wrong", the General forgives them and presents them with his daughters as brides.

These plays proved a winner - for king and country! Evening rehearsals meant there was much hanky-panky in the corridors (and afterwards for those naughty boarders as well).

THS - Pirates of Penzance

The good and the bad guys

Too many names to remember but those that came to mind included yours truly Preller Geldenhuys, Ben van As, Roy and Glen Kalil, Des van Rooyen, Neville Harcombe, Chris de Jong, Jeffrey Halkier, Reg and Ray Kaschula, Nigel McFarlane, Attie Ebersohn, Rodney McNeill, Pieter Burger, Roy Langley and Reg Wickens - plus others whose names escapes me at the time of writing.

Inside the Pirates of Penzance programme

Goodnight Vienna 1960

Goodnight Vienna is a British musical stage production.

Max is an Austrian officer in the army and son of a highly placed general. His father wants him to marry a Countess but he has fallen in love with Vicki. Attending a party given in his honour, they are informed that war has broken out. Max writes a note to Vicki and goes off to war. Unfortunately, the note is lost. Sometime after the war, Max is just a shoe shop assistant while Vicki is now a famous singer. They meet and at first she snubs him but then falls in love with him again.

The Mikado 1961

The Mikado is one of the most frequently played musical theatre pieces in history, popularised by clever adaptations by Gilbert and Sullivan. Who can forget those enduring song like "A Wand'ring Minstrel I" sung by Nanki-Poo and men with the opening scene. "Behold the Lord High Executioner" sung by Ko-Ko and men and to mention "Three Little Maids from School are We" sung by Yum-Yum, Peep-Bo, Petti-Sing and Girls come easily to mind.

Musical Productions

The Story of The Mikado

The main characters were The Mikado; Nanki-Poo the wandering minstrel in love with Yum-Yum, Ko-Ko the Lord High Executioner of Titipu, Pooh-Bah, Pish-Tush, Go-To, Yum-Yum, Pitty-Sing and Peep-Bo.

Janet Lancaster and Alwyn Strauss showing the early 60's major production programs: Pirates of Penzance, Goodnight Vienna: The Mikado and HMS Pinafore

Iolanthe 1962

Iolanthe was another comic opera by Gilbert and Sullivan musical staged by the school in 1962.

Musical Productions

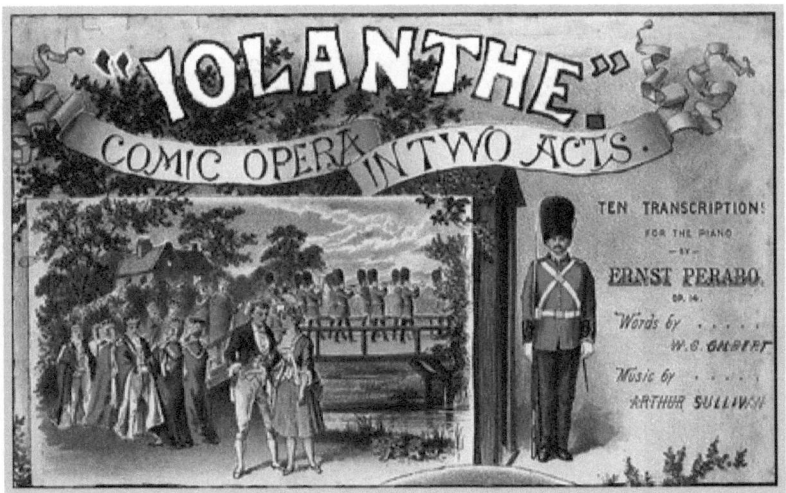

Iolanthe is the seventh of fourteen operas that Arthur Sullivan and WS Gilbert staged at the Savoy in London. When first staged it ran for nearly four hundred performances. The plot is about a band of immortal fairies who takes the Mickey out of the establishment.

Audrey Brown Chandler's Facebook page is worth repeating. Nice to see an ex-pupil using a Thornhill event as a backdrop to her Facebook page.

The King and I

This was another musical production with a very large cast, excellent costumes, and many dance routines and well received by the Gwelo public.

Musical Productions

The very large cast of The King and I

Stage settings and the quality of the costumes for all the Thornhill High School are and have been quite spectacular. Products of the Arts and Sewing classes at the school

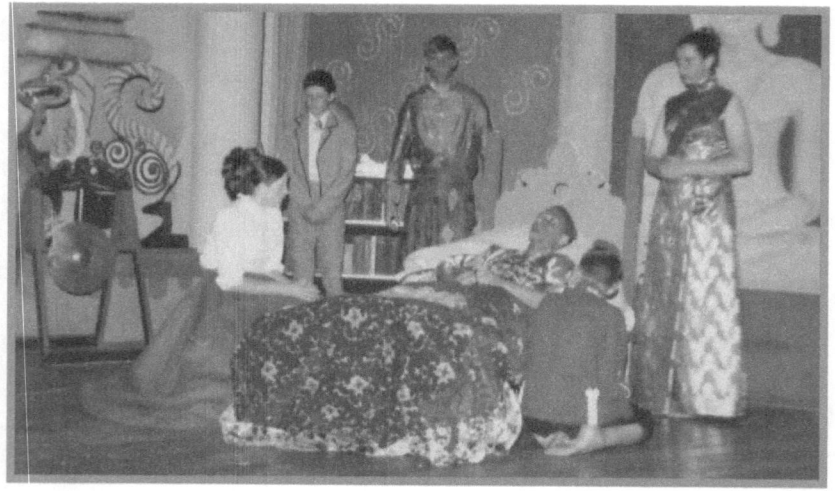

(Photo credit: Karen Johnson)

After a gap of several years, Mr Gordon Dykstra, and later Mr Bob Johnson, put on productions of South Pacific in 1971, Oliver 1973, Annie Get Your Gun 1974 and The Music Man.

Musical Productions

THORNHILL SCHOOL presents

OLIVER!

Musical Productions

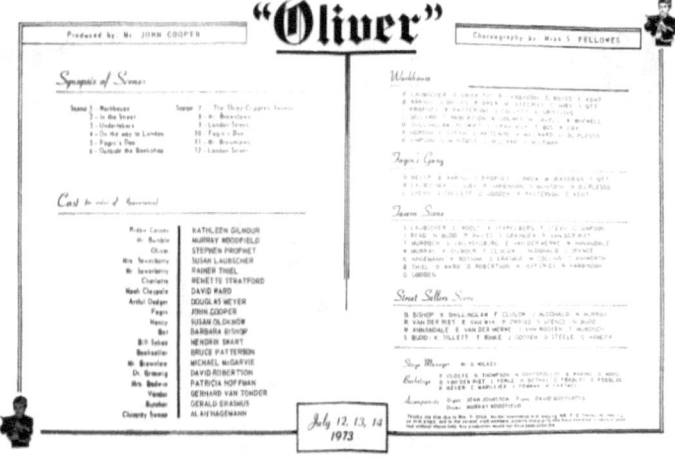

Murray Woodfield and Susan Oldknow in Annie Get Your Gun, 1974 (Photo credit: Karen Johnson)

Musical Productions

THORNHILL HIGH SCHOOL
(Photo credit: Gerry van Tonder)

Musical Productions

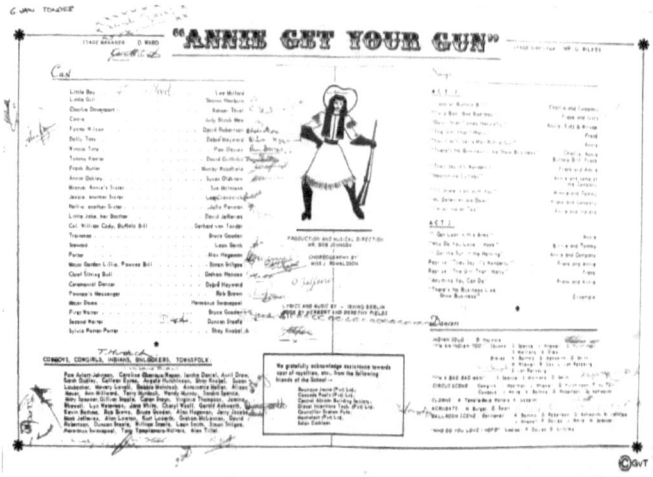

Murray Woodfield in pensive mood as Frank Butler.

Another of the main leads in the play is Buffalo Bill played by Gerhard van Tonder.

Big parade to herald school play

Times Reporter

ALL the glamour of the Wild West comes to Gwelo in a big way on Saturday morning with a parade through the city by the 70-member cast of Thornhill High School's latest theatrical production, Annie Get Your Gun.

The parade, which will include horses and a vintage car, is part of the promotion programme for the play which has its gala opening on Saturday night at 8.15 preceeded by a cheese and wine party at the school at 7.15 p.m.

For the school, producer Bob Johnson, and the actors this performance is extremely important as it is the Schools' Drama Festival entry, and on hand to adjudicate will be American Lou Salerni.

Mr. Salerni has already proved that he pulls no punches when adjudicating, irrespective of whether the productions are by schools or theatre clubs.

But Bob Johnson appeared confident this week that the production would be a credit to Thornhill.

The performance next Monday is for local schools, while those on Tuesday and Wednesday will be open to the public.

Tickets for the performances are available at the Record Centre.

Susan Oldknow who plays Annie Oakley in Thornhill's Annie Get Your Gun.

Graham Haisen, an impressive Chief Sitting Bull.

Through the grapevine we hear that this will be one of the most impressive scenes in Thornhill School's production of Annie Get Your Gun. The scene is the world shooting championships between Frank Butler and Annie Oakley and the sound effects are said to be tremendous.

(Photo credit: Gerry van Tonder)

Musical Productions

Big Parade to herald school play

All the glamour of the Wild West comes to Gwelo in a big way on Saturday morning with a parade through the city by the 70-member cast of Thornhill High School's latest theatrical production, which will include horses and a vintage car, is part of the promotion programme for the play which has its gala opening on Saturday night at 8:15 preceded by a cheese and wine party at the School at 7:15 pm.

For the School, producer Bob Johnson, and the actors this performance is extremely important as it is the Schools Drama Festival entry, and on hand to adjudicate will be American Lousi Salerni.

Mr Salerni has proved that he pulls no punches when adjudicating, irrespective of whether the productions are by schools or theatre clubs.

But Bob Johnson appeared confident this week that the production would be a credit to Thornhill. The performance next Monday is for local schools, while those on Tuesday and Wednesday will be open to the public.

South Pacific

Scene from South Pacific - photo credit from the Thornhill High School Past Pupils website,

Musical Productions

More South Pacific photo credits from the website - Annette Robb on the left and Gerald May on the right

Then there was the 15-minute Hamlet in 1979, inter-house and Inter-School productions in 1980.

The Music Man

Some anxious moments were had when Karen Hurndall (Shillinglaw) stood in for Nadine at short notice. In her own words, she recalls: "I stepped into Nadine (Budd) Evans shoes at the last gasp - no doubt a nightmare for Mr Johnson as I was no natural on stage! I remember Rainer Thiel, Dave Griffiths, PJ Holmes and Graham Juby well as they were all my year; also Judy Brooke-Mee, Sheila Maitland and the likes.

This really brings back memories."

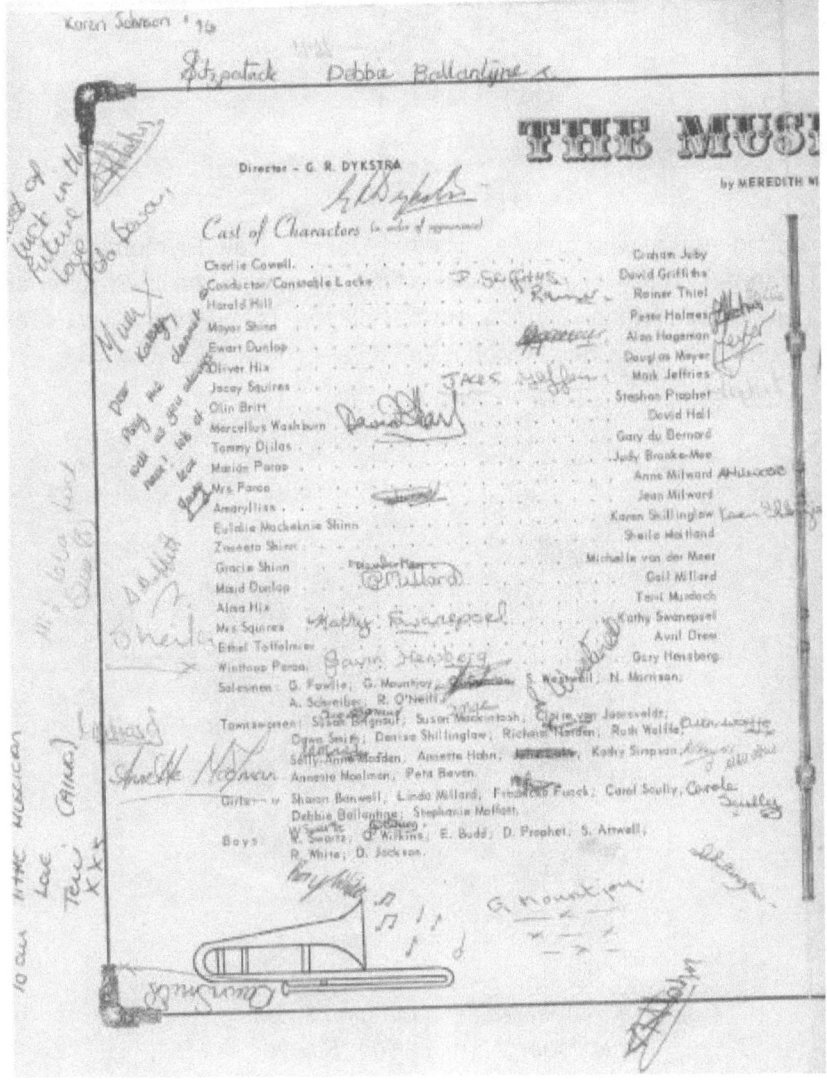

Tom Sawyer

Craig Hattle, who currently lives in Oakura, New Plymouth (Mount Taranaki area) of New Zealand, played one of the lead roles as Huckleberry Finn. Timothy Harper played Tom; Anne Millward as Aunt Polly and Craig Hepburn as Willie.

Craig Hattle is the pipe smoking Huckleberry Finn in Tom Sawyer - 1978

Musical Productions

The Music Man with Gavin Hensberg and Anne Millward

Scenes from Hamlet - 1980

(Anna-Marie Lamprecht)

Cast included Wendy Enola Gay Smith, Don Ward, Debbie Johnson, Ona Steyn, Alison Cole, Pikki Moolman, Debbie Finlay, Anna-Marie Lamprecht, Paul Rigby, Sandy Smith, Neil Burton, Craig Hepburn, Philipa Potgieter, Mark Templemore-Walters, Steve Hewitt, Rodney Drew, Gary Poole and several more.

Musical Productions

Hamlet

(Photo credit: Gerry van Tonder)

'White Sheep' a winner for Thornhill High School - - -

Following two very successful school performances, the Thornhill High School Drama Group presented the "White Sheep of the Family" to the Gwelo public in the school's Todd Hall last weekend. This hilarious comedy written by L du Garde Peach and Ian Hay and produced by staff member Mr GR Dykstra was well received by the audiences.

The Saturday Gala Night preceded by a cheese and wine party proved to be a most successful function. Mr R Hawkins Minister of Transport and Power, The District Commissioner Mr Parker and his wife and the Mayor and Mayoress Clr, and Mrs TH Blackburn attended.

It is very difficult for young actors to portray adults, particularly middle-aged adults in a convincing manner, but this the young Thornhill actors succeeded in doing. They were refreshing, clear and audible - a point commented upon favourably by Mr Tony

Musical Productions

Weave the adjudicator who is a well-known figure in Rhodesian drama circles.

Noteworthy performances were given by Murray Woodfield as James Winter worthy of a long line of crooks. Gerhard van Tonder, the wily wide boy and David Boothroyd as the amiable and absentminded vicar. Other members of the cast who also turned in good performances were Cheryl O'Connor, Fern Fuchs, Susan Laubscher, David Robertson, Robert Wermuth and Elizabeth Davies.

The set was attractive, the lighting adequate and all went smoothly so that the large number of people behind the scenes also deserve congratulations for their part in this successful presentation.

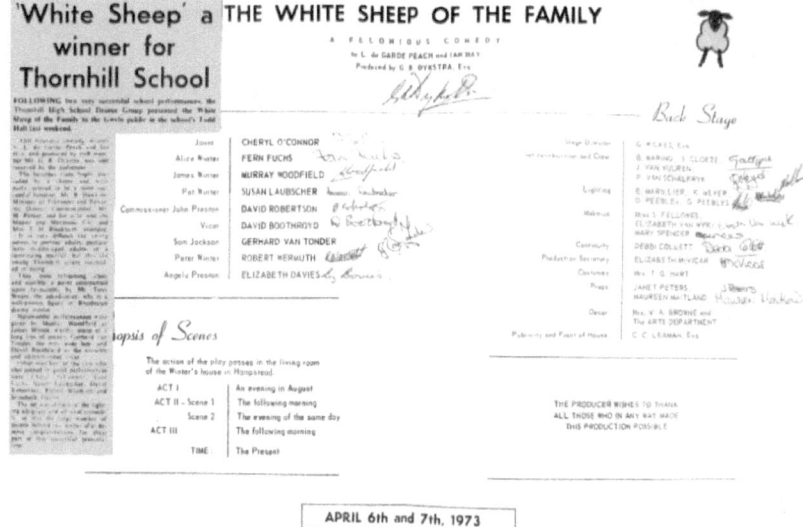

School Bands and Choirs

Karen Johnson, currently from the United Kingdom, appeared with band members in 1978 - as well as one of the Thornhill beauties - as per the photographs below.

Musical Productions

The Band

Thornhill Choir 1976

Terri Murdoch, Debbie Hahn-Dyer, Sue Armstrong Bentley, Annette Hahn, Ona Steyn, Alan Hagemann, Karen Shillinglaw, Bronwyn Smith, Nadine Budd, Gary du Bernard,, Sharon Widcombe, Gwen Bryan (Carr), Steve Prophet, Denise Shillinglaw, Heather van der Riet, Mark Jefferies, Richmal Nordin, Greg Mountjoy, Gary Fowlie, Karen Howell, Trudy Steenkamp, Martin Terence Byrne, Piet Buys, Judy Brooke-Mee, Eric Budd, Caren Howell Neethling, Kendal, Sharon Whitcombe and Richmal Nordin.

Musical Productions

Thornhill Theatre Band 1979

Craig Hepburn, Colin Till, Gavin Hensberg, Arlene Hepburn, Michael Nesbit, Alun Hart, Debbie Finlay, Bridget Hepburn, Karen Johnson, Alison Yates, Liz Forder, Paul Davidson, Matt Wightman, Andrew Semple, Eric Budd, Karen Botha.

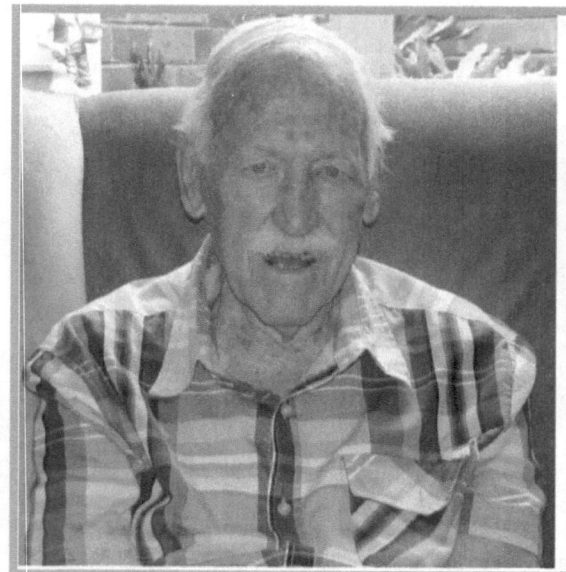

Karen and Bob Johnson toasting Mr Gordon Dykstra's good health and happiness in 2013

Karen and Bob Johnson with Gordon Dykstra in 2013

Beauty Pageants

You Beauty Miss T.H.S.

Beauty Pageants was a feature of Thornhill High School. Pupils were a happy lot. One just need to page through the following pages to note the smiling faces the vast majority have.

ABOVE: Judy Brooke-Mee (centre) was elected Miss Thornhill last Friday at a beauty contest held at the school. She is flanked by her princesses, Susan Loubser (left), the senior princess, and Bronwyn Smith, junior princess.

Beauty Pageants

Judy Brooke-Mee Scott won the 1975 title of Miss Thornhill, with her Senior Princess being Susan Loubser and Junior Princess being Bronwyn Smith.

Lyn van Heerden and Dianne Baldwin ran the first Miss Thornhill contest in 1968, to raise funds for their Hockey tour. Local businesses donated the prizes.

Carole Ward was a latter winner.

1978 - with Karen Johnson, Helen Wightman Gent and Tracey O'Connor (in the bright red dress borrowed from Viv Simpson)

Very unfortunately, a listing of some of the names has been mislaid. While beauties Carole Ward and Karen Johnson have been most helpful, the writer trusts that many of the un-named beautiful ladies will recognise themselves in the photographs.

Thornhill Beauties (Photo credits - Karen Johnson)

Beauty Pageants

Carole Ward, Lindsay Pebody and Audrey Folkertsen Nieuwenhuizen (Photo credit: Carole Ward)

A noteworthy feature of Thornhill girls are their beautiful smiles. One just need to page through the section listing past pupils to take note of the happy lot Thornhillians are. That, despite the obvious 'smile for the birdie' whenever one faces a camera lens.

(Photo credit: Gary Drew)

1982

Vanessa Robinson, Melanie Wheeler Haselwood, Sue Ballantyne, Ella Blignaut Kirstein, Elsa Taylor, unknown and Alison Yates.

Darlene van Gopel, Audrey Folkertsen Nieuwenhuizen, Jackie Maimin, and Lorna Culverwell Drew (writer not sure of order)

Cranwell Capers

Bruce Brislin writes: How times change. When I was in the third dormitory at Thornhill a bunch of us decided to bunk out one night and raid the mealie fields in what was known to all as 'Chafook' – the sewage farm that bordered the school grounds. The doors were never locked back then, 1962 I think, and getting out required only the very minimum of stealth. Off we trotted in our school gear and before long had a fire going and mealie cobs roasting on the coals. It must have been during the winter term because I remember the cobs being well dried out. We ate what we wanted and then, stinking of wood-smoke we made our way back and back to bed. In the morning we were the first to shower, something generally only done in the evenings after sport but we had to get rid of the smell of wood-smoke that seemed to cling to us like a second skin.

Unfortunately, it had also permeated all our clothing so despite us being abnormally well washed we still smelled strongly of smoke that completely smothered the delicate scent of standard issue Lifebuoy soap. We were therefore obliged to take our chances until laundry day because the routine was a rigid one and we carried no spare clothing in our lockers. I don't think anyone was actually questioned by a teacher about the miasma that accompanied all of us but on all future forays we were that little bit more careful about keeping away from the smoke.

Imagine a boarding school today that left all the doors open overnight. It would be unthinkable anywhere in Europe and in most other places too, I would imagine. It just shows the freedom we, as Rhodesian kids, enjoyed. And they call the Old World 'civilised.' I often wonder whether it was jealousy rather than media-induced morality that caused half the World to vilify us later on. I suspect it was. Still, it was we that enjoyed that freedom and that is beyond the power of any sanction to remove.

Which reminds me: We also used to raid fruit trees in the dead of night, stuffing our shirts with as much oranges that we could safely make our escape whenever we woke the households from their slumbers (often when causing the racket when falling through breaking tree branches).

Thornhill High School Golfers - July 2015

Names, not necessarily in the right order, include Steve Prophet, Neil White, Dave Griffiths, Derek Perryman, Ray Hewitt, Rob Collins, Dave and Thorn Prophet.

Thornhill (golf) hats

Large sign near one of the entrance roads to the school

Several photographs of the school and various spots and prefects' photographs appear in a five-minute segment of a Youtube titled "Rhodesia's Rebellion: 50th Anniversary of UDI - Unilateral Declaration of Independence.

The following screen-shots of the video is reproduced here, despite the poor quality pictures and sound.

A montage of the YouTube video titled Rhodesia's Rebellion: 50th Anniversary of UDI. The Unilateral Declaration of Independence occurred on the 11th November, 1965.

Immediately following the Harare Silver Jubilee celebrations in October 2015, Karen Johnson re-visited Thornhill School and posted the following photographs on Face Book.

Thornhill High School

Karen Johnson with long, still serving Wallis - in 2015

Jane Few commented appropriately "Well done, thou good and faithful servant". 35 years' service must be a record.

Karen Johnson visited Thornhill High School immediately after the October 2015 Harare reunion and posted her photographs on Facebook. The vast improvement in building maintenance and grounds upkeep attracted widespread favourable comment.

Photograph credits by Karen Johnson

P.J. Todd Hall and painting of the first Headmaster
Examinations were in progress

Hall Foyer. The far side-side door is the passage to the Principal's Office. The portrait of the first Headmaster, Mr PJ Todd, can be seen on the wall above the main entrance doors.

The School Hall as photographed by Terri Murdoch-Coyle in November 2015. The Head Boy and Head Girl boards are maintained in good condition. Terri photographed the Head Girl board and may names will be found throughout this book -

featuring time and again during various reunions - often in countries worlds apart.

Old Head Boys and Girls - Sheldon Dudley 1978, Louis de Haas 1962, Sheena Bloom 1972, Rip Kirby 1966, Ina Moolman 1979 and Lex Edy 1986. Absent: Mark Templemore-Walters 1979.

Dirk Benade, in his Colours Blazer, with some previous head boys and girls who include Mark Templemore-Walters, Janet Lancaster Marchussen, Gideon Benade, Linda Turnbull and Yolanda Coetzee MacIntyre.

Head boys and Head girls :-

Head Boy and Head Girl - 1959 to 2015

1959 - Nigel Rowlands and Ann Torry

1960 - Nigel Rowlands and Nan Winter

1961 - Bev Davidge and Lynette Palmer and Janet Lancaster (Marchussen)

1962 - Louis de Haas and Megan Winter

1963 - Colin Paterson + Nigel McFarlane and Gwen Tapson

1964 – Brian Quail and Gwen Tapson McFarlane

1965 - Gideon Benade and Linda Turnbull

1966 David (Rip) Kirby and Linda Turnbull

1967 - Vivian (Viv) Grater and Vera Voster

1968 - Patrick Young and Penny Doyle and Colleen Roselt

1969 - William (Bill) Robb and Colleen Roselt

Thornhill High School

1970 - Bill Robb and Marilyn (Mimi) Squair (deputy was Dianne Baldwin)

1971 - Gerald May and Carol Friedrichs

1972 - Pierre d'Hotman and Sheena Bloom

1973 - Robert Wermuth and Heather McEwan

1974 - Murray Woodfield and Pam Davies

1975 – Simon Stilgoe and Susan (Sue) Laubscher

1976 - Rainer Theil and Jane White

1977 - Alan Hagemann and Diane (Di) J Voyce

1978 - Sheldon Dudley and Yolanda Coetzee MacIntyre

1979 - Mark Templemore-Walters and Ina Moolman

1980 - Alex Lex Edy and B Smith

1981 – Craig Holmes and Liz Forder + Vanessa Pfaff

1982 – Ted Burns + Alun Hart and Nicky Chamberlain

1983 – Iain Chamberlain and Janet Taylor (Janet Medland Udy)

1984 – R Maumbe and Florence Samkange

1985 – L Moyo and M Munger

1986 – E Shumba and E Demister

1987 - K Elwanger and L Mavhengere

1988 – W Chikoto and D Hungwe

1989 – J Rukani and E Hungwe

1990 – S Khan and F Sithole

1991 – M Ncube and S Wutete

1992 – A Chisadza and M Mpofu

1993 – T Masusela and T Mazhindu

1994 – S Chiruka and A Gwara

1995 – G Mutubuki and L Jawona

1996 – B Maitaso and R Dzvmbunu

1997 – S Ncube   and   V Tshuma

1998 – C Mharapara   and   V Munjanja

1999 – A Battey   and   M Mpalale

2000 – E Chabata   and   J Madhaka

2001 – B Paketh   and   W Chiota

2002 – M Moyo   and   L Size

2003 – T Shuro   and   P Mhunduru

2004 – K Mavetera   and   T Ndudzo

2005 – M Kadungvre   and   T Mapuranga

2006 – J Mudungwe   and   N Chisora

2007 - V Kurebwa;   2008 - L Morgan;   2009 - C Hollington

2010 - N Mpofu;   2011 - K King;   2012 - M Masviba

2013 - T Katai;   2014 - T Muzondo;   2015 - Zisengwe

Manicured green lawns between the Hall and classrooms, with the Girls hostel, Halton House, in the background

Eastern side of Halton House Girls Hostel. Now ring fenced - because Cranwell house boys used to scale the toilet down-pipes in the dead of night during the late 1950's early 1960's. One unfortunate Cranwell lad was disturbed with his pants down!

Science classroom

Thornhill High School

Western side of Cranwell House Boys Hostel

Smart uniforms in 2015

New courts - replaced the old courts that were located in the same area. Muti-function courts with netball floor demarcations as well

Net Ball and Basket Ball Courts beyond the Tennis Courts

Thornhill High School

Manicured lawns photographed by Terri in December 2015. Tracy O'Connor and Karen Johnson had also visited Thornhill High School a few weeks earlier.

Photo credit: Terri Murdoch-Coyle

Thornhill High School

Thornhill Marriages

Neville Baldwin married Dianne Palmer

Dirk Benade married Janet Newman

Eric Bradnick married Sheila Weber

Martin Byrne married Vanessa Calder

Andrew Davidge married Glenda Rice

Louis de Haas married Audrey Brown

Rod Dixon married Chris Lloyd

Rodney Drew married Lorna Culverwell

Prop Geldenhuys married Rina Malan

Brian Hayes married Maureen McIlroy

Rip Kirby married Maureen Cosh

Elan Marillier married Alison Stokes

Alan Marshall married Lynda Scully

Nigel McFarlane married Gwen Tapson

Dave McGraw (staff) married Jenny Chivers (staff)

Ian McKie married Cheryl Spencer

Chris Pluke (staff) married Kay Jackett (staff)

Dave Porter married Sarah Dudley

Wessel Strydom married Cecelia Seymore

Blackie Swart married Janet Peters

Malcolm (Zack) Thackray married Coleen Williams

Doodles Viljoen (staff) married Derris Bowyer (staff)

Chris Viljoen married Betty van der Merwe

Joe Ward married Carole Scully

Reunions

Thornhill family Debbie Finlay, Mr Bob Johnson and Karen Johnson celebrating a Christmas together

2003 - Forty Years On Reunion in Johannesburg

Frik Nel, Bev Davidge and Run-Rabbit-Run Louis de Haas

Previous Reunions

Charles Cowie, Gwenda McFarlane, Audrey Chandler 2003

The class of 1963 held a "Forty Years On" reunion

Ron Watkinson, Sudden Bekker and wife, Jan Nysschen, Bev Davidge 2003

The class of 1963 held a "Forty Years On" reunion in Johannesburg. The guests were: Audrey Chandler (nee Alan-Brown, ex de Haas), Bev Davidge, Louis de Haas, Nigel and Gwen McFarlane), Des van Rooyen, Charles Cowie, Ron Watkinson, Japie and Ernie Venter, Frans Malan, Philip Malan, and Louis Theron.

2003 Durban Reunion

On-board the Hakuna Matata in Durban harbour: Gwen (Tapson) and Nigel McFarlane, Phil and Elcora Malan, Frik Nel, Jan Nysschen, Rina and Preller Geldenhuys.

2005 Golden Jubilee - Bluff, Durban

Credit to Beverley Nelson) who maintains the Thornhill website and sends out the newsletters.

Previous Reunions

Hank van de Weg with Mike and Clive Phillips.

Hank giving his 'speech' at Brighton Beach in April 2005, where about 150 gathered to celebrate Thornhill's Golden Jubilee. Clive Phillips (if he is still alive), was a class mate of the author.

Preller Geldenhuys, Janet Lancaster, Alwyn Strauss, Rina Malan, Jan Nysschen and Sally Struckel

John and Helen Wightman with Preller and Rina Geldenhuys, celebrating 50 years.

The reunion was organised by Marilyn (Atkinson) Darné with the venue and braai facilities arranged by Neville Fromburg. Pots of good old sadza and gravy went down well. Walls were adorned with sports pictures and school events. Coffee and beer mugs with the school logo sold like hot cakes

Salt Rock Reunion - 2009

Joan van der Merwe took several photographs of the Salt Rock reunion - some names and faces were familiar, but most are new to many old boys and old girls.

Andrew Nieuwoudt, Ray Hewitt, Delise Joubert (Swift), Joan van der Merwe, AN Other Couple

Sharon Davis (Banwell), Sharon O'Bree, Julie Lake, Joan van der Merwe and Delise Joubert (Swift).

Previous Reunions

Not Salt Rock reunion, but a get-to-gether by Chris de Jong, Frik Nell and Ian Gordon at the Suncor Stadium in Brisbane in September 2009 at the Wallaby versus Springbok Test

Auckland Reunion - 2010

Rupert and Linda van Heerden, Neil and Sharon Walker Calder, Colin Craddock and Pamela Fountain Aranyos) at the re-union in Auckland in 2010.

Previous Reunions

The Shabani Girls in 2010
Reunion held in Centurion, organised by Kendel Nordin
Heather van der Riet, Joanne Naude), Gail McGowan), Tracey O'Connor, Fiona Nuttal-Smith, Enid Kruger Mayhew, Andrew Nieuwoudt and Cheryl Linda Boyce (Photo credit: Kendel Nordin)

Previous Reunions

2011 with Steve Prophet, Ray Hewitt, Mark Templemore-Walters, Paddy Kruger, Judy Brooke-Mee, Debbie Light Jenkins and Sharon O'Bree. (Photo credit: Kendel Nordin)

Heather Frew, Tracey O'Connor, Fiona Nuttal-Smith, Judy Brooke-Mee, Joan van der Merwe, Heather van der Riet, Sue Blignaut Steyn (Photo credit: Heather van der Riet)

2010 re-unions were also held in Australia (Perth) and UK (Derby).

Mark Marais, Ray Hewitt and William Adrian McDonagh in 2013

Previous Reunions

Another 2013 get-to-gether by Ian Dunbar, musician Bill Malkin and Stu Dunbar

Terri Murdoch-Coyle's Cape braai with Barry Keats of Guinea Fowl 1972, Yolanda MacIntyre, Sheryl Low, Bob Low and Peggy

Previous Reunions

Yolanda MacIntyre with Sheryl Low and Terri Murdoch-Coyle

Terri at her braai in the Cape, as a prelude to her trip to Zimbabwe coming up soon. She said "Ears must be burning all over the globe as they recollected their Thornhill / Halton House boarding days. Wished that Barbara Robertson Keats were there too as they had a great catch-up."

Terri Murdoch-Coyle meeting up with Annette McFarlane nee Moolman

Previous Reunions

Terri sharing her 42-year friendship with Yolanda

Yolanda MacIntyre meeting up again with her Head boy of 1978, Sheldon Dudley, who lives in Cape Town. 2015 has been a great year of reconnection for Yolanda.

Previous Reunions

Karen Johnson and Tracey O'Connor with Clare Thornton in Gweru. Enjoying Dutch Oven fare. Karen used to work there, and Clare presently has Gweru as her home town.

Helene Lombard meeting up with Sue and Rodney McNeill in December 2015

Previous Reunions

Paddy Kruger, Ted Lamb, Braam Kruger and Rhodes Bezuidenhout

Ex-Thornhill High School Rhodesian Light Infantry members at the RLI's 55th Birthday Parade to unveil a duplicate of 'The Trooper'. The original statue was cast from spent cartridge cases in 1978, now standing proudly in Bedford, UK

Delise Swift-Joubert meeting up with her old friend Dors who lives in Cape Town

Previous Reunions

Elaine Knott entertaining Helga Toland, Julie Bradnick Yeatman, Joan Gibhard and at the back, Ronella Hundermark Garrod

Karen Johnson at Saint Agnes in the UK with Mark Templemore-Walters, Derek Manning, Willey Swartz, Anna-Marie Lamprecht and Cheryll Linda Boyce

Previous Reunions

Sisters unite – Drikkie Robinson and Anna Bakkes van Druten, in Port Edward / Wild Coast Water Park during April 2016

Beth Murdoch with daughter Terri Murdoch-Coyle

2015 Diamond Jubilee Re-unions

London

Murray Woodfield arranged the first re-union on the banks of the Thames River at a charming pub called the Blue Anchor. There was a good turn-out with highly complimentary remarks concerning the organisation and desire for repetitions for future events.

Juliet Robey, Steven Brown, Doris Gaye (Robey), Murray Woodfield and Veronica Steffen

Helga Toland, Elaine Evans, Ian Dunbar and Joan Manning

Diamond Jubilee Celebrations

Patricia, Helga and Elaine Evans London 2015

Christine Gird, Malcolm Woodfield and John Manning

Diamond Jubilee Celebrations

Robey sisters - Juliet and Doris Gaye

Murray Woodfield with Janet Swart, nee Peters

Diamond Jubilee Celebrations

Helga Toland with Mary Anderson and Elaine Evans - Shrewsbury, UK, in December 2015.

Informal get-to-gethers are the way to go. More of them are the sign of the times.

Thornhill High School banners and signage were prominent at the Brisbane, Harare and Paeroa re-unions

Brisbane, Australia

The Brisbane celebrations were held at the Ship Inn on Saturday 25th July 2015. The venue, once a rowdy sailors drinking den has been transferred into a civilised Gastro Pub, and ideally suited as a venue to celebrate the event. Joe Ward is credited for the Thornhill poster photograph.

Sheila Maitland was the first to post two photographs on Facebook - celebrations with a luncheon and group photograph.

Joe Ward, Suzanne Hopkinson, Sheila Maitland, Tim Wade ,Vince Manning
Terri Murdoch-Coyle, Carole Ward, Merle Scully, Elmerie Wheeler Harley, Clare Watson Robinson, Maureen Maitland, Janet Cave, Anne Arnold, Willy Robinson

Joe Ward, Suzanne Hopkinson (Scully, Sheila Maitland, Tim Wade, Vince Manning. Front row: Terri Murdoch-Coyle, Carole Ward, Merle Scully, Elmerie Wheeler Harley, Clare Watson Robinson, Maureen Maitland Dancer, Janet Cave, Anne Arnold and Willy Robinson

Diamond Jubilee Celebrations

Collage by Terri Murdoch-Coyle that was posted on her Facebook page - and which went viral! The first two photos deserve enlarging, to illustrate a celebration in full swing.

Brisbane prompted Harare and Paeroa to produce the Diamond Jubilee sign

Diamond Jubilee Celebrations

Brisbane lunch-time

and Brisbane, night-time! Party time in full swing

Diamond Jubilee Celebrations

Carole Ward, Susanne Hopkinson and Terri Murdoch-Coyle

Perth, Australia

John Wightman was the organiser of the Perth event that was held at Zebras in East Freemantle, on 31st October 2015. John was the writers neighbour when we both lived in Married Quarters at Thornhill Air Force base. He is also a great supporter of Thornhill school re-unions - - with us making a point of catching up whenever we can.

Dave and Vanessa McBain 1970 -1973 (married 1978)

Diamond Jubilee Celebrations

Vanessa McBain reported that a lovely dinner celebration was had by a diverse group that were at the school over a period of twenty years in the 60s and 70s and were all able to share stories relating to teachers. Unfortunately, John Wightman wasn't able to join the gathering. He did report that eleven attended the dinner at Zebra's in Bicton near Freemantle.

They were Anne Booker, Allen Daniel and his wife, Jenny Green, Mark and Kathleen Hodgson, Bev Huntly, Vanessa McBain, Granville (John) Nicholson and Dawn Wood.

Jenny Green with her two sisters, Dawn Wood and Anne Booker

Clockwise, Vanessa McBain (in the blue dress), Bev Huntly, Jenny Green, Dawn Wood, Anne Booker, Kathleen and Mark Hodgson, Allen Daniel, his wife and Granville Nicholson

Diamond Jubilee Celebrations

Allen Daniel, his wife and Granville Nicholson

Vanessa McBain (1970-73) and Bev Huntly, having just finished their meal at Zebra's, Perth.

Harare, Zimbabwe

"*Message from Bev in New Zealand.*

"Greetings to everyone gathered together in Harare to celebrate the Diamond Jubilee of Thornhill School.

First, a huge vote of thanks to Ray, Tracey and their committee for taking on the huge job of organising this weekend of events, and keeping up their amazing enthusiasm and drive over the past few months. Hats (or rather, bashers) off to them!

At the beginning of the year, when I first floated the idea that maybe we should do something to celebrate this important anniversary, there was initially a distinct lack of response. Nobody seemed interested, and I thought the whole thing would come to nothing. Then, slowly but surely, people began to step forward and offer to get something organised in their neck of the woods, and what a pleasure it has been to watch all these gatherings mature and come to fruition.

I think we must all agree that we were extremely privileged to have the education that we were given at Thornhill, although we may not have been all that appreciative at the time! You'd struggle to find anything similar in the state sector anywhere these days, I'd say.

I'm sure you are all going to have a truly wonderful time, and that the reminiscences and stories will flow freely. If there are any really good ones, please send them to me for the newsletter!

I wish you all the best

May your Thorns be found only on roses, and may your Hills be the gentlest of slopes,

Per Spinas Ad Culmina!"

This celebration was organised by a team headed by Ray Hewitt with Tracey O'Connor. Tracey advised their attendees included the following:- Doug and Heather Anderson, Geoff Armand, Anna van Druten (Bakkes), Penny McDonald nee Doyle, Arlene Garner, Grant Nealon, Chris Collyer, Oscar Bekker; Alet Nortje Benade, Corlette Benade Dirk Benade and Janet Benade nee Newman; Ben (Kota) Benade; , Lyn Benade, Piet Benade, Tom Benade; Cheryl Boyce nee O'Connor and her husband Daryl; Heather Brown nee Frew and her husband Jeff; BJ Coetzee; Yolanda Coetzee; Debbie Collyer nee Plews and her husband Kim (ex-Chaplin); Chris Collyer and his wife Brenda (ex-Chaplin); Flo Coughlan (Manning) and her husband Tim; Michael Delport; Grant Evans and his wife Robyn; Cindy Frew and her partner Joseph Cable; Carol Fox; Richard and Carol Garlick; Dave Griffiths; Alan Hagemann; Jeff Hagemann; Ken Hagemann; Debbie and Alun

Hart; Ray Hewitt; Mark Houghton; Jenny Hunt; Karen Johnson; Caroline Armand Kelly; Shirley Kuttner (Nourse); Anna-Marie Lamprecht and her daughters Sharlene, Bianca and grandson Tristan; Denise Maclean nee Shillinglaw and her husband Hamish; Margaret Markham Jones; Linda Marais Johnstone; Nolene Kent; Jimmy and Kath Kinnear; Patty Knox Lamb; Bill Knox; Vince Lewis; Maurice Levy; Derek Manning; John Marais; Chinky Marillier; Paul Markham; Mike Martin; Janet Marchussen nee Lancaster and her husband Peter (ex-Guinea Fowl); Gavin McLeman; Alison Meyer; Jean (Martin) Milward; John Moore; Lynda Nel; Kendel Janson Nordin; Terri Murdoch; Frik Nell; Herman Nel; Graeme O'Connor and his wife Joyce; Tracey O'Connor and partner in crime Graham Galloway (ex Sinoia); Steve and Dana Prophet; Mike Stobart-Vallaro; Mark Templemore-Walters; Basil and Lyndie Rowlands; Mike and Robin Rust; Charlie and Viv Stewart, Lyn (Houghton) Steyn; Heather and Willie Swartz; Jan and Tammy Rust; Steve Theron; Elsie (Delport) van der Merwe; Pete van Drutten; Clare (Thornton) van Jaarsveldt; Rod Tapson; Linda Turnbull; Molly Wolfe and Ruth Riley Wolfe. The final count numbered 111 persons attended the Harare re-union.

Derek Manning, Heather, Tracey O'Connor, Graham, Ray Hewitt and Vince Manning in Harare 2015.

Diamond Jubilee Celebrations

Dirk Benade, Doug Anderson and Steve Theron

Welcome to Gweru (filler for a blank space)

Derek and Flo Manning

Diamond Jubilee Celebrations

Frik Nell, Dirk Benade, Peter and Janet Marchussen, Shirley Kuttner (Nourse)

Class of 1978 in Harare 2015

Anna-Marie Lamprecht, Denise Shillinglaw MacLean, Flo Manning, Yolanda MacIntyre, Lynn Houghton and Anna Bakkes van Druten

Diamond Jubilee Celebrations

Karen Johnson's school friends forever: Beejay Coetzee, Jean Millward, Cheryl Linda Boyce, Ben Benade, Vince Lewis, Karen Johnson, Willie Swartz, Kendel Nordin and Caroline Kelly Armand

Hamish Maclean, Beejay Coetzee, Grant Evans, Rob Rust and Mike Martin, Gavin McLeman, Willie Swartz, Ray Hewitt, Steve Prophet, Mark Templemore-Walters and Frik Nell

Diamond Jubilee Celebrations

Dana Prophet, Yolanda MacIntyre, Anna-Marie Lamprecht, Tracey O'Connor, Jean Millward, Janet Marchussen, Karen Johnson, Denise Shillinglaw MacLean and Shirley Kuttner.

Lynn Houghton and Anna Bakkes van Druten)

Diamond Jubilee Celebrations

Shirley Kuttner in her element

Shirley reported on the four-ball alliance golf game. The team led by Dirk Benade (the Headmaster) was called 3 Jacks and a Jill with the other two players being Basil Rowlands and Mike. The other winning team was Linda Turnbull's team, called "Three Gills and a Dickie". Neither girl knew about the team names.

Shirley got the "Ladies Longest Drive" prize.

Three Jacks and a Jill

Diamond Jubilee Celebrations

Frik Nell, Dirk Benade, Peter and Janet Marchussen, Shirley Kuttner

Christopher Robert, ex-Churchill + Chaplin, and Brenda Collyer, celebrated Thornhill's Diamond Jubilee. They married 1983

Sharlene Wood by Anna-Marie Lamprecht

Diamond Jubilee Celebrations

Ben and Colette Benade, Gavin McLeman, BJ Coetzee, Mark 'Frog' Templemore-Walters and Aletta Benade

Dirk Benade's colour blazer for Rugby and Cricket - which still fits!

Diamond Jubilee Celebrations

Peter and Janet Marchussen

Mark Templemore-Walters, Ben (Kota) Benade, BJ Coetzee and Ray Hewitt

Diamond Jubilee Celebrations

The Harare crowd enjoying the moment and interaction

Willie Swartz and Vince Lewis in Harare

Mini reunion with the McGrady's - Janet McGrady, Kevin McGrady, Yolanda MacIntyre, Margaret McGrady, Coleen McGrady and Brian McGrady

Diamond Jubilee Celebrations

The Johannesburg get-together in October 2015 was organised by Colleen (McGrady) Lonie, who was a Que Que girl, but came to Thornhill for her M's and A's, as they did back then. She and Yolanda MacIntyre have been friends since school days. Brian McGrady was the Headmaster of QQ Junior School, where his wife, Coleen also taught.

Sign of the Times

Impromptu THS reunion at a Retirement Village: Yolanda MacIntyre, Colleen McGrady, Wendy-Lee Weir, Robert Collins, Gavin Hensberg and Fiona Collins Keys

Karen Johnson and Denise Shillinglaw MacLean had plenty reason to smile during the various functions at Harare.

Denise Shillinglaw MacLean commented "Thanks and congratulations to the organising committee of the wonderful

Diamond Jubilee Celebrations

reunion held in Harare over the weekend. From the moment assembly began, presided over by 'headmaster' Dirk Benade, to the wonderful slideshow put together by Alan Hagemann, the amazing "Bob Johnson Band" featuring Steve, Vince, Grant, Ray and Karen and an impromptu concert by Beejay - I felt incredibly proud to be a past pupil of Thornhill High School. The fellowship and atmosphere certainly made it a day to remember always."

Tracey O'Connor's feedback newsletter reads as follows: "Our week of celebrating our great schools 60th Diamond Jubilee has come and gone. And what a week it turned out to be. We the committee are sure those that did not manage to "enjoy" with us have seen many of the photos, words etc that have appeared on the various sites. I would like to stress that I did not do this all alone and thanks should be given to Grant Evans, Ray Hewitt, Debbie Collyer (Plews), Heather Brown (Frew), Steve Prophet, Vinny Lewis, Karen Johnson, Cheryl O'Connor, Robyn Evans, Debbie's daughters, Brenda Collyer, Mrs Singleton and Gavin (hope no other special people have been forgotten here). All of these lovely peeps had a hand in somewhere along the line from February right through to Saturday 17th October!

I am sure most of you have heard by now about the Rock band regeneration! Yes we got some of the members, plus a few new ones together to entertain as it was at the "old " school socials way back in the 70s. It was a great achievement as they are spread over 2 continents – 3 countries! The band members each had their music sheets allocated to them and it can't be denied that they practiced their wee hearts out. On Wednesday prior to the Reunion Karen Johnson flew in from the UK and she was not given long to catch her breath as I took her to Ray's for a quick shower and freshen up period (and yes a glass of wine!). Instructions were to be at Grant's house for the 1st band practice together, minus 1. I was so proud of Karen, Ray Hewitt, Grant Evans and Vinny Lewis. Thursday and Friday were band practicing days – and Steve Prophet joined them, along with Gavin (Vinny right hand man) and this led to the birth of the Bob Johnson Band. I am sure that those that attended the Reunion can vouch that they were superb to say the least.

On Friday afternoon we had a mini warm up for the Saturday main event. Debs Collyer (Plews) had organized a fun golf game at Wingate Club. We ended up with 9 teams of 4, each team paying $120 to enter. She made a great effort in getting some fab prizes and got some players to also bring along some goodies. We raised $1 080.00 plus a bit on "extras" and decided that we would cover the costs for the players and the hangers on for their hamburger dinners – we served 60 burgers which was great – I am sure many saw the pictures on Facebook of the warm up! We had a start off figure in our kitty on the fundraising side. At this point I want to say a big Thank You to Debs for organizing the 1st day of festivities, a great way to start what was to turn out to be a fabulous weekend. The funny part was that we had a Sinoia pupil boasting how he took home 2 Thornhill girls that night!

And so came along Saturday, the long anticipated Big Day. Some of us had late night but were up with the birds to be at Borrowdale Brooke to get things rolling! Vinny arrived with the early birds to get band equipment set up, tables placed, decorations put up plus more! A run was made to buy the flowers, collect the cake and the last forgotten things – we had many ladies doing flowers, sticking the lanterns up, "60" curtains etc. And here a huge thank you to Debs (once again), Heather Brown (Frew), Cheryl Boyce (O'Connor), Robyn (Our Bob's) Evans, Cindy Collyer (Debs' daughter), Mrs Singleton (Grant's Mom in law), Brenda Collyer and Chris Collyer (Debs' in laws) – I hope I have not forgotten anyone and sorry if I have. Before we knew it we had people standing at the registration table – it was already 12pm! If I remember Yolanda was the 1st! The band was already set up and "in hiding" as we did not want our "guests" to know the surprise event! It was not long before there was a queue at the front desk, but Cheryll, Heather and Robyn were stars in getting money in, selling shirts and caps, getting name tag written etc.

We kicked off with a speech and introduction from our Committee Chairman, Ray Hewitt. He read our very special letter from Bev Nelson (yes Bev is the heart and soul of THS). After that Ray went on and introduced our Headmaster and Assembly started – as in a normal school day, just off cue! Dirk Benade was headmaster for the day and on taking the stage he separated the Hall! Yes boys to his right and girls to his left, juniors in front! We sang our attendance hymn and then Dirk behaved like a true headmaster! We held a minute silence for those departed and those that could not share this special occasion with us. He went on to de-heading some and announce new heads. Some were fined for bringing their drinks to assembly! We ended with the Lord's Prayer and our famous 'we going home hymn" – Lord Dismiss us. Lunch was

Diamond Jubilee Celebrations

served soon after and then the Bob Johnson Band was introduced to the World. And from there the party had started. We were lucky enough to have Guinea Fowl and Chaplin waiters there but their attention to detail in serving was not there! During a band break we went ahead with our auction and raffle ticket drawing – we had a table of goodies for this! And the list of thank you's is a long one – Grant Nealon, Janet and Pete Marchussen (yes huge cheer for a GF boy), Terri Murdoch-Coyle, Penny MacDonald, Rafe – Food lovers market, Ram Petroleum – Andrew Marchussen, Shirley Nourse Kuttner, Jan Nysschen, Piet Benade, Alan Hageman, Grant Evans, Ray Hewitt, Debs Collyer Plews, Graeme O'Connor, Vince Manning, Chris Collyer (Big up Chaplin!), Brenda Collyer, Kendal Jansen Nordin, Arlene Garner, Liz English, Margaret Markham Jones, Fraser Mackay, Prop Geldenhuys, and I am sure I have forgotten someone here!

The rugby had started as we finished this part of the day and no need to say that this was when most men disappeared and girls could now behave badly! The band once again entertained us – from hostel war cries to trips down memory lane – we all had fun! We decided then to have the only team competition for the day – a pop the balloon race. I really think no further explanation is needed here! The photos on Face Book say it all. Each house was given their respective colour balloons to inflate and with teams of 5 (could have even been 6!) the race began. Now being an upstanding Graham girl I have proof that Stanard did cheat and I hear now that maybe Howie did too! Howie won and was closely followed by Graham. At this stage if Stanard had not cheated they may still be at the Brooke trying to burst their balloons! It was also a huge change from "our" school years that Stanard came in last – in my years at THS they always won the Interhouse sports trophy.

The last to leave – as normal – the party was around 12.30! Yes someone had to pick up lost property. But not bad for a 12 hour party I say and I am sure many agree with me. This was not the end to the Jubilee fun – on Sunday some of us went out to BJ Coetzee for a braai and afternoon near the dam. This was a great relaxed day. And here I want to ask us all to be upstanding to Janet Marchussen (Lancaster) and Pete Marchussen, Frik Nell (that man with the double L) and Shirley Kuttner (Nourse) who joined in right from Friday through to Sunday. What a fantastic effort from some of our school seniors. Once again the photos are on Face Book for all to see.

Diamond Jubilee Celebrations

To wind up the weekend and can I say to tie ends up, a small group went to lunch at Fishmonger on Monday. Then another small farewell gathering at the Tin on Friday!

Over all we hope to have raised about $6300.00. We still have the wine to "auction" as well as some shirts and caps to sell. If there is anyone one out there that wants to purchase a shirt and/or a cap please contact me. The shirts are $20 plus postage and caps $15 plus postage. I have visited the various homes in Gweru and we have an idea how we will help them, mainly Bogies. They are wishing to modernize their lounge area and we as Thornhill folk, I am sure will be proud to know that we have assisted in this. We have also targeted a few oldies to assist. Once we have had our final meeting and we all agreed on the next step I will keep all informed. And as the improvements are being made and we get updates we will definitely keep all concerned informed. At this point the committee can say that if it was not for the big hearts of so many, this figure would not have been reached. We can't thank you all enough for your generosity.

Way back in February when Ray Hewitt approached me with the words – let's do a party here in Zim, our main target was to make it the flagship school celebration, the one that everyone would enjoy and go back and say what fun they had. Our committee was a hard working bunch – made up of day scholars and boarders! We all came up with great ideas and supported each other when some of us had doubt. Ray's main aim was to have 100 attendees – we went over that figure. We had folk attend from just down the road, some from South Africa, UK, Aussie and USA.

I turn this page over having learnt a lot about the tightness of our school. There was no holding back with the differences in age, it was as though we were all at THS the same time. And I am sure many feel the same. We renewed old friendships and many of us added to our THS families. I am sure many did not know that somewhere on the business front we were dealing with someone that went to Thornhill. Yes many "new" faces have come out the woodwork just here in Harare alone. Many have contacted us for the Wall of Remembrance – we have a few more names to add.

I was awarded Grant's prefects badge on Sunday with a request from some that I do this again in 5 years time! I want to thank you all for the great words posted and want to stress I did not do this on my own – I want to say thank you to Ray, Grant, Heather, Debbie,

Steve, Karen and Vinny, wow what a team of lovely people you all are. Love you all! See you at 40 Cork Road in 4 ½ years time!"

Tracey with husband Graeme O'Connor, Caroline Kelley Armand, Karean Johnson, Debbie Collyer and Clare Thornton

November 2015 Reunion and Celebration - by Terri

Terri Murdoch-Coyle Scott posted on Facebook "Have had an amazing first few days in Harare, Zimbabwe. Haven't been back to Zim since 1998 and haven't been in Harare for at least 25 years. The change since then is pretty dramatic in terms of general aesthetics and functionality. My initial reaction is that it looks very neglected. But after being here a few days I got to see that everything kinda works and that through all its cracks there is a beautiful light that shines through - through its people, through its natural geography and natural beauty".

Diamond Jubilee Celebrations

Anna Bakkes

Ian and Mini MacDonald (Ianthe Macdonald on Facebook)

Diamond Jubilee Celebrations

Phillipa and Mark van Deventer with Terri

Grant and Robyn Evans

Diamond Jubilee Celebrations

Gavin McLeman, Dana and Steve Prophet, Mark Templemore-Walters and Karen Johnson in Harare - 31 October 2015

Diamond Jubilee Celebrations

Avril Drew, Alison Perryman, Rhodes Bezuidenhout, Rowene Bowker, Les Johnston and Catherine Perryman

Paeroa, New Zealand

The New Zealand celebrations were held at Beulah in Paeroa - a place where memories are made. The property is a life-style block situated between Auckland and Tauranga (Bay of Plenty) and owned by Stu and Dee McColl.

For such a small town, half the size of Gweru, there is much on offer and must do's. The 3-day, week-end event, mid-October 2015, lived up to its reputation of a place where memories are made.

Beulah, Paeroa, New Zealand

Bev wrote: "Hello to everyone gathered together in Paeroa on 17 October 2015 to celebrate the Diamond Jubilee of Thornhill School. First, a huge thank you to Prop, who took on the task of organising this New Zealand get-together. I'm sure there will be many opportunities for everyone to renew old acquaintances and to meet get to know new friends. Those of us who are far from our home country all know how comfortable it is to be able to spend time with others who grew up in the same "potting soil", and who instantly know what we mean, without needing an explanation!

I'm sure this will be a memorable weekend, full of memories and stories of school days, and also time to reflect on how far we've come since then, and by what circuitous routes!

I have been privileged to watch the growth of the community of ex-Thornhillians (or, as some say, "Thornhooligans"!) for 25 years now.

It has been such a privilege to make contact with everyone, and I get particular joy when I hear stories of people connecting with old friends, sometimes not seen since school days. That's what it's all about!"

Diamond Jubilee Celebrations

An impromptu mini-reunion was held on 2nd September 2015 when Wallaby Vince Manning flew in to Kiwi All Black country to square up with Springbok Prop Geldenhuys. Having made his way to Paeroa earned Vince automatic Beulah Facebook group membership.

Black Rock, in the distance, is a feature of Beulah

Pamela Aranyos joined Delene McColl, who attended Chaplin, to make this mini-gathering with Vince. earn Diamond Jubilee celebration status. Dee and Stu McColl kindly opened their house for another very memorable Beulah happening.

A mini-reunion in Paeroa during September 2015, Pamela Aranyos), Vince Manning and Prop and Rina.

Diamond Jubilee Celebrations

Static display - The Thornhill display presentation was quickly made up to commemorate Vince's visit to Paeroa.

Total turnout at Beulah, in Paeroa, was 20. Left to right, from the top. Are: Steve Geach, Renene Geldenhuys Jelley, Stu McColl from Oriel, Lynette Nelson nee Jessop 1975 - 1978, Pamela Aranyos (Fountain) 1979 - 1984, May Craddock from Chaplin. Paul 1967 - 1977 and Linda Friedrich from Chaplin, Vince Manning, Rina Malan Geldenhuys 1959 -1963, 'Prop' Preller Geldenhuys 1958 - 1961, Shay Geach 1973 - 1976, Gordon 1968 - 1973 and

Diamond Jubilee Celebrations

Louise Collett, Grahame Jelley from Guinea Fowl 1972 - 1977 (attended Biology, Chemistry and Physics classes at Thornhill), Lynda and Dave Peebles 1970 - 1975, Colin Craddock 1966 - 1969, Dee McColl Chaplin and Jane Few with a record 15 years 1968 - 1983.

Prop and Vince, with Rina and Pamela 1979 - 1984

Paul and Linda Friedrich (nee Bleeker), from Thornhill and Chaplin respectively, live in Tauranga, New Zealand. They were the first to arrive, albeit only stopping briefly en-route to Auckland.

Diamond Jubilee Celebrations

The next couple to arrive were Colin 1966 - 1969 and May Craddock who had travelled the 650 kilometres / eight-hour journey from Wellington.

Colin and May Craddock's dedication made a big impact on the writer

All the way from Wellington - in Rhodee

The Craddock's were followed by Dave and Lynda Peebles

Diamond Jubilee Celebrations

Dave Peebles with Pamela Aranyos) and Colin Craddock

Dave 1970 - 1975 and Lynda Peebles from Auckland

Diamond Jubilee Celebrations

Louise Collett and Gordon brought Jane Few with then - from Auckland

Lynette Nelson with her two brothers, Peter and Phillip Jessop. 1975 - 1978. Lynette had driven up from Rotorua, all by herself. Her husband Dave being away, in South Africa, on business.

The Geaches from Auckland were the next to arrive.

Diamond Jubilee Celebrations

Steve and Shay Geach (Knoble) from Auckland

The Cake Competition

Tiny Paeroa was swamped by the Harare vote riggers in the Cake competition. Both birthday cakes were masterpieces - Jane Few baking the Paeroa cake and Aletha McDonald baking the Harare cake.

Paeroa and Harare birthday cakes

Diamond Jubilee Celebrations

Happy 60th birthday, Thornhill High School. Lynette Nelson doing the honours - the youngest and oldest Thornhillian represented

Rupert and Linda van Heerden are now in Auckland. Rupert's mother is visiting from South Africa, flew back home during the reunion. They visited Paeroa later for a mini-reunion

Karangahake Gorge situated between Paeroa and nearby Waihi offering cycling, tramping, gold mining, Tunnel and Windows Walk is a bucket list item when visiting the Coromandel in New Zealand.

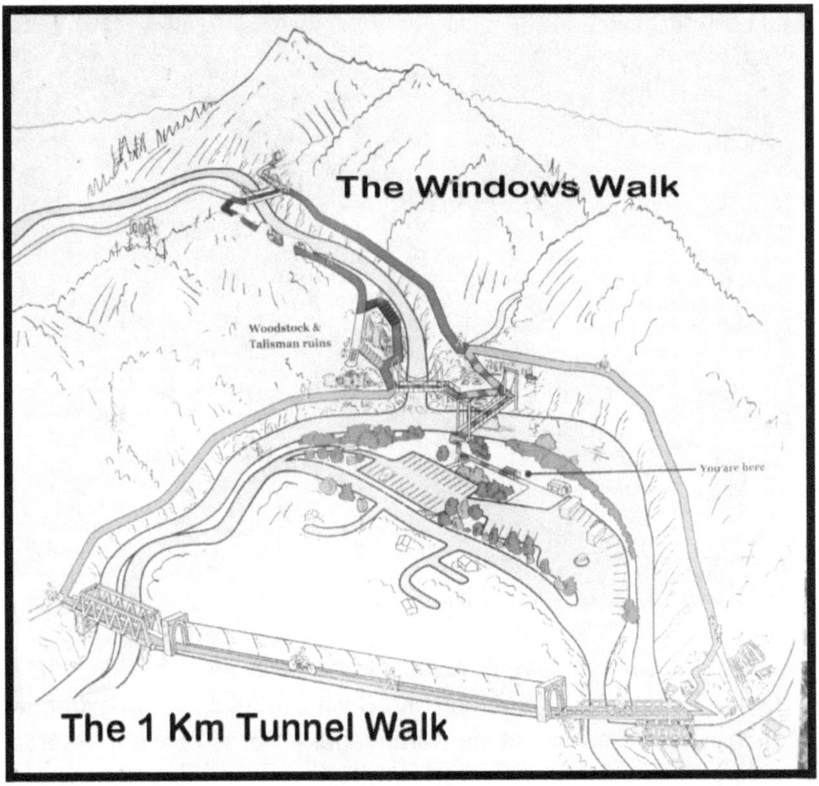

The Windows and Tunnel Walks diagram

Diamond Jubilee Celebrations

The Windows walk - old gold mining tunnels in the Karangahake Gorge, situated between Paeroa and Waihi in New Zealand

Gordon Collett, Dave Peebles, Grahame Jelley, Shay Geach, Lynda Peebles, Steve Geach and Colin Craddock at the extremity of the Windows Walk at the Karangahake Gorge between Paeroa and Waihi.

Diamond Jubilee Celebrations

Visit to the Paeroa museum - Prop Geldenhuys, Shay and Steve Geach, Lynette Nelson, Louise and Gordon Collett, Jane Few and Colin Craddock.

A toast to Bev Nelson (Matthews) to celebrate Thornhill's Diamond Jubilee - Louise Collett, Grahame Jelley, Lynda and Dave Peebles.

Diamond Jubilee Celebrations

A very special moment on top of Primrose Hill, with Jane Few reading the Roll of Honour of those Thornhillians that paid the supreme sacrifice during the Rhodesian War 1965 - 1980, so that we may live.

Bidding farewell is always a sad moment - for Gordon and Louise Collett and Jane Few. Grahame and Renene Jelley stayed behind to share more precious moments with Rina Malan Geldenhuys.

Diamond Jubilee Celebrations

Rina Malan Geldenhuys, Pamela Aranyos (Fountain), Dee McColl, Lynda and Dave Peebles

Paeroa, world famous in New Zealand for its L&P - Lemon and Paeroa drink, is now better known world wide.

Diamond Jubilee Celebrations

This noticeboard Thornhill Airbase, photographed by Karen Russel, generated quite a few comments by old pupils who joined the Joined the Air Force, or lived on Married Quarters.

Then and Now Chapter

This *"then and now"* photo gallery is for those who made contributions.

"Then and Now" photo gallery

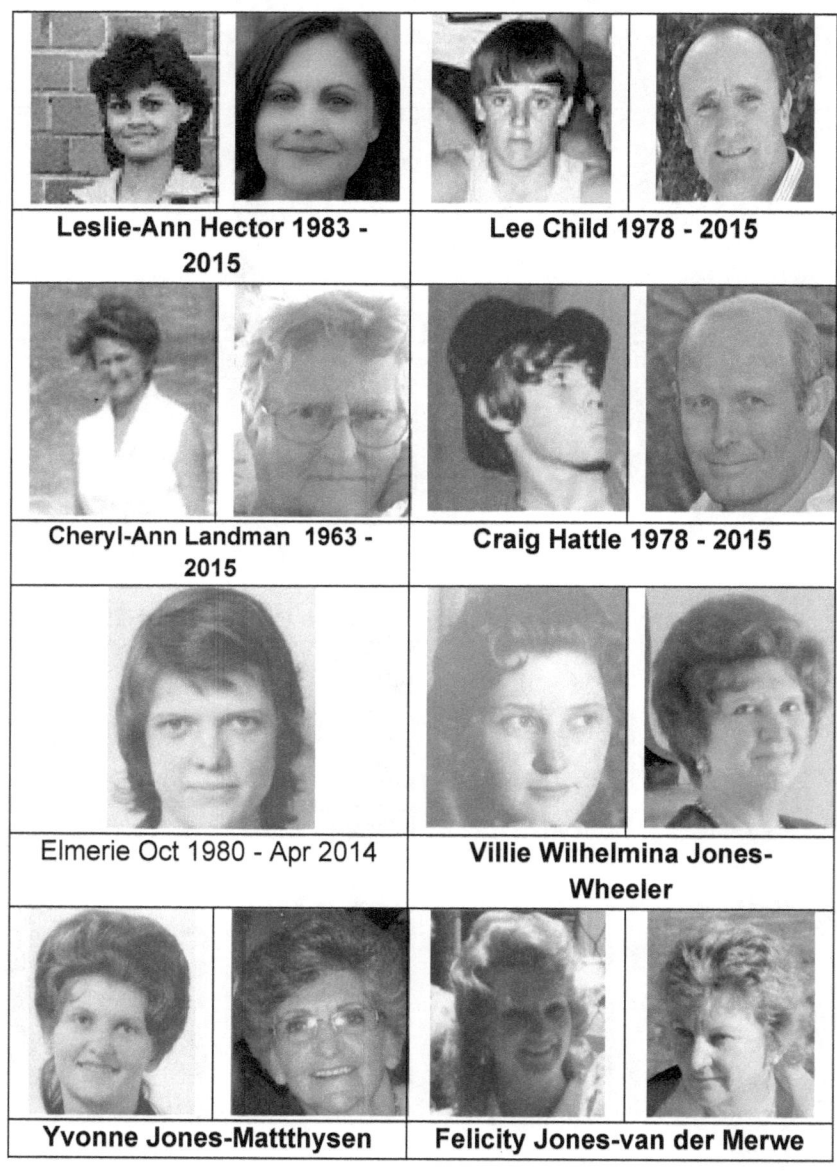

Leslie-Ann Hector 1983 - 2015	Lee Child 1978 - 2015
Cheryl-Ann Landman 1963 - 2015	Craig Hattle 1978 - 2015
Elmerie Oct 1980 - Apr 2014	Villie Wilhelmina Jones-Wheeler
Yvonne Jones-Mattthysen	Felicity Jones-van der Merwe

"Then and Now" photo gallery

Diamond Jubilee Celebrations

Diamond Jubilee Celebrations

"Then and Now" photo gallery

6th form class of 1970 :
Adele, Ann, Bean, Bev, Jim, Sue, Tom, Valerie

Adele (Carter) Koninis, Ann (Ashford) Gie, Jonathan Wilson, Bev (Matthews) Nelson) Bottom row: James Welsh, Sue (Marshall) Cunliffe), Tom Benade, Valerie (Hunt) Malcolm,

Diamond Jubilee Celebrations

"Then and Now" photo gallery

6th form class of 1970

Bill Robb (Head Boy), Carol (Friedrichs) Wilson, David Marshall and Di (Palmer) Baldwin. Bottom row: Mimi (Squair) Gillies (Head Girl), Liz English, Ray Stout and Rod Dixon.

A then and now for Hank van de Weg - sporting the school tie 60 years ago. No apologies are made for repeating the photographs because as a pioneer, Hank deserves to have the last word for this section.

Diamond Jubilee Celebrations

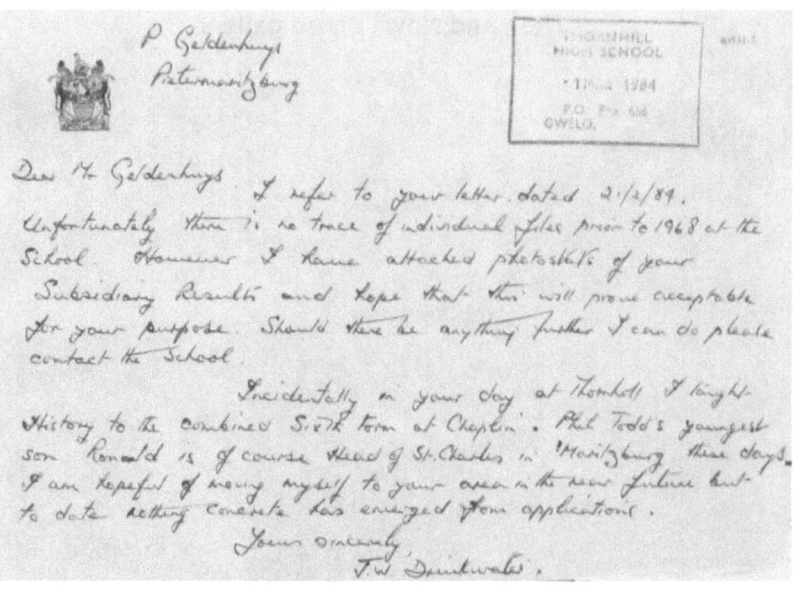

Headmaster Drinkwater was a lot more responsive in 1984, than Headmistress Muzondo in 2015.

Thornhill High School Magazine – Colour edition

Past Pupils and Staff of Thornhill High School

Editor's note: Some images and information is taken from Facebook. Apologies if there are any errors.

Beverley A'Bear (Paxton)*

Ina Aberdein (Wentzel) 1966-1970, born Gwelo and currently lives in Durban.

James Adam born 1954 is looking for 1969 - 1971 school photographs.

David Aimer 1965-1969

Tony Aimer

Bernard Alan-Brown from Bulawayo, Thornhill class of 1958 and now owner of BA Sound Studio Workshop in Durban. His has two daughters, Kirsty-Ann Leigh and Leisel Wild.

John Alexander

Donovan Alp 1966-1971

Geoff Alp, 1969-1974*

Sharon Allen (Kendal) is from Cape Town 1957, now returned where she is the Manager, Curves Women's Gym in Edge mead.

Bettie Amira (van der Poll)

Doug Anderson lives in Gwelo. He attended the Harare reunion.

Mary Anderson - see also Mary Riley. From Margate, studied at Pinetown Technical College and lives in Shrewsbury, Shropshire. Mary is from Margate, KwaZulu Natal, 1962.. Brother is John Frank Anderson.

Pamela (Fountain) Aranyos) 1979-1984 with her husband Nic are the co-owners of the Post Net stationery shop in Paeroa, New Zealand. She introduced the author to Margie Molloy.

Pamela arranged the Thornhill re-union that was held in Auckland in 2010).

Caroline Kelly Armand - married 2009, has two daughters, Amanda West and

Karen Taylor, and a son, Mark Armand.

Caroline met up with Vince Lewis by chance, sitting at the same table at a wedding.

Judy Armstrong (Marshall)

Anne Arnold attended the Brisbane celebrations. Married to Clive Arnold and they live in Toowoomba, Queensland, Australia. Works for or used to work for Globetrotters Travel Agency. Known as Anne Milward at school.

Zelda Arnott Owner operator at ZellyCo, Johannesburg. Has lived in Melbourne, Australia.

Elizabeth Ashby (Forder)

Tony Ashford

Nigel Ashby - 1977, born Gweru 1959, served in the Rhodesian Air Force, lives in Dublin, Ireland.

Denise Ashby left School mid-seventies, married Les Ashby in March 1979. They have three sons and live in Rathvilly, Ireland.

Chris with the Boxing Trophy - proudly displaying his blazer badge.

Chris Ashley was at Thornhill in 1973, came from Capetown and currently lives in Bristol, United Kingdom.

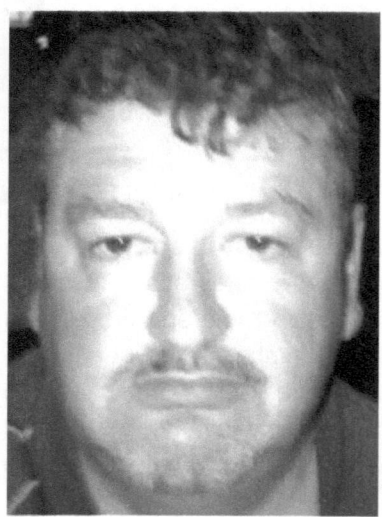

Doug Atkinson* 1975 - 1977, born 1963, lives in Stirling

John Avery born 1956, lives in Marondera and works at Nyambuya Services. He remarried in 2014 and has three daughters; Carla King, Dawn Lindsay Weare and Kerryn Townsend.

Anna Bakkes see Anna van Druten.

Hendrina Bakkes – see Drikkie Robinson

P Bakkes born Bulawayo 1952, played 1969 1st XV Rugby and 1st XI Cricket.

Cousin to Anna Bakkes van Druten)

Dianne Baldwin, born Gwelo and went to Thornhill High School from 1965 to 1970. Was known as Dianne Palmer. Dianne married Neville Baldwin.

Neville Baldwin 1963-1968, married Dianne Palmer.

Sheryl Baldwin (d'Hotman) born Gwelo 1953 lives in Mpumalanga. Sister of Pierre d'Hotman

Cindy Ball*

Gavin Ball features in a group photograph in front of Cranwell House, circa 1978.

Kathy Ballantyne friend of Valerie Malcolm, married Leo van Beurden, passed away 25 October 2013 after a lengthy illness.

Sue Ballantyne born 1967 and married 1989, friend of Sue Medland Udy.

Suzanne Bardouz (nee Robinson) attended Thornhill, class of 1975, and studied at Melton Mowbray CFE Class of 1885. From Newark Upon Trent, Nottingham, UK.

Tony Barlow 1958-1961

Alistair Barr

Gill Barr is from Gwelo and lives in Atikokan, Ontario. She recalls the rock cakes that she made under Mrs Alexander's

eagle eye (and part with, to her male classmates waiting outside)!

Eulalie Barry born Shurugwi 1967 and lives in Kadoma, Zimbabwe. She is the Manager at Spar. She played First Team Hockey in 1983 (together with her good friend Leslie-Ann Hector and Janet Medland Udy).

Her sister is Audrey Folkertsen Nieuwenhuizen, who also attended Thornhill.

Annette Barratt (Wickens)

Lee Bartlett, remembered by class mate Valerie Malcolm

Lauretta Basedow (Bothma)

Cynthia Bate (Frew) born 1954, younger sister to Adrienne, lives in Harare and has a son, Brendan Ross Bate and a daughter Candy Bate. Cindy Frew and partner Joseph Cable will celebrate Thornhill's Diamond Jubilee in Harare.

Judith Bates. - 1975, born 1958 and worked at Ariel School, Ruwa, Zimbabwe

Michael Bates - 1979. Born Perth 1964, played 2nd XV Rugby for Thornhill High School, helicopter engineer at Australian Helicopters since 2008, married Mary Davies 2010, and lives in Tolga, Queensland.

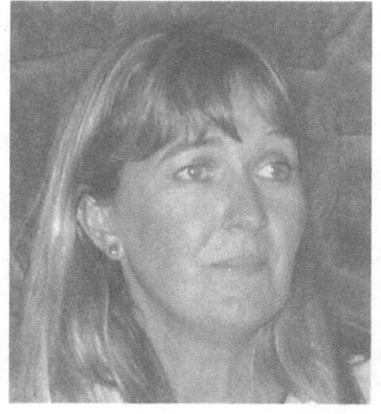

Jayne Bauwens (Weston), 1978-1982 - a very shy Facebook Thornhill friend.

Adrienne Baynham (Frew), born Selukwe 1952, elder sister to Cindy Bate (Frew), studied at Rhodes University and lives in Tzaneen, South Africa.

Pieter Beets

Oscar Bekker born Shabani 1954, married 2007, lives in Harare (younger brother to the late Sudden). Oscar has a daughter, Kym Tracey Mead. Oscar is expected at the October 2015 gathering.

Sudden Bekker (late) 1958 - 1961 was a class mate of the writer, warrants mention here as a memorial to younger brother Oscar.

Ben Benade (Kota) played 1979 1st XV Rugby. Ben and several Benade brothers attended the Harare celebrations in October 2015.

Dirk Benade. Photo taken from the Old Pupils and Staff website. Dirk was at school with the writer, and known for his ball skills playing first team rugby. He was only one of quite a few 'Benade's that went to Thornhill.

Janet Benade (Newman) - also attending Harare reunion

Piet Benade*

Tom Benade 1966-1970. One of the many Benades brothers. See the photos of the Harare reunion, 2015.

Carol Bennett , born Gweru, worked in real estate and lives in Whangarei, Northland, New Zealand.

Sue Bently (Armstrong), born Shabani, singer in the 1976 Choir, graduated Hon. B.A. Psychology at the University of Exeter in 1986, lives in Hilton, KwaZulu-Natal

Darlene Bentley (Naude) 1976 - also studied at Wits Technikon. Born 1963 and

married 2008. Lives in Oamaru, New Zealand and works at Radiology Receptionist at the Hospital.

Justin Berkowitz - 1971, born Enkeldoorn, travelled to Kenya in 2013, self employed in Middelburg, Mpumalanga.

David Berry

Truida Bester, born Gweru, went to Thornhill till 1962 and currently lives in Polokwane, South Africa. Her two brothers are Hermanus and Petrus Botha (her maiden name). Truida is also a cousin to the late Hennie Bakkes.

Ruth Bester is is from Johannesburg, self-employed in Jacksonville, Florida.

Bob Bester

Denise Beuke See Denise Norval.

Rhodes Bezuidenhout studied B,Comm Unisa. Formerley RLI and BSAP, worked at Ecotraining and now Shangani Trails.

Rhodes lives in Johannesburg and attended the Harare reunion and also the Dickie unveiling of the duplicate RLI 'The Trooper' statue.

Rebecca Bingham (staff - was Mrs Short) Facebook friend of Steve Prophet.

Mike Bischoff played 1979 1st XV Rugby. Possibly related to Marcelle Simmonds (Bischoff) 1969 - 1974?

Sue Black (Daynes) - 1959. Married and retired as the Accounts Supervisor at the Church of Jesus Christ of Latter Day Saints. Proud grandmother of Rhett and Courtney Annandale.

Ann Blanschard – see Ann Harbinson.

Hannes Blignaut (Johannes) features in a group photograph in front of Cranwell House, circa 1978.

Neels Blignaut* Neels has quite a few THS Facebook friends. He also features in a group photograph in front of Cranwell House, circa 1978.

Phyllida Bloom

Heather Blundell (Kerfoot)* - 1977. Born 1964, married Howard in 1984, graduated from the Open University 1999 and is the class teacher at the Elm Green Prep School, Chelmsford, UK.

Irene Boag

Anne Booker and her sisters Jenny Green and Dawn Wood attended the Perth reunion.

Atholl Boothroyd

Colin Boothroyd

Teresa Bos

Allan Bossert

Attie Botha 1960-1964). Born 1947 as Adrian Jacobus. Was a boarder at Cranwell House. Now doing the food and goodies supply to the old age homes as the Zimbabwe Pensioners Supporters Fund.

Beryl Venter Botha attended both Thornhill and Chaplin High Schools. She started working for Bata Shoe Company in 1968. Beryl is now divorced and and lives in Reading, England. Her brother Leon Botha worked with the writer at Masonite in Estcourt, KwaZulu Natal.

Colin Botha

Gill Boswell 1961 – 1966, born Selukwe. Studied Salisbury Polytechnic 1967 and worked at Appolo Blinds and law practice McCullough Robertson, Brisbane, Australia.

Judith Botha (Burden) Class of 1977, sister to Sheryl Burden. Her sister, Angelz Govender (Burden) also attended Thornhill, as did a third sister, Sheryl Burden.

Stacey Botha - See also Stacey Botha Lemmer, living in Klerksdorp.

Graham Bothma*

Heather Bower (Roselt)

Paul Bower*

Cheryl Linda Boyce - 1979, born Zvihavane, joined Customs on leaving School, moved to Datlabs as Shipping Manager till 1995, and then Freight Shipping Manager with Schenker International till 2003. Cheryl lives in Harare, married Daryl Boyce and have two sons, Damian and Logan. Her brother is Graeme O'Connor and sister Tracey O'Connor.

Eric Bradnick played in the

Thornhill Bands. He married Sheila Weber.

Annette Brand (Robb)*
Works at International School of Aberdeen.

Gail Bray (du Plessis) 1973. Born 1955 and lives in Auckland

Wendy Breakwell (Kerfoot) lived in Triangle, Zimbabwe and now lives in Seacroft, Leeds, United Kingdom.

Hank Bresler Class of 1962, studied Unisa and lives in Cape Town.

Herman Bresler nicknamed Mahalapye - possibly from Botswana.

Mike Brett

Pierre Briatte

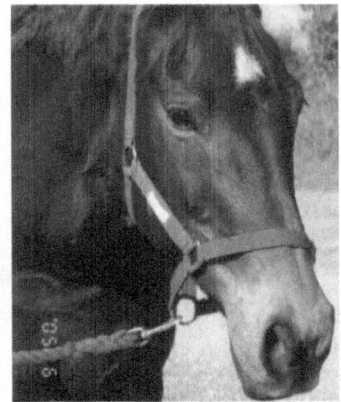

Judy Brightman 1976 attended Thornhill for one year only, 1976, from Kwekwe High

Kelvin Bruce circa 1965 - 66, played in the 1985 U-15 Rugby Team. Lived in El Salvador in 2011.

Bruce Brislin writes: It is something that you can never forget, that first day at a new school. For me arriving at Thornhill was something to be happy about, I had been sent to Guinea Fowl to begin with and had hated it, but the moment my parents saw the old prefab RAF barracks in which I was to be housed, the one for the first years with its broken window and shabby paint work, they decided to send me to Thornhill instead. It was about two weeks before the move was made, two weeks that seemed to last forever but then it happened. I found myself in the junior dormitory at Thornhill. I was given the one remaining bed, that next to the prefect, Noel 'Charlie' Bannell. When I say 'bed' people should understand that our beds were probably less comfortable than those found in most prisons. They were made of angle iron and tubing. The mattresses were coir filled and some bore stains from use by someone who must have had a weak bladder. For some reason it was bottom of the list of desirable bed sites, even lower down the list than the one beside the sock-box at the door.

From then on it was a matter of sorting where in the pecking order I stood; new-boys were always subject to some kind of scrutiny and 'test' but despite the fact that my sister Isla was in the other hostel with the girls, it did help that she had already been there for a year. As in most schools bullying did occur and the first years bore most of it but it did us little harm as far as I am aware. After all, we were Rhodesians. There were also strange protocols to observe, (standing orders in military terms); rigid meal times and the queueing for them. Then the grace and as the most junior of juniors, a duty to fetch the main course Mrs Corkery had devised for the evening meal within the constraints that the tight budget that had been imposed upon her. Those constraints had also apparently destroyed any culinary flair she might once have had. In essence her food was plain, overcooked and awful; watery stews, brown cabbage, tripe on occasions or other offal and seldom fish. There never seemed to be enough of it either, the seniors always had first shot at any left-over's and the head of each table made damn sure that the juniors down at the bottom received the smallest servings in the first place. She was a sour woman too, never a friend to any of the eighty boys whose meals she and her crew prepared and was apparently impervious to criticism. For my whole time at the school I cannot say she ever produced a meal that I would have said was passable. Still, we were all in the same boat and complaining was a waste of energy. Despite this we all somehow survived so it couldn't have been so terrible.

My two weeks at Guinea Fowl had been far more demanding and pressured regarding schoolwork, but the more laid back attitude at Thornhill was far easier to live with, and I liked it. As in every field there were good teachers who could hold your interest and others who merely presented the course-work and expected you to make of it whatever you could.

Really notable teachers included Audrey Gudath, a powerfully built woman who had already had a bit of a career in the police force behind her. She was something of a martinet but also had a sense of humour which applied even to herself. On one occasion, someone in the class had drifted off in a daydream, a foolish thing to do in Miss Gudath's class. She took the blackboard duster and with a throw that would have made a fielder on a cricket pitch proud, hurled it at the miscreant but missed, and instead it struck my good friend Phil Malan on the arm of his brand new blazer depositing a splurge of chalk onto it. Philip glanced at her with theatrical distain, removed a pocket blazer-brush and without a word, dusted off the chalk dust. His histrionics had the class in suppressed fits until Miss Gudath too burst out laughing. I think it was on that day that most of us realised what a fine and dedicated teacher she really was. Despite this I still failed Latin and it wasn't for want of any effort on her behalf.

Another great teacher who loved his subject was Mr Berry, the English teacher – not to be confused with the science teacher, Berry-Cook. Mr Berry once put on a play, 'The Monkey's Paw,' and was so pleased with the way we all performed that he shared out a pack of Benson and Hedges Cocktail cigarettes with all who had been involved – against all the rules of course, but it earned him the affection of us all. The other man I mentioned, Berry-Cook, fell out with the entire Cranwell House on his first day of duty when he picked on Barnie Olivier for some very minor misdemeanour whilst we were queueing to go into supper and knocked him to the floor. Barney was a polio victim, as thin as a rake and with the longest legs one could imagine, a likeable and harmless lad who never grumbled about his affliction. There were some darker repercussions to this and Berry-Cook didn't last too long as a teacher in our school.

I boarded at Thornhill for all my secondary schooling though for the last year the classes were held at Chaplin to which we were bussed my Mr Rowlands daily. I cannot say that at the time I enjoyed my school years much but they did me quite a bit of good and I do have many happy memories from those times. I was there between 1959 and 1963 and made many good friends. I have made contact with several of them in later life, some after almost half a century. Sadly some have now passed on but that happens to all of us so it has to be expected. We all shared a lot though, so however badly or well we have fared since, there was a time when we lived a life together very much as equals and it is those times that I, for one, still value.

Now I watch my grandchildren growing up in a highly competitive and changing world with more than a little pride. Their time is still to come and it will be a different time to the one that I have enjoyed so much. I think my time was a lot easier than the one that they will have to face. We have to let them go, however; to run free and do their best, as we were left. They will make mistakes but they will also have to make their World as close to what they would like it to be as we have tried to do for ours. They have a hill to climb and there will be thorns along the way – but there will also be delightful shady groves; just like the hill we had to climb.

Isla Prince Brislin. Yanchep, northern suburbs of Perth.

Leigh Bristow born Bulawayo 1960, lives in Louis Trichardt and is the Managing Director at Sumbandia Scholarship Trust. She was missed by her good friend Terri Murdoch-Coyle at the Brisbane jubilee celebrations.

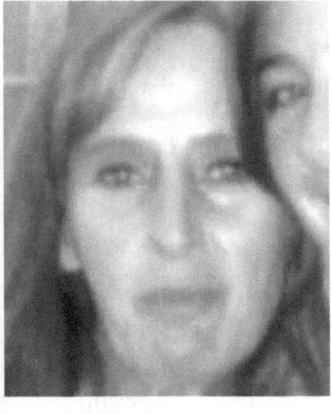

Michelle Bronkhorst studied at Ilsa College, Harare and lives in Kariba.

Judith Rautenbach Broodryk's sporting prowess at School has continued to make her a pretty good Bowls player. She presently lives in Gauteng, retired, and has had two sons, Andre and Louis.

Judy met up with Lynn Fortman, (Howden) while playing bowls at the Brakenhurst Bowling Club. Having first met at Thornhill, what a lovely 'diamond jubilee celebration' the two ladies must have had. Judy posted the chance meeting on Facebook, mentioning that she (Judy) was the Victrix Ludorum and Lynn won the Novice Single for 2015.

Judy Brooke-Mee studied at the University of Zimbabwe, lives in Benoni, Gauteng, South Africa.

Heather Frew Brown, born in 1959 and graduated from Thornhill in 1974. Was very good friends of Terri Murdoch-Coyle of Brisbane, who she is hoping to meet up with again at the Harare celebrations in October. Heather works for Cycle Tech in Harare.

Lesley Brown (Clarke)

Steven Brown 1963. Steven played 2nd XV Rugby for Thornhill High School. He attended the London celebrations. He was photographed with Gaye (Robey), Murray Woodfield and Veronica Steffen.

Kelley Bruce 1965 - 1969

Anne Buckley Venables lives in Johannesburg and still maintains her friendship with several Thornhill old-boys and old-girls

Gwen Bryan (Car) 1973 - 1977.

Lesley Brown (Clarke) born Bulawayo, has a daughter Emma Brown and lives in Hastings, Sussex, UK.

Eric Budd lives in Logan, Utah, USA.

Kim Budke (Griffiths) lives in Johannesburg. She attended the Harare 2010 reunion. Her sisters Sandy and Debra Griffiths also attended Thornhill.

Sherryl Burden is a third sister that attended Thornhill High School.

Dean Burns features in a group photograph in front of Cranwell House, circa 1978.

Gary Burns from Shurugwi attended Thornhill and

Westering High School in Port Elizabeth, South Africa. Lives in London, UK.

Tod Burns played 2nd XV Rugby for Thornhill High School

Neil Burton

Helena Burton - sister to Caroline Kelly Armand

Anneline Bushell played 1979 Hockey. Born Kadoma 1962, lives in Gaborone, Botswana. She has some good THS golden oldies.

Jennifer Bushell played 1st Team Hockey in 1960.

Juanita Maria Bushnell, Class of 1978. Lives in Portsmouth, United Kingdom.

Mark Button

Leslie-Ann Butts - see Leslie-Ann Hector

Piet Buys born Gatooma sang in the 1976 School Choir lives in Pretoria. Also known at school as Petrus. Brother to Berta Maritz).

Cathy Byrne (Budd)

Craig Byrne from Gweru, played in the 1978 Thornhill Brass Band, lives in Port Elizabeth, South Africa.

Terry Byrne

Neil Calder has given his apologies. He and his family are going on holiday to SA during October and will be attending his parents 50th Wedding Anniversary.

Neil attended THS from 1980 until he left and moved to Estcourt Natal. He played in the School band and enjoyed playing rugby for U-13. While in Estcourt he completed his schooling and then worked for Masonite Africa Ltd.

Neil has been in Auckland since 2000. He and his wife Sharon attended the October 2010 reunion in Auckland (also attended by Pamela Aranyos (Fountain)).

Neil and Sharon at the Auckland Maritime Museum.

Neil is currently employed by Frucor Beverages as their Maintenance Manager. He is married to Sharon Walker and they have a son Bailey and a daughter Samantha.

Sally Callaghan (Struckel) 1957 - 1959 is a regular contributor to to Thornhill affairs. Like Hank van de Weg, Sally is a pioneer of the 'old school' and has contributed several photographs of classrooms at the Royal Rhodesian Air Force Base.

Derrick Calvert - 1974. Born Papakura, New Zealand 1965 and currently lives in Auckland.

Norman and Titch Cape, brothers.

Alfred Carinus* 1973 - 1977, lives in Sydney, divorced, and self-employed since 2014. He is brother to Kaz Carinus Botha Nobel who is in Botswana.

Nigel Carter born Gwelo, married in 1974, worked for Air Rhodesia and now lives in Bury St Edmunds, UK.

Terry Case*

Fernando Cavalheiro

Rob Celliers.

Debbie Carter (Collett) left Thornhill in 1974 and lives in Durban

Iain Chamberlain played 1st XV Rugby for Thornhill High School. Born 1963 and living in Klerksdorp, South Africa, Iain remains a sportsman of note - cycling, running, canoeing, motor-cycling and likely several other pursuits not mentioned.

Mrs EM Chamberlain, History teacher fondly recalled by numerous Thornhill pupils.

Audrey Chandler Also known as Audrey Anne Alan-Brown, I married Louis de Haas 1966, and then married Robin Chandler in 1981 (now deceased, 2012).

We had Kerrin married to Mike Begg in 1994 - 4 sons: Matthew 17, Adam 15, Daniel 11, Timothy 8; and then Roualeyn married and now divorced in Charleston, South Carolina - 1 son: Elliot 6.

My life has been described by people from 'all walks' as the equivalent to at least three of the 'average' person! 'Varied', 'interesting', 'different' and 'full' would probably be a good heading!

Louis and I lived in Gwelo, Que Que and Salisbury, and had two great kids. A fantastic father, Louis was very hands-on. Louis went on to marry Steph around 1977, and I immigrated to South Africa, Johannesburg, at the end of 1978. I re-married in 1981, to Robin Chandler who had two children Philip and Adrienne. First living in Johannesburg for a couple of years then moved to Denyesville in the Free State, my children who were then 9 and 6 went to the local Afrikaans medium laer skool until we re-located to Cape Town in 1983.

Kerrin graduated with an MBCHB and went on to specialise in Family and Community (Public) Health and Hospital Administration and Economics all together!! This, while pregnant and aged 26, as well as running the False Bay Hospital as Superintendant and manning the Obstetrics and Childcare area of the hospital as there was no maternity section as such. She then went on to run the Southern Cross Hospital, The Groote Schuur Private Hospital briefly before finally running the Christiaan Barnard Memorial Hospital. With four sons by this time she moved on to consultancy in various fields including lecturing a module to 4th year med students at UCT.

Roualeyn graduated with a Business Degree as well as running his Executive Travel Guiding company (having begun it at school and developing it whilst studying) and gave in to the wanderlust immediately thereafter by travelling to the UK and USA. Disaster struck two days from returning home. Both Kerrin and I brought him home from the Spinal Unit in Albany, New York State, with a C6 spinal injury, on a stretcher, bagged and tubed, completely paralysed! Guess what... the pioneering spirit that runs through 'Rhodesian's' veins didn't stop him from an 85% recovery and he continued his business from his hospital bed then recovery time to go on and meet and marry an American client! Hence his living the the USA and now the senior Sales Executive for the South Carolina Aquarium.

I have had an interesting working life (considering I walked out of school at age 15, being the feisty anti-establishment, independent girl I was) ...mostly in the secretarial field until 1983 and run all sorts of offices...from building supplies to psychology practice to eventually becoming a residential consultant and commercial broker in the Realty world which is where I currently work 8 days a week (if you know the Real Estate industry!).

My home is an apartment in Wynberg, Cape Town and my office is about 2kms away! Social life is interesting. I do anything and everything (at least once) and thoroughly enjoy 'growing up' with my awesome grandsons. They entertain me with their cricket/rowing/hip-hop/music/academic prowess with Western Province and invitation team overseas touring thrown into the bag plus other interesting escapades of rock climbing/birding type interests.

I have been very fortunate to have travelled fairly extensively around Europe, Thailand, Singapore, Hong Kong, United Kingdom and Ireland, USA most states with highlights of a shuttle launch at Cape Canaveral and the John F Kennedy Space Station and very interesting exploration of Santa Fe New Mexico to name a few, as well as South America including Brazil, Peru, Bolivia, Chile, Argentina with the highlight of a trip down the Amazon on a 'boat' (of sorts!) with a peruvian manning one outboard motor and non-English-speaking, to a jungle village where we did alligator hunting at night in said boat with an equatorial thunder storm brewing overhead...scary to say the least! I have to add that the 'hunting' was not killing...merely catching and handling then returning to the swirling waters of the Rio Negro (on which side of the jungle we were camped!). Also lucky to have visited Canada, Mexico,

Jamaica and Cuba. Life is a tapestry – we do or don't weave it!

Her Facebook page features one of the Thornhill Gilbert and Sullivan's musical choir photographs, very rarely seen.

Lee Child* 1978 - 1982, born 1965 and lives in Cape Town where he worked at Qorus Software. He played 1st XV Rugby for Thornhill High School. Lee is married to Lyndsay and they have four sons, Aiden, Jordan, Malachie Lee and Ryan.

Jean Clarke (Hudgeson)

Georgina Cloete, born 1952, lives in Bulawayo. Sister to Paddy and Braam Kruger.

Rob Cloete - 1982, born Richards Bay 1965, lives in Durban. Rob has two brothers, Clutz and Steve Cloete.

Steve Cloete born 1954, Head of Cranwell House in 1973, studied at Durban Tech, worked at Iilovo Sgar and lives in Dwangwa, Nkhotakota, Malawi. Elder brother to Rob who also attended Thornhill.

Pauline Cochrane (Nelson)

Beejay Coetzee has stacks of Facebook friends. He has made a major impact at Thornhill, and continues to be a staunch supporter in Harare.

Ursula Cole (Beets)

Tim Coleman

Eduardo Gomes Coelho lived in Zvishavane in 1979 and works at Vetzone.

Ondina Codeco (Oliviera)

Gordon Collett is not on Facebook. He lives in Auckland, and together with his wife Louise (whose picture is shown) attended the Paeroa reunion. They have two sons, Keenan and Warwick.

Fiona Collins Keys lives in Johannesburg

Rob Collins, born 1960, played 1st XV Rugby in 1978, studied at the University of Natal, Durban and lives in Johannesburg, working at Bytes Specialised Solutions.

Robert played golf at the Umhlali Country Club with the rest of the Thornhill team.

Debbie Collyer (Plews) born 1963, is self-employed and lives in Harare. Debbie is part of the Harare organising team for the Zimbabwe Diamond Jubilee celebrations. Debbie has two daughters, Cindy Leigh and Linda Collyer.

'Such a very happy lot' - Tracey O'Connor with Debbie Collyer at Darwendale Dam in the Norton Area, Zimbabwe

Karen Compton (Boag) has two children, a boy and girl, and is the owner of KC Property, a real estate at Lanbert, United Kingdom.

Sandy Connolly (Smith) 1970 - 1973 had hoped to make the Paeroa reunion but gave early apologies when pressure of work made a long trip from the South Island inadvisable. Sandy was married to Charles, who sadly succumbed to cancer.

Christeen Cooke (staff)

George Cooke

George Coppen (staff) is from Edinburgh, UK, studied at University of Cape Town, graduating in 1965. He taught Geography and History at Thornhill during 1967 to 1979. He is now retired and lives in Inverness, United Kingdom. He sent the following good wishes from Scotland:
"I hope the Diamond Jubilee Celebrations go well - do give my fondest greetings to the NZ contingent and thanks to them for some great memories"

Ed Cornish 1966 - 1971, born Selukwe 1952, married 1979 and lives in Plymouth where he is the Head Gardner at Crylla Valley Cottages, Cornwall.

Rob Cornwell features in a group photograph in front of Cranwell House, circa 1978.

Tracey Cosgrove from Gwelo, also attended Chaplin, studied at Rand Afrikaans University RAU 1998 Dip.FMI and lives in Cape Town.

Steve Coster*

Flo Coughlan (Manning) is married to Tim, they live in Harare and are expected at the Zimbabwe reunion in October 2015.

Terri Murdoch-Coyle posted on Facebook -

I have had the most amazing three days in Brisbane with a really special gal - Sheila Maitland. She has managed to show me the length and breadth of Brisbane and squeeze in a school reunion! Plus we have had time to recall many of our high school year's experiences (not always with synchronized accuracy) and drink copious bottles of great Merlot. Many ears must have been burning!!! I love this gal sooooo much!!! Our only regret is that our 'gang' from Thornhill days weren't all here to share this with us. We missed you Yolanda MacIntyre, Leigh Bristow, Wendy-Lee Weir, and Dawn Midgley! But there's always a next time.

Chas Cowie was spotted at the London celebrations, with Rick Owen (Chas was with his partner, Marilyn Darling). Chas studied at Unisa and lives in Dorking, United Kingdom.

Tuxcia Cowley (Hadzigrigoriou) - Tuxcia Taxiarhia, former social worker at Cumbria County Council.

Molly Cox (McGowan) played hockey for the U/15 Team in 1958 - that was captained by Sally (Struckel) Callaghan.

Colin Craddock 'Tojo' 1966 - 1969, a boarder, hail from Wellington. He is married to a Chaplin girl, May Bright, and they have booked their attendance for the Paeroa celebrations.

Terri Crow (Budd) 1966 - 1970, from Gweru, studied Business and Accounting at Commercial Careers College, married 1971 and has four children; Alan, Darryn and Craig Crow and a daughter Paula Lee. Terri is the Human Resources Administrative Officer at the University of Utah and lives in Salt Lake City, Utah.

Sue Cunliffe (Marshall) 1966 - 1970. See also the 6th Form photo in the 'Then and Now' chapter.

Wendy Cunliffe Facebook friends with Steve Prophet, Carole Ward and Terri Murdoch-Coyle. Lives in Harare.

Deidre Cusak (Finch)

Tracy da Fonseca (Fernandes) from and lives in Harare. Studied at Gweru Polytechnic.

Maureen Dancer attended the Teachers Training College in Bulawayo after finishing at Thornhill. She attended the Brisbane re-union.

Allen Daniel studied Engineering at Bulawayo Technical College and lives in Perth Australia. He attended the October 2015 Diamond Jubilee celebration in Perth.

Ian Daniel* served British South Africa Police BSAP 1972 - 1980, left for Perth, Australia 1981 and lives on the Gold Coast.

Noreen Daniel

Sally Danse (Swaine) 1960 - 1963. Born Gwelo, now widowed. Brother is Roger Swaine.

Marilyn Darné (Atkinson) 1967 - 1969 is from Durban and lives in Durban. She married Marco Darné in 1974.

Gary Davel 1977 - 1983

Andrew Davidge was at Thornhill from 1960 to 1964, following the footsteps of his elder brother Bev. Andrew married Glenda Rice and they now live in Umkomaas, KZN Natal.

Glenda secretly sent the 'then and now' superb photos to the writer, who trusts that Andy's grandchildren will appreciate this record long after he (Andrew) pushes up daisies. The photos do reveal exceptional achievements - the much sought after Thornhill High School Colours blazer - and a magnificent Trophy award.

Bev Davidge graduated from the University College of Rhodesia and Nyasaland - UCRN - and has studied at the University of Natal. He lives in Hilton, Pietermaritzburg and is the Curator and Archivist at Hilton College and HOD History at Umtali Boys High.

Paul Davidson is from East London and lives in Ga-Mokopane, Limpopo, South Africa. Paul played in the 1978 Brass Band.

Colin L Davies* 1967 - 1971, from Cheltenham, Gloucestershire, lives in Christchurch, New Zealand.

John Neal Davies - 1970. From Wincanton, married Melaney Casper Davies and lives in George, Western Cape. Elder brother of Colin.

Sharon Davis (Banwell) born 1962 Kadoma, Zimbabwe, married 2009 and lives in Centurion, Gauteng. She attended the 2009 Salt Rock reunion

Geoff Day (staff), the Arts Teacher, was responsible for designing the first Thornhill High School magazine covers and also sketched the Library which featured in the early volumes.

Tracy da Fonseca (Fernandes) - 1984, studied at Gwelo Polytecnic and works in Harare. Facebook friends with Wayne Fernandes.

Louis de Haas will be remembered for being swift of foot, holding several athletic records for a number of years in the 100 and 220 yard heats. Louis married his school sweetheart Audrey Brown, had two talented children and then dissolved the marriage. Both remarried - with Louis now living in Cape Town with his lovely lady Diane while Audrey's partner relocated to Britain where he died shortly thereafter.

Sorry about the long time delay in replying to your face book request re- my sprint times. It all started in 1957 at Old Thornhill when I was 14 years and 4 months and ran the 100 yards in 10.4 secs, also won the 220 yds, long jump, 440 yds and relay and became middle Victor Ludorum plus won a silver spoon for the top athlete of the day. I repeated this in 1958 in the same age group. In 1959 I was by then considered a senior. On the Thursday before the athletics meeting, we had a final training session and I ran a timed 9.9 sec 100yds but could not do that at the meeting on the Saturday, but managed a 10.0 sec for the 100, won the 220, 440, long jump and the Senior Victor Ludorum.

You may recall I then left school but returned 18 months later and joined you when you were head of Cranwell. In 1962 I again won the Senior Victor Ludorum, and in that year I followed you as head of Cranwell and also School Head boy. I remember the times we went to the farm for the day with the girls in your little Morris Minor and how we had to beg Miss Lamport to let the girls out in our care as "well-respected" seniors of the school.

We have sent photos of the 1958 1st XV and 1962 farewell ceremony to Mr P.J. Todd under separate cover. The photos attached here are me with the Victor Ludorum 1957, taken by Pieter Burger, and the start of the 440, I think in 1958.

Louis's younger brother Karel also attended Thornhill as a boarder. Karel became a talented rugby player.

Nick de Klerk

Yvonne de Kock (van Niekerk), born 1952 in the City of Sunderland, UK, currently lives in Johannesburg, SA.

Gaille de Swardt (Ashby)

Christopher Dee class of 1960 – 1964.

Denise Deetlefs (Coetzee)

John Deetlefs

Lin Dell from Zvishavane, married since 1985, lives in Bulawayo and is the owner at Book and Bean.

Mark Denton features in a group photograph in front of Cranwell House, circa 1978.

Elsie Delport (van der Merwe) class of 1974. From and lives in Harare. Worked at Anaesthetic Consultants. Elsie is well known to the writer, related to look-a-like Helene Lombard who served in the Rhodesian Air Force during the war years.

Jenny Devantier (Jeremiah) 1972 - 1974, from Gweru, lives in London. Jennifer studied at Modern Business Training Centre and works at BRM Administrator at Alliance One International. Her brother, Wayne Derek Jeremiah who also went to Thornhill High School, passed away in August 2013. Her sister, Sharon Lombard, went to Chaplin High School. Jenny has a daughter, Chantelle Veale.

Sharon Dewhurst (Ashley)

- 1977, born Bulawayo, lives in Lowestoft, UK, and is the Legal Secretary at Nicholsons Solicitors.

Pierre d'Hotman

Heather Dicker (Hatt)
born Gwelo 1945, lives in Chigwell, UK and is the Legal Secretary at Yazbek Attorneys.

Christine Dixon (Lloyd)

Ian Dixon
1968 - 1971, studied at Percussion Institute of Technology, Los Angeles, married Gayle and lives in Toowoomba, Queensland, Australia.

Rod Dixon

Nita Dobson (Lawton)
born Bulawayo 1961, married Richard Dobson 1979, worked for Edgars Germiston and now lives in Margate, KwaZulu-Natal.

William Dodgen

Lulu Dormer (le Quesne)
1972 - 1977, born 1959.

Ian Doig followed his father's footsteps in the Rhodesian Air Force, qualifying as an engineer and befriended the writer in Durban. Ian married Shaina in 1973. They have three sons, David, Gary and Jared.

Jo Ann Downs (Whewell) born Amanzimtoti 1959, studied at University of London, worked at African Christian Democratic Party and lives in Amanzimtoti. Jo-Ann has a daughter, Rebecca van Niekerk.

John Dormer., past Rhodesian Air Force, works for Mercedes-Benz and lives in East London, South Africa

Marie Drakes - 1962. From Bulawayo. Studied at Hillside Teachers College, Bulawayo. Lives in Leighton Buzzard, UK.

Basil Drew - 1981 from Lesmurdie, Western Australia, lives in Perth. No photos to show on Facebook.

Lorna Drew was born in 1963, studied at Thornhill and Technikon Natal. Works for Tiger Canyons and lives in Johannesburg.

Avril Drew sang in the Thornhill Choirs. Avril has a daughter, Shelah Drew. Avril was photographed by Catherine Perryman at the reunion with Rhodes Bezuidenhout and four others.

Gary Drew posted many Miss Thornhill photographs on Face Book.

Rodney Drew played Hockey with Gary Drew and Ray Hewitt.

Roger Neil Drinkwater 1983 - 1986. Born Margate 1965. Roger rightfully claims the rare distinction of attending all the High Schools in Gwelo. Roger started at Guinea Fowl in 1978 and then went to Chaplin from 1979 - 1980. Roger then went to Fort Victoria High School from 1981 to 1983 and moved back to Gwelo to Thornhill High School from 1983 to 1986 where he wrote his O levels and finished his schooling.

Roger then studied at Wits Technikon and now lives in Durban.

John Drinkwater (Staff). A very popular Headmaster who made his everlasting impression at Thornhill High School. His impact is referenced throughout the history of the school and Alumni website. He succeeded John Eadie who retired in 1981. He coached the winning 1st XI Cricket Team in 1983.

Garry du Bernard was a singer in the 1986 Thornhill Choir. He is an excellent fisherman. He played 1st XV Rugby for Thornhill High School

Mark du Bernard singer, swimmer and water-polo player of note. Represented Midlands U-19 Water Polo at the Rhodesian Swimming Championships in Umtali in January 1978.

Maryanne Ducray (van der Poll) 1976 - 1980, born Gwelo, lives in Christchurch, New Zealand.

Sheldon Dudley played 1st XV Rugby, and appointed Head boy, in 1978. Has remained personal friend of his 'headgirl' Yolanda MacIntyre ever since. They met up again following the Harare reunion in October 2015.

Shaun du Bernard.* Class of 1982. He also played 1st XV Rugby for Thornhill High School

Mike Dubell*

Ian Dunbar 1951

Stuart Dunbar, born Harare, married Debbie in 2011, is self-employed and lives in Milton Keynes, UK.

Debbie Hahn-Dyer from Selukwe, sang in the Choir, lives in Jensen Bay, Florida.

John du Plessis 1966, left Rhodesia - Zimbabwe in 1973 for Scottburgh on Natal South Coast. Lives in Huntsville, Alabama.

Peter Dyer*born 1959, also attended Hamilton High School Hamilton and Chaplin in Gweru. His sister, Wendy Murray Dyer went to Thornhill.

Wendy Dyer Murray friend of Sheila Maitland and Delise Swift Joubert.

Rients Dykstra (staff)

Mark Edington* born Lalapanzi 1964, now self-employed and lives in Plettenberg Bay, Western Cape. Mark has two other brothers, Sean and Stewart Eddington.

Brenda Edwards, nee Landman

Chaela Edwards - see Vermaak.

Lex Edy 1979, born Gweru, studied Rhodes, married 2009.

Caroline Ehlers (van Jaarsveldt) friend of Vince Manning, Karen Johnson and Pamela Aranyos (Fountain**)** Lives in Pretoria and worked at Koningkinders Ministry. Sister to Clare Thornton. Caroline was in Jane Few's domestic science class in 1982.

Nella Ellams (Beugel)* from Horley and lives in Crawley, UK

Charles Henry Eckstein was at Thornhill High School 1963

Gavin Ellis graduated in 1978. He features in a group photograph in front of Cranwell House, circa 1978.

Liz English, from Gweru 1952, Thornhill 1965 - 1970, studied at the University of Natal, Pietermaritzburg; lives in Harare and has worked for Air Zimbabwe and African Distillers.

Gerhard Erasmus 1968 - 1973, born Harare 1954 and lives in Kerikeri, New Zealand.

Andy Evans (Staff), taught Geography and coached Hockey. Passed away in 2002.

Martha Erasmus (Berkowitz), born Enkeldoorn 1945 and lives in Blenheim, New Zealand. She has a daughter Elizabeth Ducladier and a son Jack Erasmus. Sister to Justin Berkowitz who also went to Thornhill.

Floris Esterhuizen

Elaine Evans attended the London re-union, being photographed with her good friend Helga and Murray Woodfield. Her facebook page does not reveal much but adds that she is the Financial Controller at Universal Smart Cards.

Grant Evans 1973 - 1979 was an organising team member for the Harare reunion, arranging golf for those interested. Grant was born 1961, served with the British South Africa Police - BSAP, worked at Bristle Brushware and owner / founder of Mr Sachet Enterprises and also Emacs-Evans, Grant Maintenance and Coating Solution in Harare. He is married to Robyn and they have a son Justin Evans and a daughter Lauren Ashley Whiting. His sister is Janet Evans, Grant-Windsor. Grant and Robyn attended the Harare celebrations.

Nadine Evans (Budd) - 1977, studied and graduated Brigham Young University 1994, married Mark Evans, Grant in 1998 and has a daughter, Tanya Lynn Treseler. Worked at Nebo School District / Transportation. Lives in Payson, Utah.

Phillip Evans 1960

Lynda Fagan 1963 -1969 lives in Boksburg, Gauteng.

Courtney Ferguson circa 1959 - 1962. He was a school prefect 1959. Courtney is married to Gail Watkinson Ferguson and they live in Harare.

Gavin Ferguson

Wilma Ferguson born and lives in Gweru. Has lived in Wankie and now self employed since 1988.

Wayne Ferguson

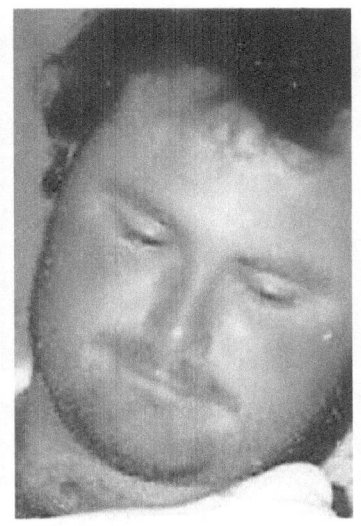

Mark Feltham was in the 1978 School Bands.

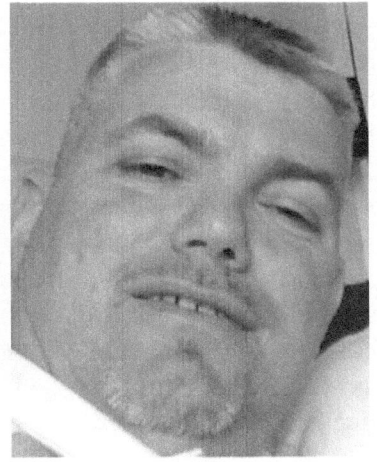

Wayne Fernandes 1982 - 1986 born Gwelo and lives in Maidstone, Kent, UK where he is the Operations Director at Leading Edge Labels (started 2012). Motor cyclist of note and adores his 'princess daughter'. Facebook friends with Tracey da Fonseca (Fernandes)

Jane Few studied at the University of Natal and obtained her Teachers' Diploma in Salisbury. She married Air Force pilot Blake Few and they had one son Athol and a daughter Valerie Klein. She taught Geography at School - and was persuaded by headmaster John Eadie to to take on the Domestic Science vacancy when the teacher Mrs Alexander died during the August 1974 school holidays. Jane reluctantly accepted this added responsibility despite having a baby on her hip at that time. She currently lives in Auckland, New Zealand.

Stephanie Field*

Debbie Finlay (Johnson) is on Facebook. She was in the 1978 Brass Band.

Rona Fisher 1979 - 1982, born Gwelo 1966, studied at Commercial Careers College, Harare, lives in London and is the Accounts Assistant at 3c Risk Ltd. Got engaged in 2013. Her brother, Robert MacDougal Fisher went to Plumtree School, class of 1986.

Colin Fitch* born Gwelo and now lives in Cape Town where he is the Regional Manager at World Surf League.

Bronwyn Fitzpatric appears in a photo with Doreen Swartz and Cathy Holmes

Daphne Fivaz is from Gwelo, studied at Thornhill and lives in Johannesburg. She travelled to Thailand and Zimbabwe in 2013.

John Fivaz

Will Flanagan has many Thornhill friends and may have attended before finishing his schooling at St. Andrews High School in Blantyre, Malawi, 1969 - 1970.

Linda Flanders lives in Brisbane and is the 'Avon Lady', Silver Executive Sales leader with Avon.

Clive Fletcher - 1979, born Gwelo, studied at the University of KwaZulu-Natal 1981 - 1984, married Cathy in 1992 and worked at the Commonwealth Bank of Australia, Sydney.

Yvonne Fortescue (du Plessis) is Facebook friends with Grant Evans, Grant

Irene Foletti

Linda Fouche (Rademeyer) - 1972, studied at Progressive College in Bulawayo and lives in Amanzimtoti, KwaZulu-Natal. Linda has a son Jason and two daughters, Kirsten Meier and Melanie Panayiotopoulos.

Patrick Ford - Patrick's Facebook picture! Obviously has a passion for wild life photography and also aircraft at air shows.

Stephen Fountain 1981 - 1983, born Gwelo, married and lives in Perth, Australia.

Diane Fourie (Neasham)*

Lynn Fortman (Howden), and Judy Broodryk (Rautenbach), both Thornhill High girls, met by chance at the Brakenhurst Bowling Club. She won the Novice Single for 2015 award. What a way to go ladies, to celebrate Thornhill's diamond jubilee!

Linda Rademeyer Fouche also studied at the Progressive College Bulawayo. She lives in Amanzimtoti. KZN Natal.

Diane Lynn Fourie 'was the quiet one' at School, leaving in 1978. She had lost her elder brother Raymond Neasham in a car / train accident with Allan Killner in 1974. Then in 1979 the family lost Colin killed in action near Mapai while serving in the Rhodesian Light Infantry. SAAF Puma 164 was shot down during Operation Uric /

Operation with the loss of three South African aircrew and fourteen Rhodesian soldiers. Diane is currently the assistant Resort Manager at Qwantani Berg and Bush Resort in the Drakensberg near Harrismith.

Harry Fowle born Durban, has a son Matthew who went to Westville Boys High School and a daughter Sarah who went to Westville Girls High School.

John Fowle - 1971, born Mutare 1955, lives in Johannesburg and works in the Security industry.

Gary Fowlie is from Bulawayo and served in the Army after school.

John Fox

Marileine Fox (Bromley)

Sue Francis (Budd) 1969 - 1973, born Gwelo, studied graphic design at Brigham Young University in Idaho and lives in Ontario, California.

Hillary Fraser (Spencer)
1966 - 1971

Lorimer Fraser

Fiona Frey* born Gwelo and lives in Winterthur, Switzerland. Fiona has a daughter, Maja Frey.

Cindy Frew - see Cynthia Bate (Frew).

Linda Friedrich (Bleeker) went to Chaplin and married Paul Friedrick from Thornhill.

Paul Friedrich was born in Chingola, Northern Rhodesia / Zambia in 1960, is a past student of Thornhill and Guinea Fowl schools, completing his GCE 'O' Levels at Specis College, Bulawayo. He is currently the Sales Engineer at Decco in Tauranga, New Zealand. He has also lived in Amanzimtoti. He married Linda Bleeker-Friedrich in 1981.

Colleen Timms Fromburg was at Thornhill in 1982. Then went to the Dominion Convent in Salisbury and returned to Gwelo ant attended Gwelo Technical College in 1984.

Presently lives in East London and married to Robin Timms in 2011.

Neville Fromburg born Gwelo 1954, has a daughter Chantelle Fromberg, and moved from Melbosstand, Cape Town in 1983 to George in the Eastern Cape.

Robert Fromburg married to Angie and lives in Port Alfred

Peter Frost

Richard Frost

Chris Fyfe studied at Rhodes University after graduating from Thornhill. He is currently a self-employed contractor and is known for his paintings.

Fiona Fynn (Clulow) born Gwelo, married Don Fynn, and lives in Hamilton, New Zealand. Has worked at Hamilton East Medical Centre and now with Sport and Spine.

Arlene Garner has lived in Pueblo, Colorado, North Carolina, and Panama City Beach, Florida.

Sharon Garlick (Cullinan) born Gwelo, also went to Chaplin, former secretary at High School for Girls, Potchefstroom 1982 - 1991, lives in Gordonsbaai, Western Cape.

Ronella Garrod (Hundermark) class of 1979

Jan Gavazzi is on Facebook.

Doris Gaye attended the London celebrations. She is from Kwekwe and now lives in Cheltenham, Gloucestershire.

Shay Geach (Knobel) from Harare, studied TTC Bulawayo, worked at Pinehurst School, New Zealand and lives in Auckland.

Preller Geldenhuys, more commonly named 'Prop', attended April 1958 till December 1961, as a boarder at Cranwell. Favourite teachers were Miss Scott for biology, Gilly Squair for Physics, Maths and Chemistry; Tommy Burgoyne for history and Doodles Viljoen for extracurricular activities. Mr Nel and Swanepoel gave us plenty stick at Rugby. I was also taught life skills by my house- and headmaster Philip Todd.

Highlights at school were meeting my future wife Rina Malan, captaining the First XV Rugby Team, Victor Ludorum at athletics and appointment as Head of House, Cranwell during my final year.

I 'dropped' out of 'A' Levels upon acceptance into the Royal Rhodesian Air Force as a pilot. Retired after 20 years service as a Wing Commander - having survived the Rhodesian War whereas at least 38 of my colleagues were killed in action. Commanded Admin Wing Thornhill, Forward Airfields 2 Kariba and 7 Buffalo Range, and Fire Force Charlie at Shabani.

Joined board manufacturer Masonite (Africa) Limited as a Personnel Superintendent in 1982, retiring after another 20 years service as their Loss Control Manager.

We settled in Durban, lived there for ten years and were persuaded by our daughter and son in New Zealand to emigrate there. I took up writing military history and researching family genealogy - as my main hobbies.

Rina Geldenhuys (Malan) - see Rina Malan later on

Richard Genocchio attended Chaplin 1982 - 1984. Lives in Aberdeen, UK.

Helen Gent (Wightman) class of 1980, studied at Kelley Greenoaks Secretarial College and is presently the PA at Pan African Resources in Cape Town. Helen has a daughter, Alice Gent and lives in Cape Town. She was neighbourly friends of the writers' daughter at Thornhill Air Base married quarters. She attended the reunion in Durban.

Joan Gibhard*

Ann Gie (Ashford) 1966 - 1970

Lester Gilbert born 1950, got married 2011 and is the Associate Professor at University Southampton.

Hedley Giles married to June, lives in Brisbane, Australia

Rod Giles 1944

Mimi Gillies (Squair) - 1970, born Gwelo 1953 and lives in Edinburgh, Scotland.

Gilly Squair (staff) was the writer Physics teacher in 1961.

Christine Gird (Weston) is from Gwelo and lives in Cambridgeshire, UK, where she works at Animal Health trust. Christine attended the London event. She was at Thornhill from 1966 - 1969.

June Gohery, from Gweru and widowed. Mother of Grant Evans, Janet Evans, Grant-Windsor and her late son Blake Evans, Grant.

Anne Gold (Thackray)* married Trevor Gold in 1979; they have two daughters Ashleigh Fincham and Nicole Gold; and two sons, Hayden Keating and Jason Gold.

Bruce Gooden born 1958 lives in Harare.

Jeremy Goosen

Ian Gordon*

Angelz Govender (Burden) went to Thornhill, like her sister Judith (Burden) Botha. She has a second sister Sherryl Burden.

Sally Graca (Spencer)

Sharyn Grainger

Viv Grater -1967, studied at Rhodes, graduated 1973, lives in Cape Town and has a son, Ross Grater.

Susanne Gratton (Robinson)

Adrian Gray, from Gwelo, born 1962, lives in Edenvale, Gauteng.

Phil Greager (le Quesne) 1964 - 1968, from Durban, at Salisbury Central Hospital studied Medical Radiography and lives in Crowmarsh Gifford, UK.

Charmaine Green, class of 1978, born 1962, worked at Baille, Koseff, Wheeler and Bornebusch, widowed and lives in Boksburg, Gauteng.

Jenny Green attended the Perth reunion in 2015. She was joined by sisters Anne Booker and Dawn Wood.

Anne and Dawn together at Zebra's in Perth.

Pam Green*

Dave Griffiths was at Thornhill from 1971 to 1976, lives in Johannesburg and is a Sales Director at Millbo Paper. His photograph is from the recent golf tournament, sporting Thornhill logoed clobber.

Helen Griffiths is from and lives in Harare, where she is the Administrator at Acorn Foundation Primary School. Her daughter is Kim Stevens

Megan Ann Griffiths is also on Facebook

Sandy Griffiths born Selukwe 1961 and lives in Centurion, South Africa. Sister to Debra Griffiths and Kim Budke (Griffiths).

Jillian Grimbeek nee Hill left Thornhill end 1964, married Hilton Grimbeek from Guinea Fowl school and settled in Perth, Australia. Her elder brother, Donald, popularised 'Patches' that made number one on the Rhodesian pop-music charts. See Jody Wayne later on.

Jimmy Gretton

Debra Griffiths studied at Thornhill and Jameson High Schools. Lives in Lakeside, Western Cape, South Africa and works at Women's Rugby Co-ordinator at Rugby Concern.

Lynn Grobler (Meyer) - no information on Facebook.

Tracy Grobler Ashley, from Bulawayo - previously Tracy Karen Ashley.

Henry Groenewald

R (Scotty) Gunn

Trudy Guy (Bower)

Ian Hadfield*

Alan Hagemann - 1977. Alan sang in the Choir and attended the School Leavers party in 1977. Lives in Belfast, UK.

Jeff Hagemann was born on the Copperbelt town of Chingola in 1955 and attended Thornhill High School from 1968 to 1972. He served in the Rhodesian Air Force where he qualified as a photographer. Jeff married Sallyann Tapson from Que Que in 1980 and then moved to Que Que 1980 and opened a photographic shop until 1999. I have 3 boys Luke, Dan and Matt. Luke is married and Jeff and Sally are proud grandparents to grandson and granddaughter.

He currently lives in Camberley, UK, where he is Managing Director of - you guessed it - Photographer. Jeff says he is happy in the UK and travels back to Zimbabwe twice a year to do his school photography.

His input into this Magazine, with enhanced photographs, is very much appreciated.

Ken Hagemann

Sharon Hall (le Roith)

Debra Hall (van Rooyen) born Gweru 1961 and now lives in Milton Keynes, United Kingdom.

Lynda Hammett (Potter)*

William Hand

Sheena Hapelt (Bloom)

Denise Hahn-Hull is a Facebook friend to a large circle of Thornhill friends, including Elmerie Wheeler Harley, Sheila Maitland, Vince Manning, Karen Johnson, Helga Toland and many others.

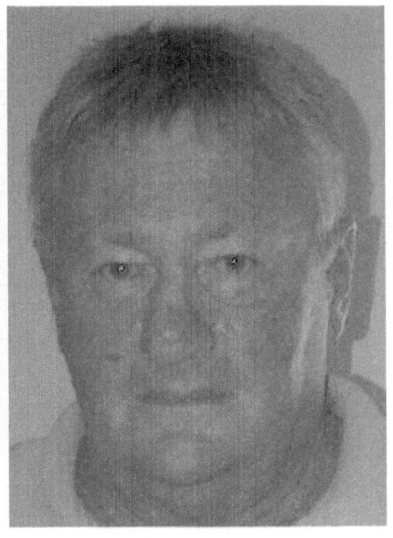

Joe Harbinson, class of 1976, born 1959, studied at the Bulawayo Technical College and currently lives in Maputo, Mozambique.

Ann Harbinson (Blanschard), born Gwelo, was class of 1979. She currently lives in Durban.

John Harbinson 1978- born Gwelo, was in the Thornhill 1978 Brass Band, lives in London.

Rob Hardy born Gwelo 1964, sang in the Thornhill choir, lives in Harare.

Shirley Anne Hargreaves (Smith)

Nicky Wilson-Harris class of 1981 - 2, born Gweru but now lives in Cape Town. Nicky (Chamberlain) was Head Girl in 1982.

Elmarie Harley (Wheeler) lives in and attended the reunion that was held in Brisbane. She married Hilton Harley in October 1984. Like Karen Johnson, Elmerie also sang in the Thornhill choirs.

She sent the following feedback report: "I am one of 3 sisters that went to Thornhill High School. Trudi, myself then Eleanor in that order. We were at Thornhill High School from 1977 - 1979 when we moved to Redcliff & went to Que Que High.

We immigrated to SA where I did my Hairdressing Apprenticeship. I left SA when I married Hilton Harley (Prince Edward (Harare) guy). We have a son & daughter.

We moved around to different countries before eventually

calling Brisbane our final home town. We were in Harare, Zimbabwe, Cardiff, UK, Auckland, New Zealand & several towns in Queensland Australia.

When we left Africa we had a 5 month old baby & 5 suitcases. When we arrived in Australia 1st time we had a 6 month old, 5 suitcases & $145.00 Australians dollars to our name. We lived in a Caravan Park which was a real eye opener on how different people lived. We left for New Zealand when our son was a year old. Didn't know anyone at all in the country, but I managed to fulfil one of my dreams of owning my own Salon whilst living there.

We lived in the Outback of Mount Isa, then Townsville where I changed my profession and studied for my Certificate in Aged and Disabled Care whilst working as a Support Worker in the Industry. I worked in an Ethnic Organisation where majority all of my clients were from Europe.

Since moving to Brisbane several of my highlights have been meeting up with several old school friends

Met up with Rupert van Heerden in Auckland, NZ in February 2010 last saw Rupert December 1979

Met up with Tracey O'Connor and her beautiful Mum in February 2013 last saw her December 1979

Went back to Zimbabwe for the first time in over 25 years to see family and friends, before heading to SA for a Wheeler Family Reunion as we had not all been together since my Wedding day.

Special Highlight has been to go to the School Reunion held now on 25 July 2015 where all my seniors were present.

This is a photo of me 10 months after I left Thornhill.

Elmarie)'s mother, Wilhelmina Jones and her mother's two sisters, Felicity and Yvonne Jones also went to Thornhill.

Alun Hart* Born Gweru 1964. Class of 1976, played in the Theatre Band and 1st XV Rugby. His sister Alison Yates went to Thornhill and both his parents were teachers at the school. Alun studied at Natal Pietermaritzburg, class of 1987, and lives in Harare.

Mr and Mrs Hart (Staff). Both taught languages at Thornhill, Afrikaans and French respectively. They were parents of Alison Yates and Alun Hart.

Yvonne Hart*

Hermien Hartman (du Plessis)*

Cookie Hartzenberg (Hundermark) 1962 - 1966, from Gweru, lives in Polokwane, South Africa.

Carey Watson Harvey is from Que Que and lives in Johannesburg

Melanie Haslewood (Wheeler) lives in Highbridge, Somerset, UK.

Craig Hattle played one of the lead roles in Tom Sawyer and in the Brass Band in 1978. He played 1st XV Rugby for Thornhill High School. Craig is from Gwelo and now lives in New Zealand, at Oakura, south-west of New Plymouth (near snow-capped Mount Taranaki)

Petra Hawes (van der Velden);

Brian Hayes joined the BSAP and settled in Greytown, KZN Natal.

Maureen Hayes (McElroy), born 1947

Ralph Hayes was born in Gwelo in 1950 and lives in Houston, Texas.

Allan Hein

Sue Hemans (Porter) 1972 - 1977 attended University of KwaZulu Natal 1978 to 1981. Sue lives in Chiddingfold, UK.

Peter Henning

Gavin Hensberg played in the 1978 Brass Band.

Leslie-Ann Hector played 1983 First Team Hockey with Eulalie Barry and Janet Medland Udy.

Sharon Hepburn (Cochrane) - kindly gave permission to use her photograph in this Magazine. Little Facebook details, except born 1962.

Deirdre Herbst (van Niekerk) 1979 - 1981, born Gweru 1966, married Michael Herbst in 1990 and lives in Johannesburg.

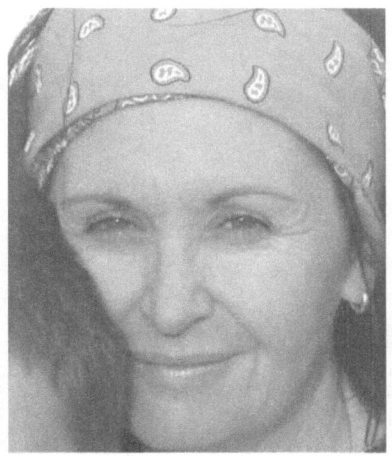

Alison Hewitt is from Shurugwi and lives in Jeddah, Saudi Arabia

Ray Hewitt together with Tracey O'Connor and team are organising the main Zimbabwe jubilee celebrations in October. Ray is self-employed and lives in Harare (born Bulawayo). He has a son, Kieran and two daughters - Stacey Fritz-Gerald and Steph Hewitt.

Ebeth Higham (van Wyk)

Cathy Hitchens (Bradnick)

Veronica Hitge (Preston)

Mark Hodgson

Margie Molloy Hoffman is the daughter of the author's drill instructor in the Air Force! Paddy Molloy has sadly passed on. This connection was only discovered my accident when the author approached the local stationery / book shop in Paeroa to arrange a book launch. Prop and bookshop owners Pamela Fountain Aranyos) lives in Paeroa, New Zealand - and Margie Molloy Hoffman living in the UK.

Harold Hofmann hails from Rotorua, just up the drag from Paeroa! He is a keen camper and fisherman, pastimes enjoyed by most New Zealanders.

Tony Holdaway 1977 - 1979, born West Nicholson 1963, studied at Unisa and lives in Polokwane, SA.

Maureen Holland (Atkinson)

Graham Holliday -1968

Ed Holloway

PJ Holmes

Mike Homan

Roy Hopkinson

Suzanne Hopkinson (Scully) attended the Brisbane function. She is from Gwelo, born 1959, married Ray Hopkinson in August 1980. They have lived in Lae, Papua New Guinea and are currently the Clinical Nurse at North West Private Hospital in Brisbane, Queensland, Australia. She and Renee Scully are sisters.

Sue Horner (Drodskie)*

Niall Houston 1964 - 1965

Rob Hoy* from Gweru and self employed in Swindon, Wiltshire, United Kingdom.

Denise Hull (Hahn)

Joseph Ernest Hundermark 1968 - 1971, born Gweru 1955, lives in Polokwane, South Africa.

Lillias Hundermark lives in Sasolburg

Jennifer Hunt One of three sisters that went to Thornhill.

Sue Hunt, studied at Thornhill, then Townsend and Teachers Training College, Bulawayo. Lives in Essaouira, Morocco and owner at Riad Lunetoile.

Bev Huntly (Ashley) Class of 1969, attended the Perth reunion.

Karen Hurndall (Shillinglaw), born Gweru 1958, went to Thornhill, class of 1976 and qualified in 1979 at the Bulawayo Teachers Training College. She currently lives in the UK where she teaches the P7 class in Cupar, Fife.

Mike David Irving

David Jackson

Peta Jacobs (Mawson) 1960 - 1962 writes "I was hitched to Roy Kalil for a while and then to Bev Davidge". Bev is married with two children and a grandchild. She says "I live in Tempe Arizona in winter, and Colorado in summer".

A. James played 1st XV Rugby for Thornhill High School.

Cave James Thornhill athletics and Chaplin Rugby. Born Durban 1965, lives in Pretoria, South Africa. His sister Tracey Carmen James also went to Thornhill.

Tracey James has a son, Sean MacLaughlin. She has a

brother, Cave James and a sister, Leslie Fourie.

Kendel Janson (Nordin)

Mark Jefferies served in the Rhodesian Air Force and is a self employed pilot in Cape Town. His dad was SWO at Thornhill base and served with the writer.

Grahame Jelley 1977. Schooled at Guinea Fowl 1972 - 1977 and attended Thornhill for his Science subjects in his final year. Studied medicine at University of Cape Town, graduated 1983. Married Renene Geldenhuys in 1992, lived in Westport and Ohope Beach, New Zealand. They have Courtney and Brendan Jelley.

Debra Light Jenkins graduated from Thornhill in 1981, went to Gweru Technical College and obtained her Masters Degree in Business Management in 1998. She married Mark Jenkins and they have two sons and a daughter - Gareth Jenkins, Greg Cottrell and Megan Amy.

Debra's parents had a huge influence on the writers' service in the Rhodesian Air Force. Jim Light was the No 4 Squadron Warrant Officer who was responsible for the exceptional serviceability in keeping the aircraft in the air. We all salute Jim and Corny Light.

Jim and Corny Light

Fifi Evans fraternising, again. Always has his hand full.

Kathy Jenkins (Tillett)

Roger Jervois features in a group photograph in front of Cranwell House, circa 1978.

Phil Jessop, born 1963, married Lorraine in 1989 and lives in Johannesburg, Gauteng. His parents, Geoff and Kay, were the writer's tennis partners at Thornhill Air Base during the early 1970's. Phil's sister is Lynette Nelson

Bob Johnson (Staff), Music teacher and director of the School musicals and bands.

Karen Johnson 1976 - 1980 - 1st year of High School was at Chaplin. Favourite teachers were Mrs EM Chamberlain

(History) Mr Barry Maytham (Science) Mr Dykstra (Geo) and Mrs Few (Domestic Science) and Mr Ninmo for English. Most of the teachers were family friends as her father was a teacher at the school for a while. Mrs Dot Cairns and Mr Alers were good mentors. Mr Newling had the patience of a saint and Karen managed to obtain a C in O level Maths...

Miss Cooke gave encouragement for hockey and swimming. All the staff made schooling enjoyable.

She played in the School Band and sang in the choir. Karen was a ember of the Pop Band Pig Factor with Greg Mountjoy, Gregory Pearce, Mark Feltham and Grant Evans and most assemblies saw her behind the piano playing the hymns and trying not to laugh at the the guys that sang out of tune. She was a keen member of the hockey and athletic teams. She was a member of the synchronised swimming team for a short while. School Musicals would have her in the Pit playing various instruments.

Karen writes "My best friend at school was Kathy Botha, but I was really good friends with Ronella Hundermark, Gail Millard, Kendal Nordin, Bronwyn and Sandy Smith, Mark Perryman, Gary Drew, Craig Joss, Les Johnston, Craig Holmes (RIP) and many more too numerous to mention."

"My last year of school I was given the honour of being appointed Deputy Head Girl and received my Honours blazer for Music and Merit."

"I had a part time job at the Dutch Oven and work briefly for Mr Alers Travel Agency as his secretary."

"On leaving school, I came over the the UK to go to college but as my parents plans to return to the UK went pear shaped and they decided to move to South Africa so I moved back to Africa. Working for Avis Rent-A-Car in Johannesburg and then for Howson Industrial Tools as their Product Manager with Les Johnston also ex-Thornhill High School."

"Moved back to the UK and worked for Birds Eye Walls, the Prudential and Cornish Coffee. My son was born in 2001 and I married Mike a couple of years later. Moved to Canada in 2005 and back to the UK 4 years ago, now working for Headforwards Solutions as PA to the Directors and in charge of HR and Recruitment."

Karen has 2 stepchildren and a step-grandson who live in Costa Rica and Italy.

Karen still plays in a Brass Band in the village. The tuba has become too heavy to march with. A few years ago a foot injury forced her to retire from playing hockey. Now-a-days Karen can be found on one of the beaches in Cornwall photographing her 14 year old surfing.

Tom Johnson (staff)

Marthinus Johnstone alias Martin features in a group photograph in front of Cranwell House, circa 1978.

Felicity Jones, sister to 'Villie' and Yvonne. (a 'then' photo)

See Felicity van der Merwe

Karen Huckle Jones, 1979 – 1981, born 1965. Mabelreign Girls High and studied Secretarial / Administration at Cape Technikon. Married 1991 and lives in North Bradley, Wiltshire, United Kingdom.

Keith Jones Is believed to be in East London, South Africa. Keith played Under 15 Rugby in 1965.

Phil Jones

Sheila Jones (Palmer)

Sheila Jones is from Suttun Coldfield, married in 1973 and lives in Birmingham, United Kingdom. Facebook friends with Jill Barnes (Air Force) and Beverley Nelson.

Wilhelmina "Villie" Jones - 1955/1956 and her two sisters, Felicity and Yvonne, went to THS. Villie married Henry Wheeler and have four children.

Elmarie Wheeler said that her mom's teachers were Doodles Viljoen, Nel and Tommy Burgoyne - the latter complaining why could her parents not have named her 'Winnifred' instead of Wilhelmina?! Her favourite subjects were Science and Geography.

Yvonne Jones, sister to Felicity and Wilhelmina. See also Yvonne Matthyser.

Delise Joubert (Swift) - 1978. Attended the London reunion. Delise was born Shabani 1960 and lives in Pietermaritzburg.

Penny Jovner (Fromburg) Penny married Rodney Dredge, but was widowed a few years ago. She has since re-married and lives in Gweru.

Joe Joubert, born 1947, Game farm manager, lives in Messina, Limpopo.

Joubert le Grange (Joe)

Lynnette Kaagman (Bugler) - 1967, from Simonstown and now lives in Cheltenham, Gloucestershire - but making her way to doing a 5-week stint in Warwickshire (from where she promises to contribute with a brief write-up).

Trevor Kalil

Reg Kaschula circa 1958 - 1961 at Cranwell with the writer. He was a noted boxer at school. He performed with the writer in the Pirates of Penzance musical.

Joanie Katchmar*

Christopher Keepin 1974 - 1976. Lives in London

Joe (Trevor) Keith* features in a group photograph in front of Cranwell House, circa 1978.

Kim Kendall 1967 - 1971, born 1954, married Debbie 1978 and has three children, Ashlee, Marc and Megan. Features in a 'Class of 1972' photograph. Got engaged in 2008.

Michelle Kenneth*

Raye Kent born in Gweru 1943. Got engaged to Penny Katz in 2014 and lives in Durban. Related to Nolene Kent?

Ina Rene Keith attended the October 2010 reunion.

Jackie King, born 1960, class of 1977, lives in Pietermaritzburg and is the owner at Pieter Rabbit Daycare and Crèche.

David (Rip) Kirby was at Thornhill the same time as the author - late 1950's early 1960's. According to Facebook, his wife, Maureen 'cosh' Kirby also went to Thornhill.

Maureen Kirby, or 'cosh' also went to Thornhill. Born Gweru and lives in Cape Town. They have a son. Jason and a daughter Kristie.

Heath Klasen, born Gweru, lives in Auckland where he is the Manager for Forbes Packaging.

Peter Kloppers* befriended the author in Durban, where he ran several successful businesses.

Bridget Kitto born 1965. No further Facebook details.

Fanie Klopper*

Lucas Kloppers*

Jock Knoetze is married to Anne and they live in Durban.

Elaine Knott went to Thornhill from 1972 to 1975 and has a very larger Facebook circle of friends. Elaine was born in Shangani, married Bobby in 1982 and lives in Thornbury, Gloucestershire, UK.

Patty Knox (Lamb)*

Willem Koekemoer

Adele Koninis 1966 - 1970. Self employed in Johannesburg. Maiden name Carter.

Andrew Krajewski is from Kwekwe and studied doctor of Philosophy Agriculture at Stellenbosch University 1993 - 1995. Lives in Albania, Western Australia.

Paddy Kruger played 1st Team Rugby in 1978. The team photograph is posted on Facebook every year. Paddy served in 2 Commando, Rhodesian Light Infantry, married Estelle in 2011, lives in Pretoria and runs his own business, Z. Lighting. Brother to Braam Kruger and Georgina Cloete.

Susie Kruger (Lamprecht);

Shirley Kuttner (Nourse), 1958 - 1962, attended the Harare celebrations. She played golf and was at BJ's braai.

Shirley established comms with the writer during August 2015, while in the UK, and having met with Colin Paterson, an old school mate of ours.

Shirley has two sons, Craig and Lance, and a daughter. She wrote "I was known as "Chirpy" as a Halton House boarder. Mrs Lamport scared the daylights out of us and whose dog, Foxy, got us into a heap of trouble.

"I excelled in tennis, netball, athletics (Victrix Ludorum) and hockey, where I captained the First Team in 1962. Head of Halton House in final year.

"Participated in all the musicals at the time - Pirates of Penzance, Mikado, and Iolanthe with music teacher Mrs Niki Antoniadis. Enjoyed St Johns Ambulance Brigade and participated in the competitions. Favourite teachers, Mrs Cairns, Miss Hague, Andy Evans, Tommy Burgoyne and Doodles Viljoen.

"On leaving school worked for the Farmers Co-Op and Barclays Bank as a teller in Fort Victoria until I met and married Felix Kuttner a Police Superintendent. We raised 3 children two boys and a girl during the Rhodesian Bush War. Then moved to Triangle and worked for Triangle Sugar Estates as the Manager of Parks & Gardens – Nursery, sports fields and golf course curator, my present job. My hobbies included gardening and floral art and continue to play tennis and golf."

Julie Lake Class of 1976, born Gweru 1962. Julie lives in

Durban, she attended the Salt Rock reunion in 2009 and married Martyn Prescott in 2014.

Lorraine Lamb is from Gwelo and lives in Durban.

Ted Lamb attended the Rhodesian Light Infantry 55th Birthday – to unveil the duplicate of 'The Trooper' statue. Photographed with Braam and Paddy Kruger

Andries Lamprecht 1974 - 1978, born Beatrice 1960, studied at Harare Polytechnic and lives in Melbourne, Australia. Andries says the good thing that he cherishes was the 1978 1st XV Rugby team that beat Chaplin after 16 years and drew with Falcon.

Anna-Marie Lamprecht from and lives in Harare. Works at Veracity Business Services.

Jan Lamprecht studied Pretoria West College of Engineering, qualified as a Certified Engineering Technician. Eskom pensioner.

Susie Lamprecht at THS 1959

Janet Lancaster attended the Durban Golden Jubilee celebration. Jan Nysschen says she is now a Marchussen, and is expected to make an appearance at the Harare Silver Jubilee reunion. If so, an extra effort will be made to establish a Paeroa Skype connection.

Jeremy Lancaster graduated from Thornhill in 1977 and worked for Saint Georges University of London,

Cheryl-Ann Landman
Cheryl-Ann lives in Tennessee (The country Music capital of the world) (Knoxville area) been here 11 years and before that 12 years in Colorado home of the famous Rocky Mountains - She jokes with everyone she meets that she is a TRUE African America, born in Africa and nationalized American. What more could she be, blue eyes and blonde hair!

With Jill Lawrence - sent by e-mail after getting N/L

Daphne Langford (staff)* from Harare, went to Girls High School in Salisbury, and lives in Nottingham, United Kingdom.

Maria Nicolaou Lapsley, friend of Yolanda MacIntyre

Tineke Laurent (van Leeuwen) born 1947, worked for African Associated Mines in Bulawayo, lives in Wieringenwerf, Netherlands and self employed as a domestic engineer. Have a son Daniel and a daughter Heidi.

Linda Lautz (Richardson)

Kevin Law is on Facebook. He features in a group photograph in front of Cranwell House, circa 1978 (photo attributed to him).

Joanne Lawrence (Naude) - see Joanne Naude (Joey) on Facebook.

Mandy Lawrence (Bull) is from Gweru and lives in Johannesburg.

Alex Leaman* born 1951, from Chelmsford

Joss Leaman ?- 1971 brother of Alex, lives in Bali, Indonesia.

Theresa Leaman from Gweru and lives in Beitbridge.

Jeanette Leeming (Andrews)*

Stacey Botha Lemmer, from Johannesburg, lives in Klerksdorp.

Paul Lewis lives in Swansea, UK and works at AtjoHuntleigh as a service engineer.

Sue Lewis (Berry) 1970 - 1975. Sue's son is getting married in South Africa, and could not make the School's reunion so close together. Also very shy Facebook friend. She is a friend of Sandy Connolly. Sue studied at the University of Pietermaritzburg and Counselling Psychology at the Australian College of Applied Psychology. She lives in Dunedin, South Island, New Zealand.

Vince Lewis* chance meeting with Caroline Kelly Armand at a wedding

Sharon Liebenberg (Lake)*

Brigitte Lindsay was one year behind her very good friend Janet Medland Udy - playing First Team Hockey 1982.

Sue Littleford (Lakelin)*

Jane Lochrie

Jennie Lolliot (Spiers)

Adrienne Andre Lombard lives in Perth, Australia.

Sylvia Long (Marshall)

Sheila Lottering (Ruffey) from White River, Mpumalanga 1960.

Nan Loveridge (Winter) was a prefect in 1958.

Sheryl Low is from Bulawayo and now lives in Kleinmond, Western Cape. She attended a braai at Overstrand with Terri Murdoch-Coyle and Yolanda MacIntyre - considered another mini-Thornhill reunion to celebrate the Schools' diamond jubilee.

Hardy Lund (Hardy)*

Sharon Lyon Mabbett, friend of Janet Medland Udi and Helen (Wightman) Gent. Sharon was in the 1978 Brass Band. Worked for Nampak Ltd and lives in Johannesburg.

Alex MacDonald played a part in the 1970's play Tom Sawyer. His sister, Janice McMillan, also attended Thornhill.

Ian MacDonald lives in Centurion, Gauteng.

Peter MacDonald, born 1953, was at Thornhill 1965 to 1970 and lives in Launceston, Cornwall, UK. He has a daughter, Tara Leigh Bird who the author thinks has blessed him with a granddaughter and a grandson. He has a third grandchild (for the record).

Rhona MacDonald (van Niekerk)*. Class of 1962. See also Rhona van Niekerk.

Yolanda MacIntyre is shy of Facebook photographs - her picture was kindly supplied (and pointed out by Bev) where Yolanda attended the London celebrations arranged by Murray Woodfield. The writer hastens to add that Yolanda is not 'shy' with the contributions made on the Thornhill Facebook page that she, together with Karen Russell makes. Thank you, ladies.

Mike MacLaughlin

Denise MacLean (Shillinglaw) studied at

Andrew Flemming School of Radiography and lives in Harare.

Jackie Maimin (Nell)* Jackie married Gary David Maimin in 1986. She is a council member at the South African Pharmacy Council since 2013. Mr Dykstra was her favourite Geography teacher.

Alistair Main

Terri Murdoch-Coyle spent three glorious days in Brisbane, with special mention made of Yolanda MacIntyre, Leigh Bristow, Wendy-Lee Weir and Dawn Midgley.

Terri commented "We missed you Yolanda MacIntyre, Leigh Bristow, Wendy-Lee Weir, and Dawn Midgley!" But there's always a next time."

Frans Malan followed his elder brother and sister to Thornhill. Being the 'quiet one' in the family, he tended to stay in the background - - but this did not deter him from becoming a Bank Manager, Financial Director and chief executive of his own company while living at Vereeniging. He retired to his daughter and son-in-laws game farm in the Polokwane area and lives near Bandolierskop, Limpopo, South Africa.

All the Form 1 girls were totally in love with blushing Frans – girls like Truidy Bester and Gill Boswell.

Hendrik Malan was the first of the Malan family to attend Thornhill High School

Phil Malan went to Thornhill from 1960 to 1963/64, is presently retired and lives in Johannesburg. He is a natural musician and plays a variety of instruments, recording his own composition on a Boeremusiek CD. Being the writer's brother-in-law and notably a twin to his sister Rina, results in constant contact. He is also noted for his humoured input to the newsletter.

Rina Malan attended January 1960 to 1963 as a boarder at Halton House, excelled at Hockey, Tennis and Athletics. Favourite teacher was Andy Evans and did well at Domestic Science. Enjoyed Music with Mrs Niki Antoniadis and participated in school musicals Iolanthe and Midsummer Nights Dream. Got plenty stick from Miss Nuttal for cuddling up and holding hands with my future husband, Prop Geldenhuys.

Left school to work for the Cold Storage Commission in Fort Victoria, where I shared a flat with Shirley Nourse who was courted by my twin brother Philip. Also worked for S.P. Burger in Chiredzi and for Civil Aviation as a Security Officer at Buffalo Range Airport (during the Rhodesian War).

Prop and I had a pigeon pair, daughter Renene and son Pey, both born in Gwelo. Contracted breast cancer early 1990's and suffered a debilitating Stroke shortly thereafter. Prop took early retirement from Masonite and we settled in a flat overlooking Durban harbour. Relocated to New Zealand three years ago.

Valerie Malcolm (Hunt) nee Hunt 1965 - 1969, born 1953, graduated from Bulawayo Teachers Training College in 1972 after leaving Thornhill. Currently living in Olney, Milton Keynes, UK.

Valerie Malcolm writes "I was at THS from 1965 to 1969. Two of my younger sisters also attended and Jennifer (Hunt) will be at the reunion in Harare, where she still lives. Sue (Hunt) now in Eassaouira in Morocco where she has a Riaad. Was a prefect in my last year - not really because I was an obvious choice but I ran the school library - Mrs Marion (I think) Richardson was technically in charge but I did a lot of 1968 and all of 1969. Was going to be a librarian - proved to be a very useful experience (as some officers in the Tower - doing their promotion exams - may remember...will say no more. At THS I was a very active member of St Johns (run by the memorable Mrs Alexander) and continued this (with breaks e.g. when I was teaching in Rusape) until my time in the Air Force when I was not only a member of the adult division, but also did First Aid classes at Thornhill (Melanie Jervois was one of the students there - subsequently met her again in 1980 when I decided to go nursing and she was a second year student and therefore senior to me!) Steve Caldwell was in my M level year. Other people who went through THS in my year: Jean Burgoyne (my friend and with whom I am still in close touch - her daughter is my god daughter - though I am a useless god mother, Angela Dallas, Liz English who is still in Harare, Billy Rob, Raymond Stout, David Berry, Roderick Dixon, Fiona Cameron and Jenny Spiers (who came in Form 3 and changed the dynamics of the class), Lee Bartlett, Howard Crooks, Beverley Paxton, Pauline Pollard, Colleen van Breda and David Wilson - both of whom I bumped into briefly in Bulawayo in the early 90s. They were in my class but there were many in that year from Riverside days too: Brenda Horn, Sylvia Palmer sister of Sheila who married Dag Jones), Dianne Palmer, Kathy Ballantyne.

Favourite teacher, Mrs EM Chamberlain who took us for Latin (after the scary Miss Baldwin left - only 100% good enough but she got me working!) and History (a huge relief as Mr Steenkamp had done it, very badly, beforehand (humiliation being the main tool which prohibited learning in my case and would have put me off the subject forever had Mrs Chamberlain not come).

Mr Geoff Lambert was head and an excellent maths teacher - would never have got through O Levels without him. Hedley Giles was there but older - think he was loved for his sporting prowess then as he was in the Air Force. He and June have been very supportive and good friends to Bugs (till he died) and to me subsequently - as I go through the Chemo process. Was at Thornhill when Douglas Bader came - he was horrified to find it was a co-ed school.

Some of the "older" ones when arriving who stuck out: Colleen Roselt (the whole family was sporty); Janice Bossert; Glenda Tapson; Rip Kirby; Rebecca Manning and Vera Vorster with whom still good friends having met at college and will be seeing in a few weeks.

Bill Malkin studied at Rhodes University and Masters Degree at the University of Cape Town and is a graduate from the School of Business. Bill formed the Thornhill High School Thyme-Agin band in 1968. The other three members of the band being Ian 'Speck' Dunbar, Eric Bradnick and Roger 'Spider' Atkinson. In 1969, Gordon Fraser replaced Eric Bradnick.

Derek Manning played U15 Cricket. Lives in Bunbury, Western Australia.

John Manning

Rebecca Manning

Tim Manning 1966 - 1969. From Melton. Mowbray, United Kingdom.

Vince Manning went to Thornhill 1975 - 1979 and currently lives in Brisbane, Australia. He has previously attended a Perth re-union arranged by John Wightman with Lorna Viljoen and Cindy Wright. Vince more recently attended the Brisbane re-union celebrating Thornhill High School's 60 year Diamond Jubilee gathering. Vince played 1st XV Rugby.

Whilst on business in Auckland, at the drop of his hat he motored or rather joined the snail-paced convoy heading south to Paeroa - were another impromptu Thornhill reunion was held with his old friend Pamela (Fountain) Aranyos). See the 'reunions' chapter later on, for photographs recording this milestone event! The visit to Beulah opens up another world where memories are made.

Andrew Marais

Ingrid Marais

Linda Marais attended the Harare reunion

Mark Marais 1976 - 1981. He played 1st XV Rugby for Thornhill High School. From Gweru and lives in Belfast, UK.

Pookie Marais

Janet Marchussen (Lancaster) 1957 - 1961 attended the Durban Golden Jubilee celebration. Janet commented on her Thornhill experience:-

"I arrived at Thornhill just after the start of the first term 1957. School was based at Thornhill Air Force base. Having been in form 1 at GHS Salisbury prior to that I found it quite daunting being at a co-ed school. I was now in form 2 and was horrified to find myself doing Latin in my first lesson. The school bell was the Air Force base siren. I loved that year as we were now doing athletics which was not done at GHS. I also enjoyed the gymnastics which Mrs. Cairns took us for. I won the Victrix Ludorum that year, running barefoot!

Mrs. Bromley ran the Girl Guides and I joined the group that year. It was a lot of fun.

HMS Pinafore was being performed and as I was doing ballet at the time I was coerced to dance with Rosalie Hughes and Veronica. It was a fun performance. The following year was Pirates of Penzance. Also good fun.

Goodnight Vienna was next and I had a minor part as one of the flower girls opposite Rodney Langley with Heather Hatt and Vic Reece. Patricia Barlow and Chris de Jong being the main characters and I always remember Anne Panton being excellent in her part.

The move to the 'new' school was exciting for us all. The fields were new and had no grass on them so athletics were something to be remembered. Running barefoot I ended up with huge blistered infected feet which could have been due to the sewage farm next door! However the fields were sorted out eventually. I won the Victrix Ludorum until my final year when I was very much 'outrun' by Carrie Russell Smith.

For the last 18 months I became a boarder. I always longed to be a boarder but once there not so sure it was my scene. I was made head girl of Halton house and then of the school in my final year.

I played tennis, netball and hockey for Thornhill and was Captain of the first hockey team, and awarded colours for playing for Midlands and going for Rhodesian trials in which I only making the probable's.

On leaving school I played for Rhodesia B two years in a row.

I married Peter Marchussen in 1964 and became a farmer's wife which suited me down to the ground. We were blessed to have 4 children all of whom are married and we have 13 grandchildren one of which is married and we have a great grandchild on the way. Time moves on! Three of our children live in Harare and one is in Nottingham road South Africa running the Notties Hotel.

With all the farm problems we moved into Harare and now live in Borrowdale Brooke on the golf estate. We love being in Zimbabwe despite the problems."

Janet's great-grandchildren and grandchildren will one day marvel at Janet's Thornhill High School achievements.

Allison Marillier, nee Stokes, married Elan who also went to Thornhill. Alison is from Newcastle, Natal and studied at the University of Pretoria.

Chinky Marillier - elder cousin to Elan Marillier.

Berta Maritz (Buys) 1976 - 1979. Also known as Alberta Buys. Sister to Piet / Petrus Buys.

Pam Markham (Scott Roger) Her son is Graeme Markham

Susan Markie (Day) 1959 - 1962

Elan Marillier married Alison Stokes. Elder cousin who also went to THS was Chinky Marillie.r

Gina Markram born 1966 and graduated from Thornhill High School in 1983. Married 2008. Also known as van der Meulen.

Victor Markram born in Centurion, Gauteng and currently lives there. He is on of the Thornhill Golfing team that were so well dressed during 2015.

Winston Markram features in the 1981 Athletics team photograph. He lives in Krugersdorp, Gauteng.

Alan Marshall Moved to Marlburg in 2014.

Lynda Marshall (Scully) works at Imperial Tobacco, Bristol, United Kingdom.

Dave Marshall

Robert Matthews

Gerald May 1966 - 1971, born Gwelo 1953, lives in Johannesburg, and has a son Andrew May.

Lynda May (Eekhout) 1966 - 1970;

Philip May*

Yvonne Matthyser, nee Jones, sister to Felicity and Wilhelmina Jones.

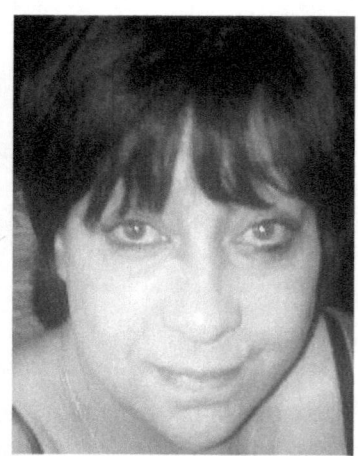

Enid Mayhew (Kruger) attended the October 2010 reunion. She works at Daot Logistics.

Barry Maytham born Bulawayo 1939, schooled at Prince Edward and graduated from the University of Natal and University College of Rhodesia and Nyasaland. He taught at Gilbert Rennie High School in Lusaka, Jameson High School in Gatooma, Que Que High School and moved to Gwelo 1974. He was the Deputy Head of Thornhill High School for five years from 1974 to December 1979, to become the Head of Fort Victoria High School. His biggest challenge was Headship of the Capricorn High School, Pietersburg north of Pretoria, 1983 to 2000.

Barry retired from teaching some 14 years ago and now lives in a little Western Cape Town between Hermanus and Betty's Bay called Kleinmond. Daughter Michelle and family live in Johannesburg and son Gary and family live in England. Barry plays as much golf as possible while his wife Martie runs their seafront house as a small upmarket Bed & Breakfast called Herds Cove.

John Mays 1958 - 1961

Shelton Shelaz Mazilawa 1998 - 2001 for 'O' and 'A' levels. Shelton is from Gweru and married Tsitsi Madzana.

Vanessa McBain (Odendaal) recognised two friends in the Brisbane group photo. She attended Thornhill from 1970 to 1973 and married in August 1978. Currently lives in Perth, Western Australia and Facebook friends of Jeff Hagemann and John Whiteman. Re-union connections resulted in Vanessa meeting up with Jillian Grimbeek again.

Lois McCleland (Dipper)
1968 - 1972, from East London. Served in the BSAP and lives in Johannesburg.

William Adrian McDonagh
Class of 1977, played water polo and features in the 1978 photograph that won the Risco Shield. William is from Ballymena, UK, and is the Quality, Environmental and Health & Safety auditor at NQA Global.

Ianthe McDonald (Daniel)*

Penny McDonald (Doyle), born Gweru 1950.

Annette McFarlane born Chakari, Zimbabwe 1958, works at Lamela Research Laboratories and lives in Johannesburg. Daughter is Kelsey McFarlane.

Nigel McFarlane and **Gwen McFarlane (Tapson)** 1959 - 1963, one of the Thornhill 'couples' that have lasted the distance. They live in Hilton, Pietermaritzburg, and have a son Stuart Andrew. Gwen's sister Sally is married to Air Force photographer Jeff Hagemann.

Dave McGaw (staff) born Bulawayo 1944, schooled at Plumtree, BA degree in Geography and Psychology at Rhodes University in 1971. Was HOD Geography at Grantleigh College till 2015, now retired to Kwabonambi, KwaZulu-Natal.

Jean McGibbon (Cowie)

Gail McGowan (Rowlands) Lives in Johannesburg, friend of Tracy O'Conner.

Rob McGowan

Ian McKie, born 1948, lives in Krugersdorp, South Africa.

Gavin McLeman from Harare, lives in Washington, Columbia.

Angela McLeod (Hutchinson)

Karen McMaster (Southey) - 1971, from Que Que, works at Caribbean and lives in Philipsburg, Netherlands Antilles.

Janice McMillan (MacDonald) - 1979, married to Dick McMillan. They have a daughter, Ellie Allison. Her brother, Alex MacDonald also attended Thornhill.

Rodney McNeill, born 1943, was a Cranwell House prefect who became very good friends with the writer during the late fifties / early 1960's. Several by chance meetings took place in KZN Natal and then contact was lost. Rodney studied at the University of Potchefstroom and currently lives in Pretoria.

Bill Meaker born Gweru and went to Chaplin. Highly likely to have attended classes at Thornhill during the Sixth Form.

Ada Meiring (Berkowitz) is from Enkeldoorn and lives in Nelspruit, Mpumalanga, South Africa. It seems she has been to New Zealand, as the photo was on board the Arahura, Wellington (ferry crossing between North and South Islands)

Clive Melton played 1st XV Rugby in 1979. He went to Guinea Fowl from 1975 - 1979.

Dalene Meyer (Carinus) married Andre Meyer, lives in Kadoma, Zimbabwe and is self employed.

Charles Meyer*

Mike Mellody* is a mutual friend of Bruce Brislin.

Dan Millard 1967 - 1972 studied at the University of Rhodesia 1977 and lives in Peoria Illinois where he is a professional anaesthesiology transesophageal echocardiogram.

David Lee Millard married in 1978 and has two children, daughter Amanda and son David.

Jeff Millard from Harare lives in Cape Town.

Alex Millar - 1966, left Zimbabwe in 1981 and now lives in Ashfield, UK.

Clover Miller (Lovell) *Studied Bookkeeping and Business, from Gweru and lives in Henley on Klip (SA), currently a self employed Bookkeeper. Have a daughter, Crystal Vale Lauren Smit and two sons, Duwayne and Kristin Smit.

David Mitchelmore

Karen Montocchio (Ellis)

J. Moore played Vice Captain of THS 1st XV Rugby.

Jane Morrison 1977. Also attended Que Que High School, UCT 1981 BA Degree and Vancouver Careers College plus Technical Web design in British Columbia.

Leanne Moser Mould, born 1964, married to Mike Mould, has three daughters, Katherine, Michelle and Nicola, and is the owner of Phambuka Dive Charter.

Greg Mountjoy runs Kites by

Design in Knysna, Western Cape.

Jamie Murdoch* born Gweru 1967, lives in Mount Isu, Queensland, Australia.

Joanne Naude (Joey) is on Facebook. She was in St. Johns and one of the 'Shabani Girls'.

Grant C Nealon was class of 1979

Beryl Neave (Swartz)* born Harare 1963, studied at Greys Hospital Pietermaritzburg, married Norman Neave in 1992 (stand corrected, could be 2010), they have a daughter, Siobhan, and live in Hluhluwe, KwaZulu Natal.

Jeff Neely 1965 - 1966. Global Design at IBM Design, Austin, Texas.

Caren Neethling (Howell) is from Gweru, sang in the 1976 Thornhill School Choir, and studied at Pinetown Technical College. She has a daughter, Chantal Neethling and a sister, Sherry Hoefnagel.

Herman Nel was born in Gwelo in 1964 and studied engineering after leaving Thornhill. He lives in Harare where he is the MD of Weldtech with an affinity for motorcycling

Patricia Nel (Barlow) 1956-1961

Frik Nel 1960 -1963, from Brisbane, is not on Facebook. However, his fishing buddy, Jan Nysschen, has given the tip-off that Frik is shortly due to fly out to Africa to join up with his Tiger Fishing mate, before both of them continue celebrating their frequent re-unions at the

Thornhill Silver Jubilee event in Harare.

The writer was indeed fortunate to get Frik's input on the day the magazine was submitted to the printers. Frik and Jan Nyscchen are expert fisherman, or so one or the other would like readers to believe. Frik reported as follows:

Kunjani. Fantastic to hear from you - your ears must've been on fire as Broekies de Jong and I had another great rugby weekend in Sydney - Wallabies vs All Blacks!

For the last eight years Broekies, Ian Gordon and I meet for a rugby weekend somewhere in Oz - unfortunately Ian has been too busy counting his potatoes in Zimms and has missed the last two years!! However, the tears were rolling as we recalled our days at Thornhill High School.

You will not find me on facebook - with my background I will get arrested and straight into "chookie"!

I have had a rather humble life since leaving school - have been picked up many times from the "gutter" - promised to go straight and then met my wife Vicki in Wankie. We married in 1982, had Claire (32yrs) and Phillip (28 yrs). Both still single but doing very well. Moved to Oz in 1986 and have never looked back. Now happily retired, travel and enjoy meeting up with Jan Nysschen and the boys for our annual Zimms fishing trip! Unfortunately Jan is getting madala so the competition is not what it was!!!

It just goes to show that you don't have to be a brilliant student (hell, I was a domkop) but with a bit of vision, good luck, the right person at your side, integrity, panache and the world's your oyster!

Matey, guess I can go on but you know me too well and I can't "bulldust" you! THS photos, I'm sure, has one of the "monster"!

(Author's licence: No worries, Mate - Jan Nysschen has beaten me to it - he sent in a photograph of *another* 'monster' you caught - see below:

Fishermans' stories - spot the 'Monster'

He claims he used it to catch his monster, as above).

Beverley Nelson) teaches French in Christchurch, New Zealand. She compiles and sends out the Thornhill High School newsletter for past pupils and staff. Beverley is the driving force to get the various Diamond Jubilee celebrations off the ground. All past pupils and staff join me in expressing our sincere gratitude for the tireless effort she puts in to keeping everyone likeminded in contact with one another.

Dave Nelson

Lynette Nelson (Jessop) 1975 - 1978 is the daughter of Geoff Jessop (Rhodesian Air Force) and sister to Phillip Jessop. Brother Peter also served in the Air Force. Lynette currently lives in Rotorua, New Zealand. Lynette says "I was at Thornhill from 1975 till 1978 and loved every minute of being there. Joined the form three class and was shocked as to how different if was from Salisbury Girls High. I swam, played hockey and was part of the Drama Club. Special teachers were Mr Dykstra and Mrs Brown, but fond memories the teachers, admin and heads at Thornhill. Long may she continue!!

Kevin Nesbitt

Lesley Ness*born Ndola, Zambia 1957.

Michele Newton (Le Quesne) from Gwelo, lives in Cowes, Isle of Wight, United Kingdom.

Mfanwy Newlands (Rowlands)* played 1st Team Hockey in 1960.

Sikhululiwe Ngwenya (Lacoste) is a past pupil at Thornhill High School and studied at the University of Zimbabwe.

Angela Nichol (Semple)

Granville Nicholson 1961 - 1964

Audrey Folkertsen Nieuwenhuizen played First Team Hockey in 1982. Audrey studied at Griffith College Dublin and is the Accountant at Abbey Healthcare, Ireland.

Andrew Nieuwoudt junior schooling at Shabani Primary School.

Sally Niland (Stening)*

Gillian Nineham (Quinlan)

Kaz Carinus Botha Nobel from Gweru, lives in Gaborone, Botswana and manages her own sign manufacturing company. Her brother Alfred Carinus also attended Thornhill 1973 - 1977.

Andrew Norman

Kevin North

Alan Northcote* born Zvishavane, graduated Thornhill 1982, married Roelien Strydom in 1987, is the Site Project Manager at Anglo Plats and lives in Lydenburg, South Africa. Alan is the elder brother to Deirdre-Ann Rahn who graduated from Thornhill in 1983.

Colin Northcote, also born Zvishavane, in 1967, went to Thornhill but finished his schooling at Highveld Park High School. Married Magda Viljoen in 2001 and works at New Denmark Colliery and lives in Standerton.

Aletta Nortje (Benade) born 1955, lives in Polkwane. Her Facebook picture shows Tom, Kota, Gideon, Piet and Dirk Benade, in a rare photo of all the Benades.

Denise Norvall (Beuke) is from Howick, attended Thornhill High School and Howick High School. She is a Bird-Wild Life Artist and lives in Howick, KZN-Natal.

Jan Nysschen tracked on Facebook, with a nine-year old Kariba fishing trip with his good friend Frik Nel. Credit to Bruce Brislin with us re-establishing comms.

Jan writes: Looking back now and with all the mates we had and friendships that followed, I must look upon those days as the best of my life. Thornhill was a great school and I still have many fond memories of those days.

After leaving school I joined Standard Bank and was posted to the Highlands Branch in Salisbury. After 8 months and some special effort, I was appointed to the Relief Staff and travelled most of Rhodesia, Zambia and finally Malawi, where I was offered a 2 year 'Tour of Duty Contract' which culminated in an 'all expensed paid' holiday on the Reiner del Mar Cruise Ship to South America, for a full month.

Whilst in Malawi, I carried on with my love for Rugby and was fortunate enough to represent the National side on 2 tours to Rhodesia.

Upon return from South America, I was sent to Shabani Branch as Teller no 1, and eventually Relief Accountant. After Shabani, I was again appointed to the Relief Staff and sent to a number of branches country wide, ending up in Gatooma, where I met my 19 year old 'bride to be', Wendy, in October 1970 and we got married on 30th January 1971.

My wife and I were immediately selected to do a 'tour of duty', in Malawi and we left shortly after our marriage. The strict dress code for women in Malawi could not be tolerated by Wendy, so we resigned and took up positions with the then, Rhodesian Banking Corporation, which was 51% owned by, Netherlands Bank of South Africa. (Later on Nedbank)

In 1978, during my 10 day R&R, my wife and I flew to Durban and I applied for a job with Trust Bank. At that time, South Africa was in a `recession` and jobs were hard to come by, so I left my CV and to my surprise, I received a telegram whilst on "Call Up" at Chiredzi, to say that they were offering me a position.

After a year with them, I was offered my job back with Netherlands Bank in 1979. I had a wonderful career with Nedbank and finally retired as Senior Manager, Corporate Banking, in 2004. "(Not bad for someone who only had C.O.P., and 2 "O Level", passes in Woodwork and Afrikaans)".

We celebrated our 44th wedding anniversary this year and still have the same love and respect for each other. We were blessed with 2 wonderful children, Sean (1980) and Chanelle (1984). Sean has a successful career here in South Africa and after Chanelle joined us on a holiday to Australia in 2003, she met a South African there, who had emigrated with his parents nine years before. They eventually got married, after a few years of 'long distance' romance and she moved to Brisbane in 2012.

Wendy Nysschen leaves in a few days, (19th August) to spend a month with Chanelle in Brisbane. After two trips to Australia, I rather elect to go fishing with Frik on the Zambezi every year when he flies out to Africa from Melbourne.

He arrives on 21st September and we are off to Kariba for 10 days and then on to the Thornhill School 60th

Anniversary Reunion in Harare on 17th October.

Frik can't wait to meet up with Shirley Kuttner (Nourse) and Janet Marchussen (Lancaster) again.

Patricia Oakman*1977 - 1980, from Gweru and lives in Harare. Works at Appropriate Technology Africa.

Sharon O'Bree, class of 1978, born 1960.

Graeme O'Connor* from Zvishavane and lives in Harare. Graeme is attending the Harare reunion.

Tracey O'Connor 1977 - 1982 has held re-union functions at her home. She lives in Norton and is from Zvishavane, Zimbabwe. Tracey attended the Golden Jubilee reunion held in Durban ten years ago in April 2005.

She, together with Ray Hewitt and team, arranged the Harare

function for mid-October 2015. With a ten-year learning curve, the bar will be set at a very impressive level, from which future organisers of re-unions will be wise to take note..

TOC, as Tracey O'Connor is more affectionately known, commented on Facebook "The 60th celebrations have one great thing about them - that I can read this about "ancient" pupils and proudly say that I know some of them now - how great is that!"

Ginny Ogborne (Thompson) Born in Bristol, U.K; lived in Rhodesia, went to Greendale Primary, then Courtney Selous, then David Livingstone and finally boarded at Macheke Primary. Thornhill High, then Queen Elizabeth High for her final year. Joined G.P.O as telephonist in Salisbury exchange. Moved back to Bristol U.K in 1977. Worked on telephone exchange in Bristol before becoming a Police Officer in Bath with Avon and Somerset Constabulary. Left to become Ambulance driver with Avon Ambulance Service. When first son Sean born worked night shift for the Automobile Association before immigrating back to South Africa. Married to Steve, and have four sons.

Charmaine Oelofse Class of 1976 lives in Fish Hoek, Western Cape and is the owner of JCE Forklift Services. Charmaine is a cousin of Vanessa McBain who attended the Perth reunion.

Kathy Olds (Gifford)

Margaret Olivier (Bossert)*

Phillip Oosthuizen features in a group photograph in front of Cranwell House, circa 1978.

Lynn Opie born 1961, studied secretarial at the Gwelo Technical College, and lives in Johannesburg.

Chris Owen*

Julie Owen (Till)

Rick Owen

Phil Palmer lives in Whitstable, UK.

Sylvia Palmer

E. Papadopoulos played 1st XV Rugby for Thornhill High School.

Stewart Papadopoulos features in a group photograph in front of Cranwell House.

G. Parkin also played 1st XV Rugby for Thornhill High School.

Judy Parkin

Nittin Patel features in a group photograph in front of Cranwell House, circa 1978.

Colin Patterson was in the same class as Shirley Kuttner (Nourse); they had an opportunity to recap the past since leaving school some 46 years ago.

Mel Paterson (Jervois); **John Patterson**

Cheryl-Ann Paul (Landman) 1959 – 1964

Connel Paul 1960 – 1964, born 1948, married Chaplin girl Aletta Ferreira and lives in Benoni, South Africa.

Alan Pawson* played Under 15 Rugby in 1985. It is believed Alan is now in Gaborone.

Philip Payne went to Thornhill. He is on Facebook – but no further details given.

Gregory Pearce*

David Peebles was at Thornhill in Class of 1976, attended Teacher Training College Bulawayo in 1979 and is currently in Auckland, New Zealand, attending Massey University (Educational Leadership - 2000), having worked at Pinehurst School and Murrays Bay School. He and his wife Lynda have been to the beautiful Milford Sound in 2006.

Graham Peebles

Chris Pelly*is a Pioneer member from the old school.

Mike Pember* born 1964, studied art at Sir John Colfox School, owner of Eye on Design and lives in Bridport, UK.

Mark Penberthy - 1969

Judy Pentz born Gwelo 1955 and lives in Rust De Winter, Limpopo, South Africa. Married with two daughters and three sons; Caileigh Kyle, Leandrie, Michael, Richard and Stephen Pentz.

Alison Perryman studied at Thornhill and Roosevelt, works at Discovery Health SA and lives in Johannesburg. Her two daughters resembles her (with triplet likeness).

Derek Perryman - 1979, born 1961, attended Thornhill and Guinea Fowl High Schools, played 1979 1st XV Rugby, lives in Johannesburg and is the Director: New Business Development, Africa at Nampak Ltd.

Petronella Pereira (Groenewald)

Ashley Peters

Mary Pettit (Spencer)* - 1974, studied nursing at Andrew Flemming and Johannesburg General, Class of 1980, lives in Nelspruit, Mpumalanga and worked at Nelspruit Medi-Clinic.

Brenda Phaup (Southey) from Bulawayo, studied nursing at Carinus Nursing College Cape Town, married 1978 and lives in Westville KwaZulu-Natal. Brenda has a daughter, Michele Herbst.

Petro Pereiro lives in Virginia, Free State, South Africa.

Roger Pinder attended Thornhill High School and the Royal Rhodesian Air Force, with the author. Roger qualified as an engineer, has travelled extensively and currently lives in Canberra, Australia. His neighbour (a couple of doors from his home) is another school mate, Chris de Jong. Roger also Skypes Frik Nell frequently. His hobby is model aircraft flying.

David Pleasants

Chris Pluke (staff), taught Physics and Chemistry. He married the English teacher / Librarian Kay Jackett.

Kay Pluke (staff) born 1941, went to Mafeking High School class of 1957 and then Bulawayo Teachers Training College 1960. Kay lives in London.

Garry Poole has a Thornhill 'Broadcasting - On The Air' photograph on his Facebook page. He also played rugby for the school - teaming up with Rupert van Heerden. Garry and Jenny are look-a-likes. Writer is guessing that they are brother and sister at the same school.

Jenny Poole played 1st XI Hockey in 1982 and 1983. Captained the team in the latter year.

Llanis Pople (Pringle)

Pat Posthumous*

Renee Potgieter (van der Merwe)

Stan Price*

Isla Prince (Brislin)

Lyn Prince (van den Berg), 1969 - 1973, married Gerald Prince in 1980 and lives in Richard Bay, KZN Natal.

Herman Prinsloo* Attended both Chaplin and Thornhill High Schools.

Colleen Proome (Roselt)

Dave Prophet, born 1962, Class of 1982, worked at Liberty.

Steve Prophet 1972 - 1977 served in the Rhodesian Air Force and is the owner of Fluid Power group of companies. He married Dana in 2006 and lives in Johannesburg.

David Pullen

Bruce Quail studied City & Guilds Telecommunications at Salisbury Polytechnic. Lives in Perth, Australia and works at LMR Strategy Manager at Vertel.

Bryan Quail born 1946 Bedfordview, South Africa; widowed. Bryan is the Product Manager at RISC Technology Integration.

Marcel Quik is a friend of Tracey O'Connor.

Ivan Radloff 1961 - 1966, from Bulawayo; married in 1972.

Gordon Radloff 1960 - 1966. From Harare, married 1972 and now retired.

Graham Radloff 1965 - 1970

Deirdre-Ann Rahn graduated in 1983 - younger sister to her two look-a-like brothers, Alan Northcote and Colin Northcote. Deirdre-Ann has a daughter, Kylie Rahn Levinson.

Eleanor Ramsay 1968 - 1972. Eleanor lives in the UK and is the Administrator and receptionist at the NHS Mental Health Team in Newmarket.

Her dad the late Bill Ramsay was a highly talented and respected engineer in the Air Force.

Carol Randles (Thompson)

Barbara Reece

Shirley Rees (Shepherd) 1968 - 1972, from Shabani, studied nursing at Bulawayo Central Hospital 1975, and lives in Geelong, Victoria, Australia.

Sylvia Rees (Powell), sister to Sheila Jones, attended Unisa, then Durban Business College 1970 - 1971 and Durban University of Technology 1996 - 1998.

Rene Regtien

Sharon Regtien (van der Merwe)

Doug Rice

Mary Riley (Anderson) See Mary Anderson (her Facebook name). Lives in Shrewsbury, Shropshire

Glenda Rice, born Amanzimtoti, married Andrew Davidge and lives in Umkomaas. Andrew's elder brother, Bev, and the writer, were school mates.

Paul Rigby*

Bill Robb was Head Boy in 1970. He lives in Aberdeen, Scotland.

Shirley Rob went to Thornhill, currently lives in Brisbane, Queensland, Australia. She has a daughter Angela and a son Stuart.

Bill Robertson

Dave Robertson

Dean Robertson lives in Kuruman and works at Barloworld Equipment. Dean has two sisters, Heather van der Riet (who went to Thornhill) and Noleen Leeuwner.

Clare Robinson (Watson) from Esigodini, lives in Toowoomba, Australia and attended the Brisbane Diamond Jubilee reunion.

Drikkie Robinson born Bulawayo 1963, sister to Anna Bakkes van Druten, went to Thornhill and lives in Mandeni, Kenya. Re-united with her sister in Port Edward / Wild Coast water park.

Gayle Robertson had a beautiful voice, playing Mabel in the 1959 production of Pirates of Penzance. She also played Hockey - where her photo is taken from.

Richard Robinson*

Mel Robson-Jervois attended Thornhill high School from 1974 to 1979. On leaving school Mel worked at the Parirenyatwa Hospital in Harare. She currently lives in Beverley, East Riding of Yorkshire, UK.

Paul Robson

Jenny Rochat

Tony Rochat, class of 1970, former owner at Jenton Monitoring Services

Juliet Roe lives in Dunfermline, Fife. On Facebook as Juliet Honey Roe.

Eryl Roselt*

Sandi Roux (Lindley)

Nigel Rowlands; popular Head Boy in 1959.

Helen Roy (Holliday)* 1965 - 1969

Jason Rust born Shurugwi 1970, divorced, brother to Mike and Rob; and lives in Bulawayo.

Kathy Weineck Rutherford from Gweru 1955 lives in Johannesburg.

Mike Rust* born 10th February 1967. His two brothers, Rob Rust and Jason Rust also attended THS. Mike is related to Doreen, Liz and Willie Swartz.

Rob Rust is from and lives in Harare and is attending the Diamond Jubilee reunion. He works at Diamond Drilling supervisor at Mississhinga Mining and Exploration.

Vera Sansbury (Jacobs)

Angela Sayers (Burden)*

Magda Sayers* sister to Rupert van Heerden

Geraldine Schoultz*

Sandie Scott

John Scullion

Dave Scully

Genny Scully lives in Brisbane, Australia. One of three sisters who attended Thornhill High School. Related to Suzanne Hopkinson and Renee Bennett.

Merle Scully is on Facebook, born Cape Town 1937 and classifies herself as granny babysitter (she is Carole Ward's mother) - she attended the

Brisbane celebrations. She was schooled at Roosevelt.

Renee Scully and Suzanne Hopkinson are sisters. Renee married in 2015 (Thornhill Silver Jubilee year).

Anne Scurry (Edwards) lives in Mississauga, Ontario.

Roy Segal

Andrew Semple played in the 1978 Thornhill Theatre and Brass Bands.

Eileen Sharp born 1962, studied at Gwelo Technical Centre, married 1984 and lives in Durban.

Marianne Shaw (Folkerston)* from Gweru, graduated with B. Comm 1979 from the University of Natal, Pietermaritzburg. Lives in Perth, Australia.

Deb Shaw-Meyer from Selukwe and lives in Perth, Australia.

Melanie Sheffield (Steinbach)

Ian Shirley

Marcelle Simmonds (Bischoff) 1969 - 1974, born Durban 1956, studied medical Radiography at Salisbury Central Hospital and currently lives in Crowmash Gifford, UK. She was known as Moz Bischoff back in her days at Thornhill, 1974. Played Basketball, as seen in the team photograph earlier on.

Gill Simpson (Vallaro)

Michael (Mick) Slater - 1965 lives in San Lorenzo, Paraguay. Former Director at Zeneth English Centre and past PTC Rhodesia 1969 -1978.

Johan Smit

Barry Smith

Carole Smith (Walkley) 1966 - 1970, born Gwelo 1953.

Eddie Smith

Fiona Nuttall-Smith was one of the St John girls at School, married in 1991 and attended the Harare 2010 reunion. Also counted amongst the 'Shabani Girls' photograph.

Leon Smith

Merlene Smith (Atkinson) - 1969 lives in Durban (like her twin sister Marilyn Atkinson Darné)). Telling the difference between the twins can be quite tricky.

Barry Snowdon, from Harare, now retired and lives in Aldershot, United Kingdom.

Stuart Solomon

Charles Southey 1966 - 1969, born Bulawayo, married to Trish, worked for Northam Platinum Mines and now retired to Polokwane, South Africa.

Bridget Sparks (Moffat)*

Roddy Speight (staff)

Len Spence

Sandi Spence - 1974

Gilly Squair (staff)*

Kevin Stals is self employed.

Allan Stals, born Gwelo 1951, lives in Johannesburg and owner at APS Consulting. Brother to Monica van Rooyen (Stals).

Cynthia Stals (Jardine) 1965 - 1969

Duncan Steele class of 1974, UCT 1978, and Virology at MEDUSA - Medical University of South Africa, class of 1980 for his PhD. Lives in Seattle, Washington.

Past Pupils and Staff of Thornhill High School

Heather Steele went to Thornhill and Hatfield Girls High in Harare. Lives in Royal Tunbridge Wells, UK.

Veronica Steffen (1956-1960) attended the London celebrations. She gave the writer permission to repeat her feedback report which reads "To celebrate the establishment of Thornhill High School's 60th Anniversary, Murray Woodfield very kindly organised a get together in a very old picturesque pub, The Blue Anchor, besides the River Thames in Hammersmith, a London suburb.

As it was a fine day when we arrived, were able to gather outside with our drinks. People began arriving from different parts the UK which was wonderful and an ex-pupil, who was over on business from South Africa, also joined us. I was lucky as I live not far away!

We were a mixed bunch of "boys and girls" with husbands, wives and family members, mainly from the 60's and 70's, with "only" two of us 'Golden Oldies' from the 50c who attended school at the Thornhill Air Base, before moving to our new premises.

It was great seeing friends meeting up and chatting about times past; old friends, acquaintances, and what we got up to and who we knew and those we didn't. Unfortunately, Pat and I from the 50's knew no one, not even one another, although we were there at the same time. I was a border, she was a day pupil, and both in a different classes. We did however recall pupils and teachers we knew, plus being in the same opera 'Pirates of Penzance' - her being a singer and me a dancer!! How very different it was for us (being pioneers), to those who arrived after the premises were established. I "mostly" enjoyed my school days, although I got into trouble a fair bit of the time.

I only know a few people I was at school with who now live in different parts of the world. It was also lovely making new friends that afternoon. What was amazing was the feeling I had, like meeting up with members of my lost family. We all share so much; all having been at the same place at different times in our formative years.

I finally said farewell to everyone, feeling a tinge of sadness of those days gone and people I knew; at the same time happy knowing that Thornhill will be there for many years to come producing fine world citizens. The celebration continued till late in the evening with others arriving.

Suzie Stephenson

Colin Steven

Juliet Stevens (Holsey)

Mike Stewart 1956 -

Minky Smith-Wright is from Harare, went to Thornhill and lives in Chiredzi, According to her Facebook page, she is a 'horsey' person who loves animals.

Irene Jack Steyn lives in Brisbane, Queensland, Australia. Irene has four children, a son Charl and three daughters, Liezel Blair, Natasha and Tanya.

Sharon Steyn (Deetlefs)

Sue Steyn (Blignaut) works at Admin with Avis Van Rentals, Richards Bay, KwaZulu-Natal. Sue is married to Japie Steyn and they have two sons, Karel and Andries.

Ray Stout played 1st XV Rugby in 1969

Annette Strachan*

Alwyn Strauss was at Cranwell with the writer - late 1950's

Mike Stobart-Vallaro from Gweru, lives in Harare, attending the Harare celebrations in October 2015.

Craig Stotter features in a group photograph in front of Cranwell House, circa 1978.

Kotie Strauss born Gweru 1943 and still lives in Gweru.

Lesley Strydom - 1964, born 1947, married Danny Strydom, worked at Semelar and lives in Ruby, Warwickshire

Roger Swaine* - 1966. Now retired. His Facebook son is Mike Swaine.

Kathy Sullivan is school friends of Neil Calder and Karen Johnson.

Ralph Sutherland features in a group photograph in front of Cranwell House, circa 1978.

Dean Swanepoel served in the Rhodesian Air Force.

Janet Swart born Bulawayo 1957 (living Harare?) was seen with Murray Woodfield in London, reminiscing about the 'Oliver' performance, way back in their past, but not forgotten.

Doreen Swartz is from Gweru, 1960. Photographed with Browwyn Fitzpatric and Michelle Holmes.

Keith Swartz

Liz Swartz

Willie Swartz class of 1980, rugby friend of Dave Ward.

Delise Swift – see Delise Joubert

Morag Swift (Waymark) 1958 - 1961

Tracy Swift worked at Mediclinic Hospital and lives in Pietermaritzburg.

Gillian Nicholson Swindells, born Kwekwe 1964, went to both Thornhill and Mount Pleasant High Schools. Studied at the University of Western Australia, class of 2008, and is the Associate Director, Business and Building Services. Facebook friend of Arlene Garner.

David Tankersley

Elsa Taylor - 1983, sister to Janet Medland Udy is an anaesthetist and lives in Auckland. She played hockey 1982 and 1983.

Gill Taylor (Lawrence)

Marion Taylor (Bishop)*

Robert Taylor participated in the 1981 Athletics Team. He lives in Brisbane, Australia.

Colleen Tegart (Swartz)

Mark Templemore-Walters attended the Harare reunion.

Don Thackray - 1977. Studied at Northumbria University Class of 1985, UK. Lives in Zuidlaren, Netherlands and works at Creative Director at Philips.

Coleen Thackwray (Williams) - waiting for the Shabani Bus for the 1975 Rhodes and Founders weekend; together with Delise Swift-Joubert and Katherine van der Walt.

Malcolm Thackwray*

Louis Theron*

Barry Thackwray - 1983. Born Gweru 1966, married Wendy Freeman in 1991, is an Auctioneer and lives in Colchester, Essex. Nicknamed Bazza.

John Thomson born Redcliff 1954, studied at the Bulawayo Tech 1974 - 1978, served in the Rhodesian Light Infantry, married 2012 and lived in Shurugwi.

Colin Till 1978 - 1981, born 1964, played in the 1978 Brass Band, studied at East London Technical class of 1985. Worked at Nestle South Africa..

Clare Thornton (van Jaarsveldt) married Trevor John Thornton in 1982. She is a Shareholder / Directorate Octance Tax and Accounting. They have three sons. She lives in Gweru and and was seen at the Dutch Oven with Tracey O'Connor and Karen Johnson

Errol Thurtell from Harare went to Chaplin (may have taken classes at THS), lives in Toronto, Ontario.

Alan Titterton

Helga Toland attended the Derby celebrations. Her Facebook reveals that she is from Selukwe now living in Wrexham, United Kingdom. Helga has a daughter Sharon van Ballegooyen and a daughter-in-law Andrea Pudge

Helga in London with Elaine Evans, Ian Dunbar and Joan Manning or Jean Barrand

Brian Tooze born 1962, married Audrey, is self employed and lives in Perth, Australia. He features in a group photograph in front of Cranwell House, circa 1978.

Janey Towell - 1978, born Gweru 1961, married Adrian Towell in 2006, has a daughter Melissa Stemmett Venter and a son Sean Michael Towell. Janey is self employed and lives in Polokwane

Lorraine Hewitt Triggs - 1983 played 1982 First X1 Hockey.

Rob Tubbs* born 1950, no details on Facebook. Married Angela Woodhouse.

Angela Tubbs (Woodhouse)* studied at the University of Pretoria. Brother is Colin Frank Woodhouse who went to Thornhill.

Linda Turnbull

Dierdre Turner (Cullinan) is from and lives in Cape Town. Friends with Sharon Grant.

Yvonne Twilley (Emslie)

Janet Udy (Medland) 1978 - 1983, head girl in 1983, with the family immigrated to New Zealand and Janet completed her degree in Computing and Mathematics at Massey University. Janet writes "I have many happy memories of the school and feel privileged to have received such a good education. We were also very lucky to have had so many sporting opportunities and my ongoing involvement with squash dates back to my days playing squash at Thornhill.

"Having completed my degree over three years, I then worked in the Computing Centre at the University of Otago until 1993, when I moved to Blenheim with my husband Allan. Since then we've run a software development company, mostly writing software for small businesses. Allan and I have three children - Isaac 21, Nerys 19 and Quinn 16.

"My sister Elsa Taylor is an anaesthetist and lives in Auckland."

Judy played First Team Hockey in 1982 and vice-Captain in 1983. She named most of the players as well.

Standing: Eulalie Barry, Claire Forder, V. Manning, Rene Jordan and Leslie-Ann Hector: Seated; LH, Janet Medland Udi), Jenny Poole, Lorraine Hewitt Triggs and Elsa Taylor

Martin Underhill*

Mike Upton, class of 1960, served in the Rhodesian Air Force and decorated for bravery with the Bronze Cross of Rhodesia. Michael Ian Upton now lives in Melbourne, Australia.

His brother, Bruce Christopher Upton went to Guinea Fowl and Chaplin High Schools.

Denise Ure born Gweru, went to Boksburg and Thornhill High Schools. Denise has a daughter, Kayley Ure, and lives in Johannesburg.

Brenda Valentine from Gwelo and lives in Dundee, UK.

Judy van Aardt (Beattie)
1961 - 1962. Judy was born in Gwelo and now lives in East London, Eastern Cape. She has a son Clint Bower and a daughter Yolanda Maqhina.

Ben van As went to school with the writer. He met up by chance with my daughter Renene Jelley, earlier this year during a trip to Zimbabwe. Ben and his good lady Beatrice live in Brisbane Australia. She was schooled at Que Que and studied at UNISA.

Hank van de Weg claims to be a retired layabout bum on his Facebook page, however, as possibly the oldest pioneering old-boy, he certainly is a foundation member responsible for starting many Thornhill traditions which are still developing now-a-days. Hank exchanged several valued experiences with the writer and was one of the first to produce an old school photograph wearing the school tie.

Hank was born in Durban in 1941. In 1949 his family moved to Gwelo and Hank enrolled at Cecil John Rhodes till 1954, becoming a pioneering member at Thornhill High School in 1955 when the new secondary school started at the old

Rhodesian Air Force base at Thornhill.

He graduated 1958. He returned to Durban with his family after a short stint in Broken Hill, Northern Rhodesia. Hank had four brothers, elder brother Paul who went to Chaplin (passed away 2014) and younger brothers Karel, Bruce and Gerald who attended Riverside Junior.

Hanks first job was as a bank clerk with the Nederlandse Bank in Durban. In 1960 he went to Port Elizabeth with Olivetti but returned to Durban 18 months later as his father had been diagnosed with lung cancer. In March 1969 he married Salisbury girl Shelagh Watson who was a nurse at Addington Hospital. They decided to relocate back to Salisbury in October of 1969 where they stayed until 1974 having worked at Lever Brothers and then The Dairy Marketing Board Head Office. They returned to South Africa where they ran a number of successful businesses in Durban until 2009.

He has a married daughter, Lara who lives in Gold Coast, Australia, with three sons and a daughter, a son Michael who recently relocated to the UK with two sons and a daughter, Wendy getting married in December 2015 and lastly Tracy who got married in August 2015.

Hank and Shelagh currently live in Swindon, United Kingdom where they retired to in April 2009.

See Hanks "The Reminiscing of a THS Pioneer" in the history chapter.

Ian van der Berg played 1979 1st XV Rugby

Gill van der Bijl

Betty van der Merwe played 1st Team Hockey in 1960. She married Chris Viljoen (Cranwell boarder).

Christo van der Merwe played 1st XV Rugby in 1979.

Felicity van der Merwe, nee Jones, is a sister to Wilhelmina Jones (nicknamed 'Villie") and Yvonne Matthyser nee Jones.

Joan van der Merwe (van Wyk)* attended the Salt Rock 2009 reunion, with Ray Hewitt, Delise Joubert (Swift), Sharon Davis (Banwell), Sharon O'Bree, BJ Coetzee and several others. She also attended the October 2010 reunion.

Brian van der Riet born 1957 Zvishavane, studied THS and Bulawayo Technical College, married Heather in 1980 and have two boys and two girls – see Heather.

Heather van der Riet, from Shabani, married Brian van der Riet in 1980. They two sons, Bruce and Craig, and two daughters, Madri and Petro.

Cheryl van der Walt (Fulton) 1974 - 1978, married Hannes van der Walt in 1987, from Gweru and lives in Johannesburg.

Anna van Druten (Bakkes) worked at Zimcool, Harare. Attended the Harare reunion, with the "Class of 1978".

Allison van Dyk (Bossert)

Maureen van Heerden (Marshall)

Rupert van Heerden born 1964, studied at Thornhill and Kwekwe Technical College. He works as a maintenance fitter with Orora Kiwi Packaging in Auckland, New Zealand. He has a daughter and son. Kerrie and Mark van Heerden (brother to Mags Sayers). Rupert kindly submitted his early days at Thornhill (see 1980's history section). In addition, he commented: "I left Thornhill High at the end of 1981 to serve an Apprenticeship at Ziscosteel as a Fitter Machinist and Qualified in 1986 stayed with Zisco for a further year then moved on to Union Carbide in Kwekwe.

"During that time I played Rugby for Zisco 1st and 2nd Teams, Selected for Midlands U-20, Seniors and Goshawks I've played against Moscow Slava from Russia and Ulster from Ireland and many games against old school friends who played for Gweru.

"1989 I went on walkabout to England (you can keep it) came home to Harare worked for Rothmans of Pall Mall and for Mashonaland Tobacco. Played rugby for Harare Sports Club and Old Georgians. Selected to play for Goshawks and also played against The Condors from the USA.

"I got married in 1990 to Linda (ex-Gweru) had my baby girl in the same year and then 1993 my son was born.

"By 2001 we had applied to Immigrate to New Zealand and were accepted. We packed our bags and moved here in August/September 2001. We live here in Auckland and have been back to Zim a few times to see my Mom and Mom in Law who still live there.

"My Daughter went to Uni and got her Bachelors and Master's degree in Art, My Son is a Qualified Fitter/Turner, My Wife works at the local Parish as a Secretary and I am a Maintenance Engineer at a Corrugated Fibre Packaging Factory."

Ann van Helsdingen (Ward) - born Gwelo; lives in Durban.

Bev van Helsdingen born Margate 1959, married, works at Personal Assistant at Hibiscus Coast Municipality. Lives in Durban and has two daughters, Kristen and Marcia Moodie. Maiden name van Niekerk.

Barbara van Kraayenburg (Reece), born Gwelo, lives in Johannesburg.

Rhona van Niekerk, class of 1962, born Port Edward 1945, qualified in accountancy, lives in Port Edward, KwaZulu Natal.

Brandon van Niekerk* born Gwelo, played 2nd XV Rugby for Thornhill High School and in the 1978 Brass Band. He lives in South Mission Beach, Queensland, Australia and works at Ramblers Drop-zone.

Connie van Niekerk (Knoetze). Connie is in her early sixties and has a cousin, Vic Auditore.

Sybrand van Niekerk known as 'Branie', born Gweru 1962, is the past Zululand Coordinator Zimbabwe Pensioner Support Fund and currently the Technical Controller at RBCT in Richards Bay, Kwa-Zulu Natal. Branie is married to Glenda and they have three daughters - Angelique van Niekerk Duvenage, Leane Lubbe de

Vries and Vicky-Lynne van Niekerk

Brian van Rooyen

Monica van Rooyen (Stals), widowed, and lives in Phalaborwa, South Africa. Sister to Allan Stals

George van Schalkwyk

Gerry van Tonder is from Bulawayo, Thornhill class of 1972-1974, University of Rhodesia 1979. Gerry is married to Tracy and they have a son, Andries and a daughter Ashleigh. Gerry is in Derby, UK, were he is self-employed as a Copy Editor / Writer.

Jo van Tonder born 1954, brother to Gerry, and lives in Kabul, Afghanistan / Vientiane, Laos.

Peter van Zyl*

Anne Venables is from Bulawayo and married Colin. See also the earlier 'Anne Buckley Venables' posting.

Bernie Venter

Ernie Venter (R.I.P.)

Late 1959 - early 60's

Ernie Venter settled in the Greytown, Natal area and managed a very successful 'day-old' Peking duck breeding business. His wife was an avid horse rider / jumper. His unexpected passing in 2014 came as a surprise to many.

Japie Venter, elder brother of Ernie, currently living in Secunda. He was a school mate of the writer - 1958 to 1961

Vivienne Verdelli, born 1961 and lives in Johannesburg. Vivienne has two daughters, Daniela and Coly Coly. She features in the Halton girls 1978 photograph.

Caela Vermaak (Edwards) born Gweru, lived in Leeds 2001, London 2004 and now lives in Mount Isa, Queensland, Australia.

Derris Viljoen (staff)

Fiona Viljoen*

Lorna Viljoen hails from Perth, Western Australia and previously attended a Thornhill re-union which John Wightman had organised. She and husband Johan attended the 2015 celebration dinner held at Zebra's in Bicton near Freemantle. Lorna is the Manager, Management Systems at Edith Cowan University.

two sons, Craig and Vaughan Voster.

Susan Vorster (Donaldson). Class of 1963, worked at Pomene View Lodge in Mozambique and lives in Durban.

Allan Voyce

DJ Voyce

Cheryll Enid Vorster (Woolf) - 1975, born Pretoria 1958, lives in Pretoria. Sister is Belinda Acott. Cheryll has a daughter Ashleigh Skipwith and

Sharon Voyce (Cornish) lives in Atherton, Queensland, Australia. Sister to Ed Cornish, and Facebook friends of Karen Johnson and Helga Toland.

Tim Wade is mutual friends with Carole Ward, Yolanda MacIntyre and Sheila Maitland.

Tim Wade-Pienaar - same person as above? He features in a group photograph in front of Cranwell House, circa 1978.

Carole Ward (Scully) studied at the University of Natal, Pietermaritzburg. She has worked at the Toowoomba Prep School but is currently Head of Boarding at Ipswich Girls' Grammar School, Queensland, Australia.

She attended the Brisbane reunion. Her input for the magazine is eagerly awaited!

Dave Ward was at Thornhill 1969 to 1974 and then joined the British South Africa Police BSAP till the Rhodesian War ended in 1980.

Dave writes: I was at THS as a boarder from 1969 to 1974. Head of House in 1974 was awarded Rugby colours, Water Polo and Drama half colours, much to my astonishment.

Played in the 1973 and 1974 Ist XV rugby sides and if my memory serves me correctly we always won more then we lost.

I have very fond memories of Thornhill and my days there,

amazing to be in contact with so many past pupils from my time, both seniors and juniors. Just missed seeing Bill Malkin when he was visiting my part of the world. I was his "skivvy". I bet there are many stories out there about how being a "skivvy" were terrible but it taught me to iron pretty well and quickly.

Bunking out was almost a "right of passage" visiting the Parrot was always top of the list. They did lock the doors but there were dorms with very loose screws in the burglar bars.

Tech Drawing, Geography, Art, woodwork, English and the Sciences were subjects I enjoyed. History, Afrikaans, French and Maths had less to no appeal during those days. The exact subjects I had to re-write in 1974.

After serving in the BSAP I left in 1980 for South Africa completing a Plumbing apprenticeship. Where I had to do math and Science again and learn Afrikaans, dit sal my leer.

I have been fortunate to travel and complete projects all over the world including being part of the team that did the initial reconstruction of Ellis Park Rugby Stadium.

When we were in New Zealand 2008/2009 I saw Gerry Erasmus, Graham and David Peebles.

Gerry had not changed at all still looked really fit and I am sure his athletics 200m record still stands to this day.

I hope to meet THS folk when I am in London (UK) early November this year, still counts as the year is not over, right.

A little known or publicized sport which featured Thornhill lads was Boxing which was practised down town at the local boxing club (GCABC). There were several national boxers and champions - the Ashley, Krause and Ferguson brothers come to mind. While the school did not award colours for the sport, Rhodesia did.

BOXING TEAM 1957
Back Row: L to R
Reginald Kaschula ; EvansHundermark ; Chris Viljoen
Middle Row: L to R
Terrence Smith ; Chris de Jongh; John Gordon ; Jannie Olivier
Bottom Row L to R
Roger Scales; Ronald Cousins; Edward Doughman

The 1957 Boxing Team - Reg Kaschula, Evans Hundermark, Chris Viljoen, Terrence Smith,

Chris de Jong, John Gordon Jannie Olivier, Roger Scales, Ronald Cousins and Edward Doughman

(Photo Credit: THS Past Pupils website)

(Insert by the author: Reg Kaschula was one of the 'boxers' who challenged the author to a fist fight outside Cranwell. With honour at stake, and to save face, the challenge was duly accepted. This fight attracted quite a hostel audience - and quite surprisingly the fight went against all odds, with yours truly's reputation for standing up to 'bullies' duly restored. This reminder prompts a photo of the Boxing Team).

There were a number of us who did the training and had a few fights but the aforementioned were really good.

I have nearly every class photo from my time at THS and Cranwell photos plus some sports pictures.

I know that Gerry van Tonder has a 1974 Magazine. I could ask him to scan something from that magazine and send to you.

You are probably wondering what this odd car is. Well it was named 'Bitzov' owned by Athol Boothroyd. Gerry Erasmus (wing), Athol and I (No) travelled to Fort Victoria to play a rugby game in 1973.

The 'Bitzov' - painted in Thornhill colours

We nearly froze to death on each valley but it made it there and back, it was painted Thornhill Gold and Black.

Don Ward features in a group photograph in front of Cranwell House, circa 1978 and also part of an athletics or swimming team.

Joe Ward 1971 - 1976 attended the Brisbane function, and is credited for the photographs that Sheila

Maitland posted on her Facebook page; especially the THS signage at the venue - and its usage thereof is greatly appreciated.

Brian Waring from Zvishavane lives in Vista, California. He is the Operations Manager at E3 Audiometrics.

Bruce Waring* lives in Ramona, California. Also goes by George Bruce.

Joe Watkinson (Wilson) 1960 - 1965, lived in Kloof but moved to Howick in 2015. Daughter is Sera Delene Glaus.

Chunky Watson

Colin Watson 1960 - 1963

Jody Wayne, alias Donald Hill, was a class mate of the author. He popularised the ballad 'Patches' which made the top of the 'Hit Parade'. He is the brother of Jillian who married Guinea Fowl's Hilton Grimbeek.

Darell Watt

Kathy Wayland (Gilmore) lives in Tsitsikamma, Eastern Cape, South Africa.

Sheila Weber married Eric Bradnick

Patti Weeden (Parrat)

Lizzie Weeden (Caldwell) 1966 - 1968. Finished her schooling at Queen Elizabeth High School in Harare. Has been a teacher at Chisipite Junior School, Harare, since 2001.

Albert Weidemann served in the Grey Scouts.

Kathy Weidemann (Holmes)

Wendy-Lee Weir (Whewell), played 1978 Hockey and enjoyed a mini reunion with Yolanda MacIntyre in 2015.

Shirley Jovner Weir born Gwelo 1963, self employed in Polokwane, South Africa.

Nolene Welch (Kent)* from Gweru 1961, married Clifford Welsh 1989 and lives in Harare.

Jim Welsh, 1967 - 1970.

Vivian Wentzel (Bethell), class of 1977, lives in Durban.

Sandy Westphal (Naude)*
1964 - 1968)

Syd Wheeler (OCA) (Sydney Bailie-Barry Wheeler), born 1948, studied Chaplin and Teachers Diploma at TTC Bulawayo.

Syd is known as 'Mama Chaplin' as she keeps their database and sends out newsletters and information to the OCA. She and Bev Nelson are often in touch about people from one school or the other, so we consider her an honorary Thornhillian.

Jenny Whelehan 1965 - 1970 lives in Tackley, United Kingdom. Daughter of Val Celliers who served with the writer on No 4 Squadron. They used to live at MQ 2 then posted to New Sarum.

Jenny Whelehan (nee Celliers) wrote: "I guess THS formed the foundation of the person I am today. Memories drift in and out of my mind and I have to admit I do wonder after all of these years if some of them are actual or given the mists of passing time just creations in my mind! No matter they are mine and they are treasured.

"Travelling on the Thornhill Air Force bus and driving through the gates sometimes feeling elation at the thought of seeing friends sometimes with a gut wrenching dread knowing you were heading into a day of exams. Morning assembly juggling for a spot near to your buddy or in later years because boys and girls were split and stood on separate sides of the hall, juggling for a spot where you could see the young gentleman of your current affections. To save my blushes I will refrain from mentioning the names of my amores in those days!

"Mr Geoffrey Lambert followed by Mr John Eadie both great heads and dear Mr Nick Holman.

"I think a great favourite of all the girls (and boys because of the delicious products that flowed from her class room) had to be Mrs Alexander. I adored her when we had cooking lessons but dear heaven not when we had to tackle sewing or knitting. I heard the words "cats teeth Jeanette" more times than I care to remember when handing in my apology for sewing! Mr Neil whose vain attempts at getting me to understand maths resulted in a comment on my end of year report - "tries hard but has little ability at this subject!" Mrs Cairns was a dream of a teacher I loved her classes ditto Jenny Chivers (she married one of the teachers but for the life of me I can't remember his name) the Viljoen's (my Mom was at school with Doodles!). Very fond memories of the Mrs Smith who taught music but not the same Mrs Smith who taught Afrikaans. Her ruler connected with the back on my lower legs a couple of times!

"Too many more teachers to mention but all deserve credit for their dedication in parting their knowledge to the little sponges (the students) waiting to soak it all up.

"I still see Di Rowe (Dewsbury) if she comes to the UK or on the odd occasion we are in the same town when I return to visit my parents who I am still blessed to have around living in Pennington KZN. Then via the joy of Face Book I have been lucky enough to re connect with a few dear friends again. Peter, Shaz, Gilly, Ele and Bev x 2. I do wonder what has happened to so many of the students but hopefully some of them will re surface with the publication of the Magazine."

Irene Whincup (Ellaby) 1970 - 1974, lives in Perth, Western Australia.

Ellen White born Wankie 1960, lives in Germiston, Gauteng, South Africa.

Neil is one of the Thornhill High School golfing team that played at the Umhlali Country Club.

Tara Ann Duffy-White born Harare 1966, lives in Harare and works at Kennan property sales.

Neil White 1974 - 1978, born Aliwal North 1959, graduated from Rhodes University 1984 and is the Pharmacist in Aliwal North. Neil's sister is Lorraine En Willem Blom.

Sussie Wickham studied at Damelin, lives in Jeffrey's Bay, Eastern Cape.

John Wightman arranging a 60th celebration at Zebras in East Fremantle, Perth, Western Australia on 30th October.

Stacey Wilke (Lipp) is from Perth, Thornhill class of 1976, served in the Rhodesian Air Force, married Gary, they have a son Ross J and a daughter Tamla McKay, currently living in Dubai. UAR.

Brian Peter Wilson played in the 1978 Brass Band.

Richard Wilson 1961 - 1966 writes "You will not remember me as I was about three years behind you. I was at Thornhill High School from 1961 to 1966 (Form 1 to Upper VI). I just wanted to let you know that your jubilee book as well as your other books brought back many memories and if you will allow me to waffle, you and I have some connections.

I was the eldest of the four Wilson boys and in 1966; all four of us were at THS together! That must be a record of some sort. I was not in your sporting league at school and in today's terms would have been called a nerd. All brains and no muscle! I can remember playing rugby (we had to) in Form 1 and being given the gears by Furve Steenkamp who was a useless coach for me. I was tall and lanky for my age (like the

Davidges) and so where did Furve put me?........lock. I was *donnered* from one end of the scrum to the other because I was not heavy enough. But I had to be there for the line out! My moment of glory came in a game against Chaplin when I was kicked off the field by the ref for being off side too many times. Furve never explained the rules of off side and so how was I to know! Anyway, in Form 2 we could choose between rugby and hockey and I played hockey for the next 20 years. However, I have always enjoyed watching rugby and am really looking forward to the World Cup next month. I was at the World Cup in RSA in 1995 and I went to the 2007 World Cup in France.

I was never good at sports at school but when I went to university, I discovered a good talent for squash which I played league and still play to this day, two or three times a week. Golf is an occasional social sport.

You mention Mrs. Antoniadis and the musicals of 1961 and 1962 and I remember them well (Iolanthe and The Mikado). We lived for 20 years in Stellenbosch (my wife is a South African) and who lived down the street from us? – John Antoniadis from Gwelo! He was a music lecturer at the university. His wife went on to give my daughters violin lessons and I did meet Nikki Antoniadis at their house. She did not remember me even though she had sent me to Geoff Lambert for correction during one singing lesson! Sam McGee and Geoff Day were also stalwarts of the theatre scene.

Other teachers who made an impression on me were Miss Reynolds and Nick Holman (maths), Andy Evans (Geography), Audrey Gudath (Latin), Chris Pluke (chemistry) and Gilly Squair (physics). I was good at maths and science but useless at languages. There were many other teachers such as Miss Nuttal, Mr. Harley, Mrs. Cairns, Miss Scott (of the lovely MGA), and Mr. Parker who registered lower on the impression scale. I was a day scholar and so did not have the connection with staff that you would have had as a boarder.

My school mates were John Fox, David Bromley, Tony Aimer and Ian Shirley. I won't expand on this as I am sure you would not know them. David was killed when 19 years old in a traffic accident and I am still in contact with the other three. Girls did not feature for me at high school - that came later.

Another connection I have with you is the Rhodesian Air Force. I was already married and had a child when I was called up in 1974 to the army. I was living in Shabani at the time and in our squash league were players from the Thornhill Air Base. I spoke to a Squadron Leader Peter Knobel and he arranged to get me into the Air Force for my national service. I thought this was going to be a cushy number. To back track, when I left Thornhill High School, I went to Natal University and got a degree in civil engineering. So, when I was in the RAF at New Sarum, the government was incredibly short of engineers for work in the war zone and so I was taken out of the RAF and sent to Centenary to build the new FAF (Forward Air Field) under the Ministry of Roads. I was then also involved in the FAFs at Sipolilo and Mt Darwin. I am sure you know them all. I was also seconded to the Army to build the road over the Alpha Trail to Hoya, Gutsa and Musengezi. Busy and dangerous times. The final connection with the RAF comes via my father who, as an aircraft technician in RAF Bomber Command, came out to Gwelo during World War II on a training mission. He was based at Thornhill and I have photos of him on the air base during the war. After the war, he made his way from the UK back to Gwelo as he could not stand post war England. That is why we grew up in Gwelo.

My other connection to you goes even further back. I was interested to read that your great-grandfather had ridden in the Kroonstad commando. Well, my great-grandfather was in the Royal Horse Artillery of the British Army stationed in Hong Kong quelling the Boxer Rebellion. When the Anglo-Boer War broke out, his regiment was sent to South Africa. I can trace his battles from his medals which I have. I know he was at Paardeberg, the Relief of Kimberley, Driefontein, Belfast and Diamond Hill. Who knows, maybe he and your Oupa grootjie almost got to know each other!! As you know, after the war, the British disbanded the ZARPs and asked for volunteers from the British Army to start up the new SAP. My great-grandfather transferred and was stationed in Zeerust in the Groot Marico (H C Bosman country) as a policeman. When the First World War broke out, he was called up and went chasing Germans and rebels around SWA. So, all in all, he had quite an adventurous life and lived the remainder of his life quietly in Pretoria where he died in 1956.

So, where am I? Well I have followed work eventually to Calgary, Alberta, Canada and have been here about 15 years now. The reason I mention this is that every year, the Calgary Stampede is held and it is a show case of everything cow boyish. If you want to see what a Boer Commando looks like, there is a society here which keeps up the tradition and a whole commando is seen in the parade. The reason is fascinating. The British Army needed good scouts in the Boer War and so they recruited cowboys from the Wild West because they could ride like the Boers. When the Canadian cowboys got to South Africa they adopted the Boer uniform and small horses because they said the only way to catch a Boer was to ride like him. So the commando you see in the Calgary Stampede parade is actually a corps of Canadian cowboys dressed up in khaki, *bandoliere* and felt hats. The first time I saw this, I was astounded to see a Boer-like commando in the parade!

I am still working as a civil engineer building things. My wife and I were in Oz in November last year visiting our daughter in Perth. I need to get to NZ sometime because my mother was born in Wellington and I have relations in NZ who I have never met. They live in Hamilton, Wellington, Dunedin but most of them are in Invercargill.

I could reminisce for a while longer on Thornhill, Gwelo and Rhodesia but it would be about things that I suspect you have no connection with and so I will leave it at that.

I hope you found these titbits of my version of life at Thornhill a bit interesting (Author's note: The 'non THS relevant' input are left intact - readers may find it just as fascinating as what the author found).

Eileen Williamson (McGarvie) - 1978, married Keith Williamson in 1985 and known to have had two sons and living in Bulawayo.

Geraldine Williamson (Bowley)

Carol Wilson (Friedrichs) was Sixth Form in 1970.

Dave Wilson*

Jenny Wilson (Doyle)

Jonathan Wilson 1966 - 1970. Jonathan is a fine product of Thornhill High School. He qualified MBA at the University of Cape Town in 1986 and followed up with a PhD in Strategic Management at the University of Surrey in 2000. He has been the Adjunct Professor at Liberty University, Lynchburg, Virginia; and Consultant 1086 - 1990 at Pricewaterhouse Coopers, London.

Ray Wilson - 1968. Born Gwelo 1950, self employed in Johannesburg.

Richard Wilson

Sheila Windridge (Penberthy) 1966 - 1968, lives in Amersham,

Buckinghamshire, UK. Friend of Rick Owen, Christene Weston and John Manning

Sheila was in the same class as Christine Gird (Weston) and Mark Penberty. She still sees Rick Owen, John Manning, Chas Cowie and Christene regularly. She attended Chaplin for 'M' levels and was made a prefect in her final year.

Janet Winsor (Evans, Grant) sister to Grant Evans, also attended Thornhill High School, playing Basket Ball in 1971

Ruth Wiseman - self employed, Facebook friend of Debbie Collyer.

Dawn Wood and her two sisters, Jenny Green and Anne Booker attended the Perth reunion.

Lina Woodard (Pretorius) (Staff)

Malcolm Woodfield attended the London celebrations.

Murray Woodfield was the organiser of the London celebration. Murray is London based and currently the Managing director of the UK Film Festival.

The school photo shows Murray as Head boy, seated between Sandy Connolly and Headmaster John Eadie

Colin Frank Woodhouse, retired and lives in Cape Town. Brother to Angela Woodhouse Tubbs.

Marie Woolf (Burger)*

Cindy Wright (Bredenkamp)*, from Perth, married 1999, lives in Mandurah, Western Australia, and works at Cindy Wright Artist & Workshops.

Alison Yates (Hart) has given permission to publish her Facebook picture.

Meryl Yefet (Coleman) 1975 - 1979. Also known as Merle Coleman-Yefet on Facebook.

Julie Yeatman (Bradnick), 1972, Rhodesian Army 1981, now employed as Chief Executive Officer of Jill of All Trades. Lives in Newmarket, Suffolk, UK.

Lesley Young (Ashby)* 1978, also went to Chaplin. Lives in Reviersonderend, Western Cape.

Robin Younghusband

Past Pupils and Staff of Thornhill High School

The names in this listing were taken from a variety of sources, including the Thornhill newsletter address list, Facebook, and personal submissions.

© Vic McKenzie 2014

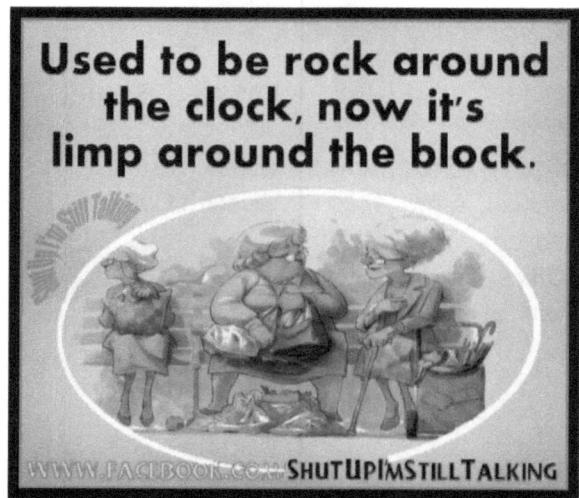

Appreciation for the Thorny Issue

So lovely you did this - Lynette Nelson (Roscoe?) x+x

Hi Bev
Good to chat to you last night on skype. It has been a superb weekend of celebration. So pleased we have been able to be part of it all and so grateful to the Lord for you and Prop for flying the flag for us all. We look forward to many more get togethers.
All the best
Dave & Lynda Peebles

Dear Bev
Thank you for all your hard work in getting the Thornhill group together. Sorry you couldn't come.

Thanks Beverley for all that you have done for our group. Great to chat to you last night. Best wishes
Gordon Gelfand, Israel

Bev
How special to be able to Share with you.
Many thanks
Dee Mocori (Chaplin-Hogg)

Hi Bev, so great to meet you Michele, hope you can one day! xx

Dear Bev
Have enjoyed the newsletters over the years. Many thanks for all your efforts lately to see you on Skype.
Pamela Aranyos (nee Fountain) 1930-1934

Dear Bev
Your email & well wishes were read out a few hours during the celebration - lovely words and sharing
Grahame & Renene Jelley

Dear Bev
Greetings! You are such an important part of the Thornhill Old Pupils' group & I truly salute you for all the hard work over many years, keeping staff & pupils in touch. I have so enjoyed all the Thorny Issues over so many years.
Bless you
Jane Fox

Great to have shared time with good old Rhodies!
Jan

What a great weekend of fellowship with a special group of people
Thanks
Grahame Jelley

RINA

Bev
We have not met. My name is Laura & I am Gordon's wife. I went to MGHS in Salisbury. Thank you for all the work you have done to build these Thornhill relationships. It is wonderful to see from this distance.

Bev
Thank you for Thorny Issue thanks to Tom from whom I have stolen most of the content of this magazine. Much appreciated
Prop 18 October 2015

In Memoriam

(Extracted from the Thornhill High School Past Pupils and Staff Website - http://freewebs.com/thornhillhigh.)

Lest we Forget

P.J. Todd, Thornhill's first Headmaster, died in October 1970.

Peter Siebert, former deputy head, died in Switzerland after receiving treatment for a brain tumour.

Lynne Smith died tragically in a car accident on 4 November 1973.

Jeff Collett   [See Roll of Honour]

Russell Poole   [See Roll of Honour]

Colin Neasham   [See Roll of Honour]

Kevin Botma   [See Roll of Honour]

Edward Benzies was murdered in Zimbabwe in the 1980's.

David Benzies passed away from a heart attack whilst in Cape Town on a training course. He was resident in Zimbabwe.

Howard Moffat   [See Roll of Honour]

Tony Templemore-Walters [See Roll of Honour]

Vaughan Burden died in a work-related accident in January 1987.

Stephen Hewitt was tragically killed in a motor bike accident on his way to work on 3rd July 1987.

Anthony (Tony) Owen passed away tragically in March 1990.

Derek Ritchie died in an accident on 9th May 1991.

Maarten van der Velden (known as "Dutch") was tragically killed in a car accident in 1991.

Joy Dicker (nee Ferguson) died of cancer on 19th April 1991 aged 44.

Olivier Celdre died in an accident on 2nd November 1991

Hendrik "Blackie" Swart passed away in 1993

Richmal Nordin born 23rd June 1960, died 9th November 1993, aged 33.

In Memoriam

Mrs Alexander, Domestic Science teacher, died during the August 1774 school holidays.

Sylvia Moraine died of cancer in 1995.

Ingrid Marais, died in 1997, the victim of a bee sting.

Norman Graham died in a motorbike accident in May 1997.

Brenda Ann Light born 10th May 1968, died 8th October 1999, aged 31.

Jan Nel, born 30th January 1968 and died 4th February 2001

Andy Evans (staff) passed away in 2002.

Barry Jovner, born 19th December 1964 and died 6th November 2002, aged 38.

Gillian Atkins (formally Blyth, le Roith), at Thornhill School in the 1960's, passed away in the UK on 11th November 2002.

Terry Hart, French teacher and Cranwell House Superintendent, died of cancer in 2002.

Nick Holman, former Maths master, hockey coach and deputy head, died on 28th November 2002 in Edinburgh, Scotland.

Janice Watkinson (nee Bossert) at Thornhill until 1966, died in 2003 after a long battle with cancer.

Mary Noddy Warrington Purdon , born 20th May 1959, died 23rd October 2003, aged 44.

Lynette Fineal (nee Palmer) passed away on 17th September 2003. She was head girl in about 1960/61.

Wayne Robertson, born 4th April 1961, died 24th September 2003, aged 42.

Ken van Blerk, biology teacher in the 1960's, passed away in Hillcrest, Durban on 12th December 2003.

Eileen Ingle (nee Bayne) passed away suddenly in Johannesburg on 9th January 2004.

David Boothroyd, Thornhill 1970 to 1975. Died in Scotland 7 October 2004.

William Trevor (Wally) Patterson passed away on 2nd September 2004 from a heart attack. He was at Thornhill 1958 to 1961.

In Memoriam

Doodles Viljoen (founder member of staff) died suddenly on 25 March 2005 at his home in Gweru.

David Palmer died suddenly on the 15th April 2005 in the South of England.

Gladys Smith, who taught Music and Afrikaans at Thornhill for many years, passed away in April 2006 after a short illness.

Nella Reece passed away on 15 April 2006. She was the cook matron at the girls' hostel in 1981/82 before moving to Chaplin.

Sue Kelley (nee Duffin) passed away in Buckinghamshire, England, on 20th March 2006 after a brain haemorrhage.

Alexander Charles Blackadder, at Thornhill late 1950's/early 60's, passed away on 25 May 2006 aged 63.

Des van Rooyen passed away in 2006. He attended Thornhill High from 1958.

Kevin Cornish died on the 20th February 2007 in Plumtree.

Keith Swartz passed away on 14th April 2007.

Philip Adcock passed away on 8th June 2007 at Claybank Hospital, Gweru.

Miranda Bloom passed away in July 2007.

Edith Lamb passed away suddenly on the 27th November 2007.

Tony Bothma born 29th September 1960, died 1st January 2008, aged 48.

Graham Weaver, teacher of Maths and Physics at Thornhill in the mid-seventies, passed away in May 2008.

Leslie Stout died in a motorbike accident in Pretoria on the 6th October 2008.

Mike Collins passed away on 28th April 2009.

Alan Rowe was ambushed and shot dead on his farm in Natal midlands during the evening of the 13th May 2009.

Murelle Hayes died suddenly in Harare on 14th June 2009.

Hennie Bakkes passed away on Thursday 16th June 2009.

In Memoriam

Gail Handy (nee Millard) passed away on the 22nd August 2009 from breast cancer. She was living in Palm Bay, Florida, USA. She was at Thornhill until moving to the US in 1978.

Deanne van Huyssteen (nee van Heerden) died suddenly in Pretoria, on the 29th August 2009. She left Thornhill in 1964.

Reg Wickens passed away in September 2009.

Roger (Spider) Atkinson died suddenly on the 15th March 2010 at the age of 57. He was at Thornhill from 1965 till 1969.

Roy Kalil died on the 9th April 2010 from cancer of the stomach.

Angela Gregory (nee Houshold) passed away in October 2010 after a battle with liver cancer.

Don Lawrence died 12th March 2011 of a heart attack in Somerset West, Cape.

Brian Authers died 9th June 2011 aged 63.

Karen Byrne, at Thornhill 1972 to 1975, passed away in August 2011 after a battle with cancer.

Shelley Knott passed away 21st October 2011

Carol Foster (nee Shirley) died of cancer on 10th February 2012.

Esme Smith, the School Secretary in the 70's and mother of Lynne, Sandy, Bronwyn and Pony, passed away on the 16th February 2012 in Howick, KwaZulu Natal.

Penny Graham (nee Ford) passed away in the UK on the 19th February 2012 after a long battle with cancer.

Gillian Harbour (nee Flake formerly Lewis) passed away in Ireland on 14th June 2012 after suffering from Chronic Obstructive Pulmonary Disease.

Kathy Jenkins (Tillett) passed away on 28th July 2012 aged 56.

Dot Cairns (teacher and hostel superintendent) passed away on 4th January 2013 in Queensland, Australia, after a long illness.

Graham Bothma, born 10th June 1964, died of cancer 19th February 2013, aged 49.

Darryl Pfaff died suddenly in March 2013.

In Memoriam

Philip Alp passed away on 5th April 2013 aged 67.

Sharon Gregson-Allcott (nee Hayes) passed away on 9th July 2013, at her home in Centenary, Zimbabwe, aged 59.

Jenny McGaw (nee Chivers) (teacher) passed away on 9th July 2013 after a battle with cancer.

Wayne Derek Jeremiah, born Gwelo 17th February 1961 passed away in Stevenage UK on 5th August 2013, aged 52.

Theunis de Klerk passed away in Witbank on 5th October 2013 after a heart aneurism. He was 66.

Kathy van Beurden (nee Ballantyne) passed away on the 25th October 2013 after a lengthy illness.

Shirley Lamb passed away 8th November 2013.

Brenda Alderson (nee Budd) passed away on 23rd November 2013 after a tough fight with cancer.

Blair White passed away in November 2013 after a battle with cancer.

Rory Harbinson, born 26th September 1960, passed away on the 12th December 2013 after a long battle with cancer. He was 53.

Margie Cunliffe (teacher) passed away 12th January 2012 after a battle with cancer.

Peter Barlow passed away on 5th March 2014, aged 66.

Pam Bates (nee Davies) passed away on 6th March 2014.

Lynette Wells (nee van Heerden) passed away on 13th March 2014 after a long illness.

Michael Brett Smith passed away 15th April 2014.

Donovan Burden passed away tragically on 4th May 2014 as a result of a motor-bike accident.

Aileen Bothma (nee van Breda) passed away in South Africa on 15 October 2014

Piet Rautenbach passed away on 16 October 2014 after a four year struggle with Steele Richardson Syndrome.

In Memoriam

Sudden Bekker passed away on 16th October 2014 after a short illness.

Wyndom Dallas who left Thornhill in 1972, died in Cape Town 26th October 2014

Ernie Venter passed away on 6th November 2014 after suffering a stroke.

Annette Hahn passed away in Florida on 19th November 2014 after a 5-year struggle with breast cancer which spread to her brain and lungs.

June (Juanita) Badenhorst (Swart) passed away in November 2014.

Andy Nimmo (teacher) passed away in UK on 27th January 2015.

Lilian Matthews, passed away peacefully in Christchurch, New Zealand, on Sunday morning 2nd August 2015. She lived in Gwelo/Gweru from 1927 to 1984 and worked at Bata, Housing Dept, Income Tax and Thornhill School (Bursar).

Trevor Wiesner passed away 4th August 2015, aged 61.

Rob Tubbs passed away in Pretoria on 6th December 2015.

Details for the following are still incomplete at the time of submitting this edition to the printers. Dates of passing still need to be determined,

Christopher Belstead

Graham Ball

Karen Burn

Mrs Barbara Coventry

Neil Engelbrecht

Blake Evans

Craig Holmes

Angela Household

Collin Kent

Ingrid Marais

Peter McDonald

In Memoriam

Celdre Olivier

Connie Oosthuysen

Derek Tyne

Robert "Skippy" Tyne

Thornhill High School

Wall of Remembrance

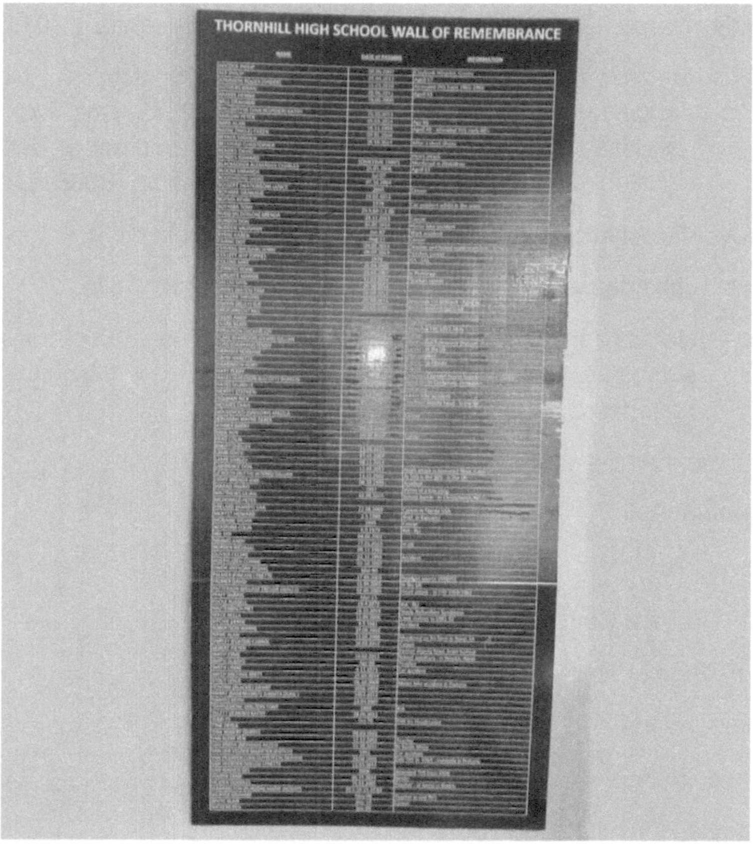

Thornhill Roll of Honour
(Rhodesian War Casualties)

Lest We Forget

Anthony John Charles "Tony" Scott-Rodger, Service Number 7871 Patrol Officer, Uniform Branch, BSAP, Killed On Active Service, 11th March 1973, Killed in an electrical accident, aged 27 years (born 14 April 1946 in Bulawayo). Educated in Blantyre and at Thornhill High School, Gwelo, Tony served in Bulawayo and Matabeleland district for his initial three years, before leaving the force with the intention of travelling the world. He re-attested in January, 1968, continuing his service in Bulawayo and was with the city's Traffic Section for the last five years. He spent much of this time attached to Highway Patrol. Described as being a willing member of the force with a sense of humour, he had considerable knowledge of traffic matters. Attested 9 June 1964.

Alasdair Ian Murray Scott, 8344, Patrol Officer, Uniform Branch, BSAP KOAS, 9th March 1977. Off duty at the time in Burnside, Bulawayo, Alisdair was electrocuted whilst trying to repair a heater at his parents' house, aged 25 years (born 21 November 1951 in Edinburgh, Scotland). Upon leaving school at the end of 1968, he applied to become a cadet in the Force and he spent the next year in this capacity at Gwelo Urban. Upon full attestation and training, Alasdair was stationed at Kezi, Nkai, Filabusi and Beitbridge, before transferring to Bulawayo Central where he was a B-Car driver. Alasdare's semi-military funeral service was held in Bulawayo on 14 March 1977. Source: Outpost (BSAP journal) and Guy Halls, who attended the accidental death.

Jeff Collett (Jeffrey Donald "Jeff"), service number 729660, Lance Corporal C Squadron, Special Air Service, Killed in action on Operation Gatling in Zambia on the 19th October, 1978. The attack was against the ZIPRA Camp at Mkushi.

Russell Forbes Poole, 729752 Mortar Troop, Support Commando, I Battalion Rhodesian Light Infantry, killed in action in a contact during a Fire Force action on 19th April

1979, in the Chiduku TTL, Makoni district (Rusape), Op Thrasher. Source: Rhodes Bezuidenhout and *The Saints*. Formerly a Patrol Officer with BSAP

Peter McDonald 110764 Patrol Officer Support Unit BSAP, Died on active service 5 May 1979. Died of leukaemia in Andrew Fleming Hospital, Salisbury, aged 19 years (born 2 April 1960 in Newcastle-upon-Tyne, England). His semi-military funeral was held at Warren Hills Cemetery, Salisbury, on 18 May 1979. Attested Jan 1979. Source: Outpost (BSAP journal) and Shaun Hodgson.

Kevin Peter Botma 105791 Rifleman. 4th Bn ('Q' Cars) Rhodesia Regiment, Died from injuries sustained in a vehicle accident. He was serving with B troop Special Forces at the time of his death. Source: Steve Lunderstedt, ex 'Q' Cars. Killed On Active Service 4th June 1979

Colin Graham Neasham, 123027 Trooper 1 Commando, 1st Battalion Rhodesian Light Infantry, killed in action 6th September 1979, Operation Uric / SA Operation Bootlace when shot down by an RPG7 in a SADF Puma helicopter at Mapai, Mozambique. The SADF Puma, call-sign Hotel 4, was hit behind the pilot's seat, causing it to crash and burst into flames. 9 of the dead were RLI, 5 from Engineers and the SAAF air crew of 3.

Howard Moffet was shot and killed at Kamativi Mine on 2nd May 1980.

Anthony Carl Michael Henry Maurice "Tony" Templemore-Walters, service number, 109431W, Cadet, National Service, Internal Affairs, Killed In Action, 25th August 1980 Died in Andrew Fleming Hospital, as a result of medical complications from a gunshot wound received in a vehicle ambush in the Mt Darwin area four years earlier on 9 April 1976. He was wounded on his 19th birthday (b. 9 April 1957 in Northern Rhodesia). He was in a convoy with police when the ambush took place, and from there Tony was casevaced to Karanda Mission. Tony was subsequently hospitalised on several occasions, but never recovered from the wound. At the time of his death Tony was serving an apprenticeship in moulding and pattern making, He was cremated at Warren Hills Crematorium.

This Roll of Honour compiled with input from Thornhill old boy Gerry van Tonder, author of the official Rhodesian War Roll of Honour.

Index

A

A'Bear (Paxton), Beverley 175
Aberdein (Wentzel), Ina 175
Acott, Belinda 336
Adam, James 175
Adcock, Philip 358
Aimer, David 175
Aimer, Tony 175, 347
Alan-Brown, Audrey*See* Audrey Chandler
Alan-Brown, Audrey Anne 201
Alan-Brown, Bernard 175
Alderson (Budd), Brenda........... 360
Alers, Mr 255
Alexander, John 15, 175
Alexander, Mrs 11, 17, 180, 273, 344, 357
Alexander, O 37
Alp, Donovan 175
Alp, Geoff 175
Alp, Philip 360
Amand, Caroline Kelly 268
Amira (van der Poll), Bettie........ 176
Andersen, Mr *41*
Anderson, Doug 133, 135, 176
Anderson, Heather 133
Anderson, Mary 125, 176, 308
Andy Evans 26, 347
Annandale, Courtney + Rhett 186
Antoniadis, Niki 11, 16, 17, *23*, 67, 262, 272
Aranyos (Fountain), Pamela 112, 155, 156, 157, 159, 167, 176, 198, 221, 249, 275
Aranyos, Nic 176
Archer, Nora 15
Armand, Caroline Kelly 134, 137, 176, 197
Armand, Geoff 133
Armand, Mark 177
Armstrong (Marshall), Judy 177
Armstrong Bentley, Sue 45, 87
Arnold, Anne 127, 177
Arnold, Clive 177
Arnott, Zelda 40, 177
Ashby (Forder), Elizabeth 177
Ashby, Denise 178
Ashby, Les 178
Ashby, Nigel 177
Ashford, Ann 35
Ashford, Tony 177
Ashley - the boxer 338
Ashley, Chris 178
Atkins (formally Blyth, le Roith), Gillian 357
Atkinson, Doug 178
Atkinson, Roger (Spider) 42, 359
Auditore, Vic 333
Authers, Brian 14, 359
Avery, John 179
Aylett, Miss 11

B

Badenhorst, June (Juanita)(Swart) 361
Bader, Douglas 29, 30, 274
Baier, Eleanor 15
Baker, Mr *38*
Bakkes, Anna*See* van Druten, Anna Bakkes
Bakkes, Hendrina*See* Drikkie Robinson
Bakkes, Hennie 185, 358
Bakkes, P 32, 179

Index

Baldwin, Dianne 31, 90, 100, 179
Baldwin, Miss 274
Baldwin, Neville 106, 179
Baldwin, Sheryl 180
Ball, Cindy 180
Ball, Gavin 50, 180
Ball, Graham 361
Ballantyne, Kathy 31, 180, 274
Ballantyne, Sue 92, 180
Banwell, Sharon ....See Sharon Davis
Bardouz, Suzanne 180
Bares, Michael 55
Barlow, Patricia 15, 277
Barlow, Peter 360
Barlow, Tony 180
Barnes, Jill 257
Barr, Alistair 180
Barr, Gill 180
Barratt (Wickens), Annette 181
Barry, Eulalie 60, 181, 248, 327
Barry, Felicity 15
Bartlett, Lee 181, 273
Bartlett, Mrs...................................17
Basedow (Bothma), Lauretta 181
Bassi, Barbara 44
Bate (Frew), Cynthia 181, 182
Bate, Brendan Ross + Candy 181
Bates (Davies), Pam 360
Bates, Judith................................182
Bates, Michael 56
Bates, Mr..11
Battey, A 101
Bauwens, Jayne...........................182
Baynham (Frew), Adrienne 182
Beets, Pieter.................................182
Begg, Kerrin........................201, 202
Begg, Matthew, Adam, Daniel &
 Timothy 201
Begg, Mike 201
Bekker, Oscar 39, 133, 183
Bekker, Sudden 183, 361
Belstead, Christopher 361
Benade (Newman), Janet...........183
Benade (Nortje), Alet 133

Benade, Aletta 141
Benade, Ben (Kota)54, 133, 137,
 141, 142, 183
Benade, Colette 133, 141
Benade, Dirk98, 106, 133, 135, 136,
 139, 140, 141, 145, 146, 183,
 295
Benade, Gideon.......98, 99, 133, 295
Benade, J................................49, 53
Benade, Janet.................... 133, 183
Benade, Lyn.................................133
Benade, Piet 133, 147, 184, 295
Benade, Tom 32, 133, 172, 184, 295
Bennet, Eve 20
Bennett, Carole 184
Bennett, June 15, 20
Bennett, Renee 312
Bentley (Naude), Darlene 184
Bently (Armstrong), Sue.............184
Benzies, Ben 15
Benzies, David 356
Benzies, Edward..........................356
Benzies, Ronnie 15
Berkowitz, Justin 185, 223
Berry, Dave 35
Berry, David.........................185, 273
Berry, Mr......................................192
Bester, Bob..................................185
Bester, Robbie 15
Bester, Ruth 185
Bester, Truida..............................185
Bester, Truidy..............................271
Beuke-Norval, Denise...........43, 185
Beverley Paxton See A'Bear,
 Beverley
Beverley, Tom 4
Bezuidenhout, Aletta 15
Bezuidenhout, Rhodes44, 119, 153,
 186, 217, 364
Bingham, Rebecca......................186
Birch, Connie................................15
Bird, Tara Leigh 270
Bischoff....................See Simmonds
Bischoff, Mike 53, 186

Index

Bischoff, Moz 314
Black (Daynes), Sue 186
Blackadder, Alexander Charles 26, 358
Blackburn, Clr and Mrs TH 85
Blankenberg, Jennifer 15
Blanschard, Ann 186
Bleeker, Linda 231
Blignaut, Hannes 50, 53, 186
Blignaut, Neels 50, 54, 187
Bloem, S 26
Bloom, Miranda 358
Bloom, Phyllida 187
Bloom, Sheena 98, 100
Blundell (Kerfoot), Heather 187
Boag, Irene 187
Boddington, Lawrence 15
Booker, Anne 131, 187, 239, 351
Boothroyd, Athol 187, 339
Boothroyd, Colin 187
Boothroyd, David 86, 357
Bos, Teresa 187
Bossert, Allan 187
Bossert, Janice 274
Boswell, Gill 188, 271
Botha (Burden), Judith 238
Botha, Annette 15
Botha, Attie 187
Botha, Beryl Venter 188
Botha, Colin 188
Botha, Ernest 15
Botha, Hermanus & Petrus 185
Botha, Judith 188
Botha, Karen 88, 255
Botha, Leon 188
Botha, Mary 23, 26
Botha, Stacey 188
Botha, Truida ......See Bester, Truida
Bothma (van Breda), Aileen 360
Bothma, Graham 188, 359
Bothma, Tony 358
Botma, Kevin 356, 364
Bott, Enid 15
Bower (Roselt), Heather 188

Bower, Clint 328
Bower, Paul 188
Bowker, Rowene 153
Bowman, T 56
Bowyer, Derris 11, 106
Boyce, Cheryl Linda 113, 137, 188
Boyce, Cheryll 133
Boyce, Cheryll Linda 120
Boyce, Damian + Logan 188
Boyce, Daryl 133, 188
Boysens, A 56
Bradnick, Eric 42, 43, 106, 189, 274, 341
Brand (Robb), Annette 189
Bray (du Plessis), Gail 189
Breakwell (Kerfoot), Wendy 189
Bresler, Hank 189
Bresler, Herman 189
Brett, Mike 189
Briatte, Pierre 189
Bright, May 208
Brightman, Judy 189
Brislin, Bruce 92, 169, 190, 295
Bristow, Leigh 48, 193, 207, 271
Bromley, Cathy 30
Bromley, David 347
Bromley, Muriel 11, 17, 276
Bronkhorst, Michelle 193
Broodryk (Rautenbach), Judy 12, 26, 193, 229
Broodryk, Andre and Louis 193
Brooke-Mee, Judy 45, 48, 81, 87, 114, 194
Brown (Clarke), Lesley 194, 195
Brown Frew, Heather 145, 146
Brown, Audrey 73, 106, 212
Brown, Emma 195
Brown, Heather Frew 133, 194
Brown, Jeff 133
Brown, Mrs 291
Brown, Steven 49, 56, 122, 194
Browne, R 37
Bruce, Kelley 195
Bruce, Kevin 190

Index

Bryan (Car), Gwen 87, 195
Buckley Venables, Anne 195, 334
Buckley, Brian 15
Budd, Brenda .*See* Alderson, Brenda
Budd, Eric 43, 45, 87, 88, 196
Budd, Nadine 45, 87
Budke (Griffiths), Kim...................196
Bugler, Lynette..............................30
Burden, Donovan 360
Burden, Sherryl 188, 196, 238
Burden, Vaughan 356
Burger, Pieter 69, 213
Burgess, Kevin 39
Burgoyne, Jean...........................273
Burgoyne, Tommy11, *23*, *67*, *68*, *234*, 257, 262
Burkett, Rob 32
Burkett, Robert 35
Burn, Karen 361
Burnett, Robert 35
Burns, Dean 50, 56, 196
Burns, Gary 196
Burns, Ted 100
Burns, Tod 55, 56, 197
Burton, Helena 197
Burton, Neil......................83, 197
Bushell, Anneline 197
Bushell, Jennifer...................23, 197
Bushnell, Juanita 197
Button, Mark...............................197
Butts (Hector), Leslie-Ann 197
Buys, Piet...............45, 87, 198, 278
Byrne (Budd), Cathy 198
Byrne, Craig 43, 58, 198
Byrne, Karen 359
Byrne, Martin 106
Byrne, Martin Terence 45, 87
Byrne, Terry 198

C

Cable, Joseph 133, 181
Cairns, Dot...................37, 255, 359
Cairns, Mrs 262, 276, 347
Calder, Bailey, Samantha + Sharon 199
Calder, Neil...........43, 112, 198, 320
Calder, Vanessa..........................106
Caldwell, Steve...........................273
Callaghan (Struckel), Sally12, 16, 20, 22, 110, 199
Callow, Winifred 15
Calvert, Derrick 199
Cameron, Fiona..........................273
Campbell, Maria...........................44
Candy Bate 181
Cape, Norman & Titch...............199
Carinus, Alfred 199, 294
Carmel, Gordon............................39
Carol Bennet 184
Carruthers-Smith, Miss 11
Carter............................*See* Koninis
Carter, (Collett), Debbie.............200
Carter, Nick 15
Carter, Nigel...............................200
Case, Terry 38, 200
Cavalheiro, Fernando.................200
Cave, James...............................252
Cave, Janet.................................127
Celliers, Rob 200
Celliers, Val 343
Chabata, E 101
Chalmers, C 37
Chalmers, Dave 15
Chamberlain, EM37, 57, 58, 200, 254, 274
Chamberlain, Iain 56, 100, 200
Chamberlain, Nicky 60, 100, *244*
Chandler, Audrey 73, 108, 201
Chandler, Philip & Adrienne 201
Chandler, Robin 201
Chase, Colin................................39
Chikoto, W 100
Child, Lee 55, 56, 170, 203
Chiota, W 101
Chiruka, S 100
Chisadza, A................................100

Index

Chisora, N 101
Chivers, Jenny 106, 344
Owen 299
Churney, Julie 44
Cindy Frew *See* Bate (Frew), Cynthia
Clarke (Hudgeson), Jean 203
Clint Bower 328
Cloete, Georgina 203, 261
Cloete, Hendrik 49, 51, 54
Cloete, Rob 203
Cloete, Steve 40, 41, 203, 204
Cochrane (Nelson), Pauline 204
Cochrane, Sharon 43
Codeco (Oliviera), Ondina 204
Coelho, Eduardo 56, 204
Coetzee, BJ 53, 54, 133, 137, 141, 142, 145, 147, 204, 330
Coetzee, Debbie 46
Coetzee, J 49
Coetzee, Karel 20, 22, 25, 27
Coetzee, Yolanda ... 48, 98, 133, *See* Yolanda MacIntyre
Cole (Beets), Ursula 204
Cole, Alison 83
Coleman, Tim 204
Collett, Gordon ... 156, 160, 164, 165, 204
Collett, Jeff 41, 356, 363
Collett, Keenan + Warwick .. 160, 204
Collett, Louise 157, 165, 166
Collins Keys, Fiona 205
Collins, Mike 46, 48, 49, 51, 358
Collins, Rob . 48, 49, 51, 94, 144, 205
Collyer (Plews), Debbie ... 145, 147, 148, 205
Collyer, Brenda ... 133, 140, 145, 146, 147
Collyer, Christopher Robert ... 133, 140, 146, 147
Collyer, Cindy 146
Collyer, Cindy Leigh and Linda ... 205
Collyer, Debbie 133, 205, 351
Collyer, Kim 133
Columbine, Michael 15

Compton, Karen (Boag) 205
Connolly, Charles 206
Connolly, Sandy 206, 352
Connor, M 26
Cook, Berry 192
Cooke (staff), Christeen 206
Cooke, George 206
Cooke, Miss 255
Coppen (staff), George 206
Corkery, Mrs 191
Cornish, Ed 206, 336
Cornish, Kevin 358
Cornwell, Rob 50, 54, 206
Cosgrove, Tracey 206
Cosh, Maureen 106
Coster, Steve 206
Coughlan (Manning), Flo 133, 207
Coughlan, Tim 133
County, Karlynn 15
Courtney Annandale 186
Cousins, Daphne 15
Cousins, Reggie 15
Cousins, Ronald 15, 339
Coventry, Barbara *11*, *57*, 226
Coventry, S 17
Cowan, Peter 15
Cowie, Charles 108
Cowie, Chas 207, 351
Cowley (Hadzigrigoriou), Tuxcia . 208
Cowper, Reginald *11*, 14, *17*
Cox (McGowan), Molly 208
Craddock, Colin 'Tojo' ... 157, 158, 159, 164, 165, 208
Craddock, May 156, 158
Craddock, Tojo Colin 112
Cranswick, Leigh 48
Crookes, Howard 32, 273
Crow (Budd), Terri 208
Culverwell Drew, Lorna 92
Culverwell, Lorna 92, 106
Cunliffe (Marshall), Sue 172, 208
Cunliffe, John 15
Cunliffe, Margie 37, *38*, 360
Cunliffe, Wendy 209

Index

Cupido, Jan 25
Cusak (Finch), Dierdre 209

D

d'Hotman, Pierre 100, 180
d'Hotman, Sheryl 35
da Fonseca (Fernandes), Tracy ... 209, 212
Dallas, Angela 273
Dallas, Wyndom 39, 361
Dancer, Maureen 209
Daniel, Allen 131, 132, 209
Daniel, Ian 210
Daniel, Noreen 40, 210
Danse (Swaine), Sally 210
Darné (Atkinson), Marilyn ... 30, 110, 210, 315
Darné, Marco 30, 210
Darwin, Mr 11
Davel, Gary 210
David, Palmer 358
Davidge, Andrew 106, 210, 308
Davidge, Bev ... 10, 15, 25, 27, 99, 107, 108, 169, 210, 211, 252
Davidson, Paul 43, 88, 211
Davies, Colin L 211
Davies, John 15
Davies, John Neal 211
Davies, Melaney Casper 211
Davies, Pam 100
Davis (Banwell), Sharon ... 111, 212, 330
Davis, Roy 15
Day, Geoff ... 10, 11, 17, 18, 19, 212, 347
Daynes, Susan 15
de Bernard, Shaun 49
de Haas, Diane 212
de Haas, Karel 21, 25, 213
de Haas, Louis ... 21, 24, 25, 27, 28, 38, 98, 99, 106, 107, 108, 201, 212
de Haas, Roualeyn 201
de Haas, Steph 201
de Jong, Chris 112, 303
de Jong, Chris Broekies ... 15, 69, 277, 290, 339
de Klerk, Nick 213
de Klerk, Theunis 360
de Kock (van Niekerk), Yvonne .. 213
de Reuck, Karen 59
de Reuk, Karen 54
de Swardt (Ashby), Gaille 213
de Vries, Leane Lubbe, ... 334
de Wet, Phil 44
Dee, Christopher 213
Deetlefs (Coetzee), Denise 213
Deetlefs, John 213
Dell, Lin 214
Delport (van der Merwe), Elsie .. 214
Delport, Michael 133
Demister, E 100
Denton, Mark 50, 214
Devantier (Jeremiah), Jenny 214
Dewhurst (Ashley), Sharon 215
Deysel, Dux 56
d'Hotman, Pierre 215
Dicker (Ferguson), Joy 356
Dicker (Hatt), Heather 215
Dippenaar, Gerry 15
Dippenaar, Marie 15
Dippenaar, Sarah 15
Dixon (Lloyd), Christine 215
Dixon, Gayle 215
Dixon, Ian 215
Dixon, Rod 106, 173, 215
Dixon, Roderick 35, 273
Dobson (Lawton), Nita 215
Dobson, Richard 215
Dodgen, William 215
Doig, David, Gary, Jared & Shaina 216
Doig, Ian 216
Dormer (le Quesne), Lulu 40, 216
Dormer, John 216
Doughman, Edward 339
Downs (Whewell), Jo Ann 216

Index

Doyle, Jenny 27
Doyle, Penny 31, 99
Drakes, Marie 217
Drew, Avril 45, 153, 217
Drew, Basil 217
Drew, Gary 61, 91, 217, 255
Drew, Lorna 217
Drew, Rodney 83, 106, 218
Drew, S 56
Drinkwater, John 7, 57, 63, 174, 218
Drinkwater, Roger Neil 218
du Bernard, Gary 48, 56, 87, 218
du Bernard, Mark 51, 55, 219
du Bernard, Shaun 54, 56, 58, 219
du Garde Peach, L 85
du Plessis, 'Dup' 15
du Plessis, John 220
Dubell, Mike 15, 219
Ducladier, Elizabeth 223
Ducray (vd Poll), Maryanne 219
Dudley, Sarah 106
Dudley, Sheldon 49, 51, 98, 100, 117, 219
Dunbar, Ian ... 42, 115, 122, 219, 324
Dunbar, Stu 115
Dunbar, Stuart 220
Duvenage, Angelique van Niekerk 333
Dyer, Debbie Hahn 54, 220
Dyer, Peter 220
Dyer, Wendy Murray 220, 221
Dykstra, Gordon 33, 37, 57, 58, 74, 85, 88, 255, 271, 291
Dykstra, Rients 221
Dzvmbunu, R 100

E

Eadie, John 7, 29, 35, 37, 55, 57, 218, 226, 344, 352
Ebersohn, Attie 69
Eckhardt, Michael 15
Eckstein, Charles Henry 222
Edington, Mark 221
Edwards, Brenda 221
Edwards, Chaela 221
Edy, Lex 53, 55, 98, 100, 221
Eekhout, Linda 31, 39
Ehlers (van Jaarsveldt), Caroline 221
Ehlers, Caroline 59, 221
Ellams (Beugel), Nella 222
Ellis, Gavin 50, 222
Elwanger, K 100
Emslie, Yvonne 15, 66
Engelbrecht, Neil 361
English, Liz 29, 30, 31, 35, 147, 173, 222, 273
Erasmus (Berkowitz), Martha 223
Erasmus, Gerhard 223, 338, 339
Erasmus, Jack 223
Esterhuizen, Floris 223
Etherman, Maura 54
Evans (Budd), Nadine 81, 224
Evans, Andy 23, 26, 223, 262, 272, 357
Evans, Blake 237, 361
Evans, Elaine 40, 122, 123, 125, 223, 324
Evans, Fifi 254
Evans, Grant 53, 133, 137, 145, 147, 148, 151, 224, 228, 237, 255, 351
Evans, Janet 38
Evans, Mark 224
Evans, Philip 224
Evans, Robyn 133, 145, 151, 224
Evans, Robyn + Justin 224

F

Fagan, Lynda 31, 224
Feltham, Mark 225, 255
Ferguson - the boxer 338
Ferguson, Courtney 21, 22, 169, 225
Ferguson, Gavin 225

Index

Ferguson, Gavin, Wilma + Wayne 225
Ferguson, Ian 48
Ferguson, Wayne 225
Ferguson, Wilma 225
Fernandes, Wayne 212, 225
Few, Athol and Valerie Klein 226
Few, Blake 226
Few, Jane37, 38, 57, 59, 96, 157, 160, 161, 165, 166, 222, 226, 255
Field, Mr...11
Field, Stephanie 226
Fincham, Ashleigh 238
Fineal (Palmer), Lynette .15, 23, 357
Finlay (Johnson), Debbie 54, 226
Finlay, Debbie...43, 83, 88, 107, 226
Fisher, Robert 226
Fisher, Rona 226
Fitch, Colin 227
Fitzpatric, Bronwyn 227, 321
Fivaz, Daphne..............................227
Fivaz, John 228
Flanagan, Will....................38, 227
Flanders, Linda 54, 227
Fletcher, Clive 44, 228
Fletcher, R 27
Foletti, Irene 228
Folkertsen Nieuwenhuizen, Audrey 92
Ford, Patrick 39, 228
Ford, Penelope..............................35
Forder, Claire 60, 327
Forder, Liz 88, 100
Fortescue (du Plessis), Yvonne...228
Fortman (Howden), Lynn ...194, 229
Foster (Shirley), Carol.................359
Fouche (Rademeyer), Linda 228
Fountain, Stephen......................229
Fourie (Neasham), Diane 229
Fowle, Harry...............................230
Fowle, John 230
Fowle, Matthew +Sarah 230
Fowlie, Gary 45, 87, 230

Fox (Bromley), Marileine 230
Fox, Carol 133
Fox, Carolyn 31
Fox, John 230, 347
Francis (Budd), Sue 230
Fraser (Spencer), Hillary.............231
Fraser, Gordon 32, 43, 274
Fraser, Lorimer...........................231
Frew, Cindy 39, 133, 231
Frew, Heather 114, 133, 194
Frey, Fiona 231
Friedrich, Linda (Bleeker)156, 157, 231
Friedrich, Paul 156, 157, 231
Friedrich, Stella 52
Friedrichs, Carol 35, 100
Fromberg, Chantelle 232
Fromburg, Neville.........39, 110, 232
Fromburg, Robert 232
Frost, Mr A 25
Frost, Peter 232
Frost, Richard 232
Fuchs, Fern 86
Funck, F 52
Fyfe, Chris.....................49, 54, 232
Fynn (Clulow), Fynn 233

G

Galloway, Graham 134
Garlick (Cullinan), Sharon..........233
Garlick, Carol 133
Garlick, Richard 133
Garner, Arlene....133, 147, 233, 322
Garrod, Ronella (Hundermark) ..233
Gatiss, Judith 15
Gavazzi, Jan 234
Gaye, Doris 122, 124, 234
Geach (Knoble), Shay156, 161, 164, 165
Geach, Steve 156, 161, 164, 165
Geldenhuys (Malan), Rina156, 166, 167

Index

Geldenhuys, Preller 20, 23, 24, 25, 27, *69*, 109, 110, 147, 156, 169, 234, 272
Geldenhuys, Prop 106
Geldenhuys, Renene and Pey 272
Geldenhuys, Rina 21, 22, 109, 235, 272
Genocchio, Richard 236
Gent (Wightman), Helen 90, 236, 269
Gent, Alice 236
Geoffrey Lambert 29
Gibbons, Mr 11, 17
Gibhard, Joan 120, 236
Gibson, Donad 15
Gie (Ashford), Ann 172, 236
Gihhard, Joan 40
Gilbert, Lester 236
Giles, Hedley 236, 274
Giles, Rodney 15, 25, 236
Gillies (Squair), Mimi 237
Gird (Weston), Christine 123, 237, 351
Glenda, Glenda 210, 308
Gocha, Noel 61
Goddard, Dave 15
Godsmark, Lorraine 31
Gohery, June 237
Gold (Thackray), Ann 238
Gold, Nicole 238
Gold, Trevor and Jason 238
Gooden, Bruce 238
Goosen, Jeremy 238
Gordon, Allan 15
Gordon, Ian 15, 112, 238, 290
Gordon, John 15, 339
Govender (Burden), Angelz 188, 238
Govender, Angelz 188
Graca (Spencer), Salley 238
Graham (Ford), Penny 359
Graham, Norman 357
Grainger, Sharyn 238
Grant, Kennedy 29
Grater, Ross 238

Grater, Viv 99, 238
Gratton (Robinson), Susanne 238
Gray, Adrian 239
Greager (le Quesne), Phil 239
Green, Charmaine 52, 239
Green, Colin 15
Green, Jenny 131, 187, 239, 351
Green, Pam 240
Gregory (Houshold), Angela 359
Gregson-Allcott (Hayes), Sharon 360
Gretton, Jimmy 241
Griffiths, Dave 81, 94, 133, 240
Griffiths, Debra 196, 240, 241
Griffiths, Helen 240
Griffiths, Megan Ann 240
Griffiths, Sandy 240
Grimbeek (Hill), Jillian 241, 282
Grimbeek, Hilton 241, 340
Grobbelaar, Johannes 44, 49, 53, 54
Grobler (Meyer), Lynn 241
Grobler, Tracy 241
Groenewald, Henry 241
Gudath, Audrey 17, 191, 347
Gunn, R (Scotty) 241
Guy (Bower), Trudy 241
Gwara, A 100

H

Hadfield, Ian 241
Hageman, Dan, Luke + Matt 242
Hagemann, Alan 45, 46, 48, 87, 100, 133, 145, 242
Hagemann, Jeff .. 133, 242, 282, 283
Hagemann, Ken 133, 242
Hague, Miss 262
Hahn, Annette 45, 52, 87, 361
Hahn-Dyer, Debbie 87
Hahn-Hull, Denise 243
Haines, Mr 11
Halkier, Jeffrey 69
Hall (le Roith), Sharon 242
Hall, Debra (van Rooyen) 242

Index

Halstead, Arthur 51
Hammett (Potter), Lynda 242
Hand, Billy 39
Hand, William 242
Handy (Millard), Gail 359
Hapelt (Bloom), Sheena 242
Harbinson (Blanschard), Ann 243
Harbinson, Ann 186, 243
Harbinson, Joe 243
Harbinson, John 243
Harbinson, Rory 360
Harbour (Flake formerly Lewis), Gillian 359
Harcombe, Neville 68, 69
Hardy, Rob 45, 244
Hargreaves (Smith), Shirley Anne 244
Harley (Wheeler), Elmarie .. 244, 246
Harley, Hilton 244
Harley, Mr 347
Harper, Timothy 82
Harris, Nicky Wilson 244
Hart, Alun .43, 56, 88, 100, 134, 246
Hart, Debbie 133
Hart, Mr 61
Hart, Mr and Mrs 246
Hart, Terry 37, 58, 357
Hart, Yvonne 37, 246
Hartman (du Plessis), Hermien .. 246
Hartzenberg (Hundermark), Cookie 246
Haselwood, Melanie Wheeler 92
Haslewood (Wheeler), Melanie .247
Hatt, Heather 15, 277
Hattle, Craig 55, 56, 82, 170, 247
Hawes (van der Velden), Petra ..247
Hawkins, AVM Harold 14
Hawkins, Mr R 85
Hay, Ian 85
Hayes (McElroy), Maureen 247
Hayes, Brian 106, 247
Hayes, Murelle 358
Hayes, Ralph 247
Heath, Miss 17
Hector, Leslie-Ann 60, 170, 181, 248, 327
Hein, Allan 247
Hemans (Porter), Sue 248
Hendrik, Hendrik 272
Hendry, Rob 32
Hendry, Robert 35
Henning, Peter 248
Hensberg, Gavin 43, 83, 88, 144, 248
Hepburn, Arlene 43, 88
Hepburn, Bridget 60, 88
Hepburn, Craig 43, 82, 83, 88
Hepburn, Sharon 44, 248
Herbst (van Niekerk), Deirdre 248
Herbst, Michael 248
Hewitt Triggs, Lorraine 60, 327
Hewitt, Alison 249
Hewitt, Kieran, Stacey and Steph 249
Hewitt, Ray 5, 49, 51, 53, 54, 94, 111, 114, 133, 134, 137, 142, 145, 146, 147, 148, 218, 249, 297, 330
Hewitt, Stephen 50, 53, 356
Hewitt, Stephen 83
Higham (van Wyk), Ebeth 249
Hill, Donald 340
Hilton Barber, Gp Capt Jock 14
Hitchens (Bradnick), Cathy 249
Hitge (Preston), Veronica 249
Hodgson, Kathleen 131
Hodgson, Mark 131, 249
Hoefnagel, Sherry 289
Hoffman, D 53
Hoffman, Jacobus 15
Hoffman, Margie Molloy 249
Hofmann, Harold 250
Holland (Atkinson), Maureen 250
Holliday, Graham 250
Hollington, C 101
Holloway, Ed 250
Holman, Nick 11, 17, 31, 344, 347, 357

Index

Holmes, Cathy 227
Holmes, Craig .54, 56, 100, 255, 361
Holmes, Jenny 38
Holmes, PJ 81, 250
Homan, Mike 250
Hopkinson (Scully), Suzanne 250
Hopkinson, Ray 250
Hopkinson, Roy 250
Hopkinson, Susanne 130
Hopkinson, Suzanne127, 250, 312, 313
Horn, Brenda 274
Horner (Drodskie), Sue 250
Houghton, Lynn 136, 138
Houghton, Mark 134
Household, Angela 361
Houston, Niall 250
Howell Neethling, Caren 87
Hoy, Rob 251
Hughes, Rosalie 15, 27, 277
Hull (Hahn), Denise 251
Hundermark Garrod, Ronella 120
Hundermark, Evans 338
Hundermark, Grant 15
Hundermark, Joseph Ernest 251
Hundermark, Lillias 251
Hundermark, Ronella 255
Hungwe, D 100
Hungwe, E 100
Hunt, Jennifer 134, 251, 273
Hunt, Sue 251, 273
Huntly (Ashley), Bev 131, 251
Huntly, Bev 131, 132, 251
Hurndall (Shillinglaw), Karen81, 252

I

Ingle (Bayne), Eileen 357
Irving, Mike David 252

J

Jack Steyn, Irene 318
Jack, Miriam 20, 26
Jackett, Kay 106, 303
Jackson, David 252
Jacobs (Mawson), Peta 252
James, A 56, 252
James, Cave 253
James, Tracey 252
Janson (Nordin), Kendel 253
Jawona, L 100
Jefferies, Mark 45, 87, 253
Jelley, Brendan + Courtney 253
Jelley, Grahame ..157, 164, 165, 253
Jelley, Renene (Geldenhuys)156, 253
Jenkins (Tillett), Kathy 254, 359
Jenkins, Mark, Gareth, Greg and Megan 253
Jenkins,Debbie Light 114
Jeremiah, Wayne Derek 214, 360
Jervois, Melanie 273
Jervois, Roger 50, 254
Jessop, Geoff 254, 291
Jessop, Peter 160, 291
Jessop, Phillip 160, 254, 291
Jize, L 101
Joanne Lawrence (Naude)*See* Joanne Naude
Johnson, Bob43, 74, 79, 88, 107, 254
Johnson, Debbie 83
Johnson, Karen43, 45, 54, 55, 64, 74, 76, 86, 88, 90, 95, 96, 107, 118, 120, 134, 137, 138, 144, 145, 152, 171, 221, 243, 244, 254, 256, 320, 324, 337
Johnson, Tom 51, 256
Johnston, Barry 15
Johnston, Les 153, 255
Johnstone, Linda 134
Johnstone, Lyndsay 52
Johnstone, Marthinus 50, 256
Jones (Palmer), Sheila 256
Jones Markham, Margaret 147
Jones, Craig 46

Index

Jones, Dag 274
Jones, Felicity 170, 256, 257
Jones, Karen Huckle 256
Jones, Keith 256
Jones, Margaret 134
Jones, Phil 256
Jones, Sheila 256, 257, 307
Jones, Wilhelmina 170, 246, 280, 330
Jones, Wilhelmina "Villie" 257
Jones, Yvonne 170, 246, 257
Jordaan, Petronella 39
Jordan, Rene 60, 327
Joss, Craig 53, 54, 255
Joss, Simone 43
Joubert (Swift), Delise 111, 221, 257, 330
Joubert, Delise 321
Joubert, Joe 257
Jovner (Fromburg), Penny 257
Jovner, Barry 357
Juby, Graham 45, 81

K

Kaagman (Bugler), Lynnette 258
Kadungvre, M 101
Kalil, Glen 22, *69*
Kalil, Roy 15, 20, 25, *69*, 252, 359
Kalil, Trevor 258
Karel Coetzee 25
Kaschula, Ray 15, 69
Kaschula, Reg .15, 69, 258, 338, 339
Katai, T 101
Katchmar, Joanie 258
Keats, Barbara Robertson 116
Keats, Barry 115
Keepin, Christopher 258
Keith, Joe (Trevor) 50, 258
Kelley (Duffin), Sue 358
Kendall, Kim 39, 258
Kendel 87, 255
Kennedy, John 25
Kenneth, Michelle 259
Kent, Collin 361
Kent, Nolene 134, 259
Kent, Raye 259
Keth, Ina Rene 259
Keys, Fiona Collins 144
Khan, S 100
Kilpatrick, Sharon 54
King, Carla 179
King, Jackie 259
King, K 101
Kinnear, Jimmy 134
Kinnear, Kath 134
Kirby, David (Rip) 259
Kirby, Jason + Kristie 260
Kirby, Maureen 260
Kirby, Rip 98, 99, 106, 274
Kirstein, Ella Blignaut 92
Kitto, Bridget 260
Klasen, Heath 260
Klopper, Fanie 260
Kloppers, Lucas 260
Kloppers, Peter 260
Knobel, Peter 348
Knoetze, Jock 260
Knott, Bobby 261
Knott, Debbie 38
Knott, Elaine 38, 120, 261
Knott, Shelley 359
Knox (Lamb), Patty 261
Knox, Bill 134
Koekemoer, Willem 261
Kolbe, Peter 32
Koninis, Adele 172, 261
Kraan, A 58
Krajewski, Andrew 261
Krause - the boxer 338
Krause, Dave 32
Kriek, Johan 15
Kruger (Lamprecht), Susie 262
Kruger Mayhew, Enid 113
Kruger, Braam 119, 203, 261, 263
Kruger, Estelle 261

Index

Kruger, Paddy 49, 114, 119, 203, 261, 263
Kung, Bernard 55
Kurebwa, V 101
Kuttner (Nourse), Shirley 21, 22, 23, 26, 134, 136, 138, 139, 140, 147, 262, 272, 297, 299
Kuttner, Craig & Lance 262
Kuttner, Felix 262

L

Lake, Julie 111, 262
Lamb, Edith 358
Lamb, Lorraine 263
Lamb, Patty 39, 134
Lamb, Shirley 360
Lamb, Ted 119, 263
Lambert, Geoff 7, 274, 344, 347
Lambrecht, Andries 49
Lambrecht, Bianca + Sharlene ... 134
Lamport, Miss 17, 213, 262
Lamprecht, Andries 263
Lamprecht, Anna-Marie 83, 120, 134, 136, 138, 140, 141, 263
Lamprecht, Jan 264
Lamprecht, Susie 264
Lancaster, Janet 15, 23, 72, 98, 99, 110, 169, 264
Lancaster, Jeremy 264
Landman .... *See* Brenda Edwards
Landman, Cheryl-Ann 170, 265
Langford, Daphne 265
Langley, Rodney 277
Lapsley, Maria Nicolaou 44, 266
Larkworthy, D *37, 38*
Laubscher, Roger 49, 51, 54
Laubscher, Susan 86, 100
Laurent (van Leeuwen), Tineke .. 266
Lautz (Richardson), Linda 266
Law, Kevin 39, 50, 266
Lawrence (Bull), Mandy 266
Lawrence (Naude), Joanne 266

Lawrence, Don 14, 359
Lawrence, Jill 265
le Grange, Joubert (Joe) 257
Leaman, Alex 266
Leaman, C *37*
Leaman, Joss 267
Leaman, Theresa 267
Lee, Enid 15
Leeming (Andrews), Jeanette 267
Leeuwner, Noleen 309
Lemmer, Stacey Botha 188, 267
Levinson, Kylie Rahn 306
Levy, Maurice 134
Lewis (Berry), Sue 267
Lewis, Paul 267
Lewis, Vince 134, 137, 143, 177, 268
Lewis, Vinny 145
Liebenberg (Lake), Sharon 268
Light Jenkins, Debra 253, 254
Light, Brenda Ann 357
Light, Jim and Corny 253, 254
Lindsay, Brigitte 268
Littleford (Lakelin), Sue 268
Lloyd, Chris 106
Lochrie, Jane 268
McCleland (Dipper) 282
Lolliot (Spiers), Jennie 268
Lombard, Adrienne Andre 268
Lombard, Helene 118, 214
Lombard, Sharon 214
Long (Marshall), Sylvia 268
Lotter, Denise 15
Lottering (Ruffey), Sheila 268
Loubser, Susan 90
Loveridge (Winter), Nan 269
Low, Bob 115
Low, Sheryl 115, 116, 269
Lowe, Hennie 46
Lund (Hardy), Hardy 269
Lynn Fourie, Diane 229

Index

M

Mabbett, Sharon Lyon 269
MacDonald (van Niekerk), Rhona 270
MacDonald, Alex 269, 284
MacDonald, Ian 269
Macdonald, Ianthe 150
MacDonald, Penny 147
MacDonald, Peter 270
MacIntyre, Yolanda 36, 98, 100, 115, 116, 117, 136, 138, 143, 144, 146, 207, 266, 269, 270, 271, 337, 342
Mackay, Fraser 147
MacLaughlin, Mike 270
MacLaughlin, Sean 252
MacLean (Shillinglaw), Denise 134, 136, 138, 144, 270
Maclean, Hamish 134, 137
Madhaka, J 101
Madzana, Tsitsi 281
Magness, Nell 11
Maimin (Nell), Jackie 271
Maimin, Gary David 271
Maimin, Jackie 92, 271
Main, Alistair 271
Maitaso, B 100
Maitland Dancer, Maureen 127
Maitland, Sheila 81, 127, 207, 221, 243, 337, 340
Maja Frey 231
Malan, Elcora 109
Malan, Frans 108, 271
Malan, Hendrik 20
Malan, Phil 21, 22, 25, 108, 109, 191, 272
Malan, Rina 23, 26, 106, 110, 156, 157, 166, 167, 169, 235, 272
Malcolm (Hunt), Valerie 273
Malcolm, Valerie ..29, 172, 180, 181
Malkin, Bill 32, 42, 43, 115, 274, 338
Manning, Derek ..120, 134, 135, 275

Manning, Flo 44, 52, 135, 136
Manning, Joan 122
Manning, John 123, 275, 351
Manning, Rebecca 274, 275
Manning, Tim 275
Manning, Vince 53, 127, 134, 147, 155, 156, 157, 221, 243, 275
Mapuranga, T 101
Maqhina, Yolanda 328
Marais, Andrew 275
Marais, Ingrid 44, 276, 357, 361
Marais, John 134
Marais, Linda 134, 276
Marais, Mark 56, 114, 276
Marais, Pookie 276
Marchussen (Lancaster), Janet 22, 26, 27, 134, 147, 169, 276, 277, 297
Marchussen, Andrew 147
Marchussen, Janet 27, 98, 99, 136, 138, 140, 142, 276
Marchussen, Peter 134, 136, 142, 147, 277
Marillier, Allison 278
Marillier, Chinky 134, 278
Marillier, Elan 106, 278
Marillier, H 32
Marillier, Hilton 32
Maritz (Buys), Berta 198, 278
Markham (Scott Roger), Pam 278
Markham, Paul 134
Markie (Day), Susan 278
Markram, Gina 279
Markram, Victor 56, 279
Markram, Winston 279
Marshall (Scully), Lynda 280
Marshall, Alan 51, 106, 279
Marshall, Dave 32, 280
Marshall, David 35, 173
Marshall, Judy 38
Marshall, Susan 35
Martell, Sonya 60
Martin, Brenda 31
Martin, Mike 134, 137

Index

Maskill, Sqn Ldr Batt 14
Masusela, T 100
Masviba, M 101
Matthews, Lilian 361
Matthews, Rob 32
Matthews, Robert 280
Matthyser, Yvonne 257, 280, 330
Maumbe, R 100
Mavetera, K 101
Mavhengere, L 100
May (Eekhout), Lynda 280
May, Gerald 80, 100, 280
May, Philip 280
Mayhew (Kruger), Enid 280
Mayhew, Enid 113
Mays, John 281
Maytham, Barry 255, 281
Mazhindu, T 100
Mazilawa, Shelton Shelaz 281
McBain (Odendaal), Vanessa 281
McBain, Dave 130
McBain, Vanessa130, 131, 132, 281, 298
McCabe, Cindy 60
McColl, Dee 154, 155, 157, 167
McColl, Stu 154, 155, 156
Mcdonagh, William Adrian51, 114, 282
McDonald (Daniel), Ianthe 282
McDonald (Doyle), Penny ..133, 282
McDonald, Aletha 161
McDonald, Penny 282
McDonald, Peter 361, 364
McDowell, B *37, 38*
McEwan, Heather 100
McFarlane (Tapson), Gwen99, 108, 109, 283
McFarlane, Annette 116, 282
McFarlane, Kelsey 282
McFarlane, Nigel25, 69, 99, 106, 108, 109, 283
McFarlane, Stuart Andrew 283
McFarlane, William 15
McGarvie, Eileen 44

McGaw (Chivers), Jenny 360
McGaw, D & J *37*
McGaw, Dave 283
McGaw, Mrs *38*
McGee, Sam 11, 17
McGibbon (Cowie), Jean 283
McGowan (Rowlands), Gail54, 113, 283
McGowan, Molly 15, 20, 27
McGowan, Rob 15, 283
McGrady, Brian and Coleen 143
McGrady, Colleen 144
McGrady, Janet, Kevin + Margaret
 143
McGraw, Dave 106
McHugh, Louis 39
McIlroy, Maureen 106
McKay, Tamla 346
McKie, Ian 106, 283
McLean, Laureen 39
McLeman, Gavin134, 137, 141, 152, 283
McLeod (Hutchinson), Angela 284
McMaster (Southey), Karen 284
McMillan (MacDonald), Janice ...284
McNeill, Rodney20, 25, 27, 69, 118, 169, 284
McNeill, Sue 118
Mead, Kym Tracey 183
Meaker, Bill 284
Medland Udy, Janet60, 181, 248, 268, 322
Meier, Kirsten 228
Meiring (Berkowitz), Ada 285
Mellody, Mike 15, 285
Melton, Clive 53, 285
Meth, Eddie 32
Meyer (Carinus), Dalene 285
Meyer, Alison 134
Meyer, Charles 285
Mharapara, C 101
Mhunduru, P 101
Michael, Michael 182
Midgley, Dawn 207, 271

Index

Millar, Alex 286
Millard, Amanda + David 286
Millard, Dan 286
Millard, David Lee 286
Millard, Gail 255
Millard, Jeff 286
Miller (Lovell), Clover 287
Miller, JW 49, 53
Millward, Anne 45, 82, 83
Millward, Jean 52, 137, 138
Milner, Peter 32
Milward (Martin), Jean 134
Milward, Anne ...... *See* Arnold, Anne
Mitchell, Beverley 15
Mitchelmore, David 287
Moffet, Howard 356, 364
Molloy, Margie 176, 249
Molloy, Paddy 249
Wolfe 134
Monge, R 49
Montocchio (Ellis), Karen 287
Moodie, Marcia 332
Moolman, Annette 116
Moolman, Ina 98, 100
Moolman, Pikki 83
Moore, J 56, 287
Moore, John 134
Moore, Pam 60
Moore, R *37*
Moraine, Sylvia 357
Moren, John 15
Morgan, L 101
Morrel, M *37*
Morrison, Jane 287
Moser Mould, Leanne 287
Mould, Katherine, Michelle + Nicola 287
Mould, Mike 287
Mountjoy, Greg 45, 87, 255, 288
Moyo, L 100
Moyo, M 101
Mpalale, M 101
Mpofu, M 100
Mpofu, N 101

Mudungwe, J 101
Munge, P 49
Munger, Fred 15
Munger, M 100
Munjanja, V 101
Murch, Sheila 15
Murdoch, Beth 121
Murdoch, Jamie 288
Murdoch-Coyle, Terri ... 45, 87, 97, 105, 115, 116, 117, 121, 127, 128, 130, 134, 147, 149, 193, 194, 207, 209, 269, 271
Murphy, Spud 32
Murray, Steven 35
Mutubuki, G 100
Muzondo, T 101
Myers, Mrs 11

N

Naude, Joanne (Joey) ... 54, 113, 266, 288
Ncube, M 100
Ncube, S 56, 101
Ndudzo, T 101
Nealon, Grant 133, 147, 288
Neasham, Colin 229, 356, 364
Neasham, Raymond 229
Neave (Swartz), Beryl 288
Neely, Jeff 289
Neethling (Howell), Caren 289
Neethling, Chantal 289
Nel (Barlow), Patricia 289
Nel, Bassie 13
Nel, Claire & Philip 290
Nel, Frik ... 25, 107, 109, 134, 289, 290, 295
Nel, Herman 134, 289
Nel, Jan 357
Nel, Jannie 15
Nel, Lynda 134
Nel, Mr 11, 16, 17, 235

Nell, Frik112, 136, 137, 140, 147, 303
Nelson (Matthews), Bev4, 10, 14, 109, 132, 146, 165, 172, 257, 291, 343
Nelson, Beverley4, 10, 31, 35, 109, 291
Nelson, Dave 160, 291
Nelson, Lynette156, 160, 162, 165, 254, 291
Nesbit, Michael 43, 88
Nesbitt, Kevin 291
Ness, Lesley 292
Newlands (Rowlands), Mfanwy26, 292
Newling, Mr 255
Newman, Janet 106, 133
Newton (Le Quesne), Michele ... 292
Ngwenya (Lacoste), Sikhuluiwe .292
Nichol (Semple), Angela 293
Nicholson, Granville ... 131, 132, 293
Nieuwenhuizen, Audrey Folkertsen 91, 171, 181, 293
Nieuwoudt, Andrew ... 111, 113, 293
Nieuwouldt, Mrs 11
Niewenhuizen, Audrey Folkertsen 60
Niewoudt, Andrew 49
Niland (Stening), Sally 293
Nimmo, Andy 361
Nineham (Quinlan), Gillian 293
Nish, Margaret 15
Nobel, Kaz Carinus Botha ... 199, 294
Noel, Bannell 190
Nordin, Kendal 45, 147, 255
Nordin, Kendel ... 113, 114, 134, 137
Nordin, Richmal 45, 87
Norman, Andrew 15, 294
North, Kevin 294
Northcote, Alan 294, 306
Northcote, Colin 294, 306
Nortje (Benade), Aletta 295
Norvall (Beuke), Denise 295
Nuttal, Miss 272, 347

Nysschen, Buddy 15
Nysschen, Chanelle & Sean 296
Nysschen, Ena 15
Nysschen, Jan109, 110, 134, 147, 264, 289, 290, 291, 295
Nysschen, Sophia 15
Nysschen, Wendy 296

O

O'Bree, Sharon46, 62, 111, 114, 330
O'Connor, Cheryl52, 86, 133, 145, 146
O'Connor, Graeme 134, 147, 188
O'Connor, Tracey60, 90, 113, 114, 118, 133, 134, 138, 145, 188, 205, 245, 249, 297, 298, 306, 324
Oakman, Patricia 297
O'Connor, Graeme 297
O'Connor, Joyce 134
Oelofse, Charmaine 298
Ogborne (Thompson), Ginny 298
Oldknow, Susan 76
Olds (Gifford), Kathy 298
Olivier (Bossert), Margaret 298
Olivier, Barnie 192
Olivier, Celdre 362
Olivier, Jannie..................... 15, 339
Oosthuizen, Phillip 299
Oosthuysen, Connie 362
Oosthuysen, Mrs 11
Oosthuysen, P 49
Oosthuysen, Phillip 50
Opie, Lynn 299
Orsmond, Mrs 17
Ould, Mr 17
Owen (Till), Julie 299
Owen, Anthony (Tony) 356
Owen, Rick 207, 299, 351

P

Paketh, B 101
Palmer, Dianne 30, 31, 35, 106, 179, 274
Palmer, Lynette 15, 23, 99
Palmer, Phil 299
Palmer, Sheila 274
Palmer, Sylvia 30, 274, 299
Panagiotopoulos, Melanie 228
Panton, Anne 15, 277
Papadopoulos, E 56, 299
Papadopoulos, Stewart 49, 299
Parker, Mr 85, 347
Parker, Ray 15
Parkin, G 56, 299
Parkin, Judy 299
Patel, Nittin 49, 299
Paterson (Jervois), Mel 299
Paterson, S 26
Patterson, B 41
Patterson, Colin 99, 299
Patterson, John 299
Patterson, William Trevor (Wally) 357
Paul (Landman), Cheryl-Ann 299
Paul, Connel 300
Pawson, Alan 300
Paxton, Beverley 273
Payne, Philip 300
Pearce, Gregory 255, 300
Pebody, Lindsay 91
Peebles, Dave 157, 159, 164, 165, 167
Peebles, David 300
Peebles, Graham 300
Peebles, Graham and David 338
Peebles, Lynda 157, 158, 159, 164, 165
Pelly, Chris 15, 300
Pember, Mike 301
Pemberthy, Mark 32
Penberthy, Mark 301

Penberty, Mark 351
Pentz, Caileigh Kyle + Leandrie ..301
Pentz, Judy 301
Pentz, Michael + Richard + Stephen 301
Pereira (Groenewald), Petronella 301
Pereiro, Petro 302
Perie, John 25
Perry, John 27
Perryman, Alison 153, 301
Perryman, Catherine 153, 217
Perryman, Derek 55, 94, 301
Perryman, Garry 43
Perryman, Mark 255
Peters, Ashley 302
Peters, Janet 106
Pett, Sheila *11*
Pettit (Spencer), Mary 302
Pfaff, Darryl 359
Pfaff, Vanessa 60, 100
Phaup (Southey), Brenda 302
Phillips, Clive 109, 110
Pieters, Piekie 15
Pinder, Roger 302
Pleasants, David 303
Plenderleith, Sheila 15
Plews, Debbie 133
Pluke, Chris *37*, 106, 303, 347
Pluke, Kay *38*, 303
Pluke, Mr 32, *38*
Pollard, Pauline 35, 273
Poole, Garry 50, 56, 303
Poole, Gary 83
Poole, Jenny 60, 303, 327
Poole, Russell 51, 356, 363
Pople (Pringle), Llanis 304
Porter, Dave 106
Porter, Mrs 17
Posthumous, Pat 304
Potgieter (van der Merwe), Renee 304
Potgieter, Philipa 83
Preller Geldenhuys 155

Index

Pretorious, Ben 32
Price, Stan 15, 304
Priest, Susan 15
Prince (Brislin), Isla 193
Prince (van den Berg), Lyn 304
Prince, Gerald 304
Pringle, Llanis 15
Pringle, Virginia 15
Prinsloo, Herman 304
Proctor, Charmane 52
Proome (Roselt), Colleen 304
Prophet, Dana 134, 138, 152, 305
Prophet, Dave 94, 305
Prophet, Steve 45, 87, 94, 114, 134, 137, 145, 149, 152, 186, 209, 305
Pudge, Andrea 324
Pullen, David 305
Purdon, Mary Noddy Warrington 357
Pyatt, J *37*

Q

Quail, Brian 99
Quail, Bruce 305
Quail, Bryan 305
Quik, Marcel 306
Quincey, Dawn 15

R

Rademeyer Fouche, Linda 229
Rademeyer, Linda 38, 229
Rademeyer, Wendy 26
Radloff, Elaine 38
Radloff, Gordon 306
Radloff, Graham 306
Radloff, Ivan 306
Rahn, Deirdre-Ann 294, 306
Ramsay, Bill 307
Ramsay, Eleanor 307
Ramsey, Allan 39

Randles (Thompson), Carol 307
Rautenbach .... *See* Broodryk
Rautenbach, Judy 15, 23
Rautenbach, Piet 360
Rawstone, Anne 23
Redman, Robert 15
Reece .... *See* van Kraayenburg
Reece, Barbara 307
Reece, Nella 358
Reece, Vic 25, 277
Reece, Victor 15
Rees (Powell), Sylvia 307
Rees (Shepherd), Shirley 307
Reeve-Johnson, Mr 40, 41
Regtien (van der Merwe), Sharon 308
Regtien, Rene 307
Respond, Caroline Cheneau 44
Reynolds, Miss 347
Rice, CP 49
Rice, Doug 308
Rice, Glenda 106
Richardson, Marion 273
Richie, D 49
Richie, Derek 51
Rigby, Paul 48, 51, 53, 83, 308
Riley (Anderson), Mary 308
Riley, Mary .... *See* Mary Anderson
Ritchie, Derek 356
Rob, Angela & Stuart 309
Rob, Billy 273
Rob, Shirley 309
Robb, Anette 39
Robb, Bill 173, 308
Robb, Elizabeth 12
Robb, William 32, 35, 99, 100
Roberts, Christine 11
Robertson, Barbara*See* Keats, Barbara
Robertson, Bill 309
Robertson, Dave 309
Robertson, David 86
Robertson, Dean 309
Robertson, Gayle 15, 16, *68*, 310

Index

Robertson, Heather 45, 52
Robertson, Wayne 357
Robey sisters 124
Robey, Gaye 122
Robey, Juliet and Gaye 122
Robinson (Watson), Clare 309
Robinson, Drikkie 121, 179, 309
Robinson, Richard 310
Robinson, Suzanne 180
Robinson, Vanessa 92
Robinson, Willy 127
Robson, Paul 310
Robson-Jervois, Mel 310
Rochat, Jenny 310
Rochat, Tony 310
Rochester, Mrs 17
Roe, Juliet, ... 310
Roselt, Colleen 99, 274
Roselt, Eryl 310
Roselt, Heather 31
Roux (Lindley), Sandi 310
Roux, Nicky 59
Rowe (Dewsbury), Di 344
Rowe, Alan 358
Rowe, Michael 14
Rowlands, Basil 134, 139
Rowlands, Bucky 15, 20, 25
Rowlands, John 6, *16*, 21, *38*, 192
Rowlands, Lyndie 134
Rowlands, Myfanwy 23
Rowlands, Nigel10, 15, 17, 19, 99, 311
Rowlands, Norma 15
Roy (Holliday), Helen 311
Rukani, J 100
Rumball, Alan 15
Russell Smith, Carrie 277
Russell, Karen 270
Russell, Mike 255
Russell-Smith, Noelene 15, 23
Rust, Jan 134
Rust, Jason 311
Rust, Mike 134, 311
Rust, Rob 137, 311, 312

Rust, Robin 134
Rust, Tammy 134
Rutherford, Kathy Weineck 311

S

Salerni, Louis 79
Samkange, Florence 100
Sanders, Peter 46
Sansbury (Jacobs), Vera 312
Sayers (Burden), Angela 312
Sayers, Magda 312, 331
Scales, Roger 339
Scheepers, Andre 39
Schoeman, Danie 39
Schoultz, Geraldine 312
Scott, Alasdair Ian Murray 363
Scott, Judy Brooke-Mee 90
Scott, Miss 234, 347
Scott, Sally 15
Scott, Sandie 312
Scott-Roger, Anthony John Charles "Tony" 363
Scullion, John 312
Scully, Carole 106
Scully, Dave 312
Scully, Genny 312
Scully, Lynda 106
Scully, Merle 312
Scully, Renee 250, 313
Scurry (Edwards), Anne 313
Segal, M *38*
Segal, Roy 313
Semple, Andrew 88, 313
Sercombe, Ruth 15
Seymore, Cecelia 106
Sharon Allen (Kendal) 176
Sharon Heburn (Cochrane) 248
Sharon O'Bree 297
Sharp, Eileen 313
Shaw (Folkerston), Marianne 313
Shaw-Meyer, Deb 314
Geach (Knobel) 234

385

Index

Sheffield (Steinbach), Melanie ...314
Sheldon, Dudley 48
Shentall, R 56
Shillinglaw, Denise 45, 87
Shillinglaw, Karen 87
Shirley, Ian 314, 347
Short .... *See* Bingham
Short, Becky 43, 44
Shumba, E 100
Shuro, T 101
Siebert, Peter 37, *38*, 356
Simmonds (Bischoff), Marcelle38, 314
Simpson (Vallaro), Gill 314
Simpson, Viv 52, 90
Singleton, Mrs 145, 146
Sithole, F 100
Skinner, Chris 15
Skipwith, Ashleigh 336
Slater, Michael (Mick) 314
Smit, Crystal Vale Lauren 287
Smit, Duwayne + Kristin 287
Smit, Johan 314
Smith - Bronwyn, Lynne, Pony and Sandy 359
Smith (Atkinson), Merlene ...30, 315
Smith (Walkley), Carole 314
Smith, A......................................26
Smith, A......................................37
Smith, Alfie 15
Smith, B 100
Smith, Barry 314
Smith, Bronwyn 90, 255
Smith, Colin 15
Smith, Eddie 314
Smith, Esme 359
Smith, Fiona Nuttal 54
Smith, Fiona Nuttall ...113, 114, 315
Smith, G 32
Smith, G. 37
Smith, Gladys 358
Smith, Leon 315
Smith, Lynne 356
Smith, Michael Brett 360
Smith, Sandy 83, 255
Smith, Terrence 338
Smith, Wendy Enola Gay 83
Smith-Wright, Minky 318
Smithy, Bronwyn 45
Smithy, Browwyn 87
Snodgrass, Dorothy 15
Snowdon, Barry 315
Snyders, Susanna 23
Solomon, Stuart 315
Southey, Charles 315
Southey, Trish 315
Sparg, Wendy 15
Sparks (Moffat), Bridget 315
Speight, Roddy 315
Spence, Len 315
Spence, Sandi 316
Spencer, Cheryl 106
Spencer, Hilary 35
Spiers, Jenny 273
Squair, Gilly 234, 237, 316, 347
Squair, Marilyn 35
Squair, Mimi 100
Stals (Jardine), Cynthia 316
Stals, Alan 32
Stals, Allan 316, 334
Stals, Kevin 316
Steel, Duncan 41
Steele, Duncan 316
Steele, Heather 317
Steenkamp, Johan 16, 17
Steenkamp, Mr 274
Steenkamp, Trudy 87
Steffen, Veronica15, 20, 122, 195, 317
Stephenson, Suzie 318
Steven, Colin 318
Stevens (Holsey), Juliet 318
Stewart, Charlie 134
Stewart, Mike 15, 16, 318
Stewart, Viv 134
Steyn (Blignaut), Sue 319
Steyn (Deetlefs), Sharon 318
Steyn (Houghton), Lyn 134

386

Index

Steyn, Charl, Liezel, Natasha and Tanya ... 318
Steyn, Liz ... 40
Steyn, Ona ... 45, 83, 87
Steyn, Sue (Blignaut) ... 114
Stilgoe, Simon ... 100
Stobart-Vallaro, Mike ... 134, 319
Stoddart, Fiona ... 52
Stokes, Alison ... 106, 278
Stotter, Craig ... 50, 319
Stout, Leslie ... 358
Stout, Ray ... 32, 173, 319
Stout, Raymond ... 35, 273
Strachan, Annette ... 319
Strauss, Alwyn ... 15, 20, 25, 72, 110, 319
Strauss, Fred ... 15
Strauss, Kotie ... 319
Struckel ... *See* Callaghan
Struckel, Sally ... 15
Strydom, Danny ... 320
Strydom, Lesley ... 320
Strydom, Wessel ... 106
Sullivan, Kathy ... 45, 320
Sully, Merle ... 127
Sutherland, Ralph ... 50, 320
Swaine, Roger ... 320
Swanepoel, Dean ... 320
Swanepoel, Kathy ... 44, 52
Swart, Blackie ... 106
Swart, Hendrik ... 356
Swart, Janet ... 321
Swart, Mae ... 38
Swartz, Doreen ... 227, 321
Swartz, Heather ... 134
Swartz, Keith ... 321, 358
Swartz, Liz ... 321
Swartz, Willey ... 49, 120
Swartz, Willie ... 134, 137, 143, 311, 321
Swift (Waymark), Morag ... 321
Swift, Delise ... 52, 221, 323, *See* Delise Joubert
Swift, Tracy ... 321
Swift-Joubert, Delise ... 62, 119, 323
Swindells, Gillian Nicholson ... 322

T

Tankersley, David ... 322
Tapson, Glenda ... 274
Tapson, Gwen ... 99, 106
Tapson, Rod ... 134
Tapson, Sally ... 283
Tapson, Sallyann ... 242
Tasker, B ... *68*
Taylor (Bishop), Marion ... 322
Taylor (Lawrence), Gill ... 322
Taylor, Elsa ... 43, 60, 92, 171, 322, 327
Taylor, Frank ... 11, 16, 17
Taylor, Gill ... 14, 322
Taylor, Janet ... 100
Taylor, Karen ... 177
Taylor, M ... 26, 41
Taylor, Robert ... 322
Tegart (Swartz), Colleen ... 322
Templemore-Walters, Anthony Carl Michael Henry Maurice "Tony" ... 364
Templemore-Walters, Mark ... 43, 44, 49, 53, 83, 98, 100, 114, 120, 134, 137, 141, 142, 152, 322
Templemore-Walters, Tony ... 356
Temple-Walters, Mark ... 54
Thackray, Don ... 323
Thackwray (Williams), Coleen ... 323
Thackwray, Barry ... 323
Thackwray, Malcolm ... 323
Theil, Rainer ... 100
Theron, Louis ... 108, 323
Theron, Steve ... 15, 134, 135
Thiel, Rainer ... 81
Thomson, John ... 323
Thomson, John Campbell ... 171
Thornton (van Jaarsveldt), Clare ... 324
Thornton, Clare ... 221, 324
Thurtell, Errol ... 324

Index

Till, Colin 43, 88, 324
Timms Fromburg, Colleen..........231
Timms, Robin 232
Timveos, Maria Nicola 52
Titterton, Alan..............................324
Todd, Mrs......................................*29*
Todd, P.J.6, 7, 11, 17, 27, 28, *29*, 96, 97, 213, 235, 356
Todd. P.J..27
Toland, Helga40, 120, 122, 123, 125, 243, 324, 337
Tooze, Audrey 325
Tooze, Brian 50, 325
Torry, Ann 99
Towell, Adrian 325
Towell, Janey...............................325
Towell, Sean Michael 325
Townsend, Roy..............................21
Treseler, Tanya Lynn 224
Triggs, Lorraine Hewitt.........60, 325
Tshuma, V 101
Tubbs (Woodhouse), Angela......326
Tubbs, Angela Woodhouse 352
Tubbs, Rob 325, 361
Turnbull, Linda98, 99, 134, 139, 326
Turner (Cullinan), Dierdre 326
Twilley (Emslie), Yvonne 326
Twilley, Yvonne (Emslie) 66
Tyne, Derek..................................362
Tyne, Robert "Skippy" 362

U

Udi, Janet Medland 60, 269, 327
Udy (Medland), Janet..........326, 327
Udy, Allan + Isaac + Nerys + Quinn 326
Udy, Janet Medland 100
Underhill, Martin 327
Upton, Bruce Christopher 327
Upton, Michael Ian 327
Upton, Mike 327
Ure, Denise 327
Ure, Kayley 327

V

Valentine, Brenda 327
Vallaro, Mike Stobart 39
van Aardt (Beattie), Judy 328
van As, Beartrice 328
van As, Ben..............................*69*, 328
van Ballegooyen, Sharon 324
van Beurden (Ballantyne), Kathy360
van Blerk, Ken 357
van Blerk, Thomas.........................15
van Breda, Colleen 273
van de Poll, Leslie.........................15
van de Weg, Hank11, 12, 14, 15, 109, 171, 173, 199, 328
van der Berg, Ian 329
van der Bijl, Gill 329
van der Burgh, I...........................53
van der Merwe (Delport), Elsie ..134
van der Merwe (van Wyk), Joan 330
van der Merwe, Betty20, 23, 106, 329
van der Merwe, C........................53
van der Merwe, Christo 329
van der Merwe, Felicity 256, 330
van der Merwe, Joan..111, 114, 330
van der Meulen, Gina 279
van der Pol, Ben...........................15
van der Poll, Bettie*See* Amira, Bettie
van der Riet, Brian 330
van der Riet, Brian, Bruce, Craig, Madri + Petro 330
van der Riet, Heather87, 113, 114, 309, 330
van der Velden, Maarten 356
van der Walt (Fulton), Cheryl.....331
van Deventer, Mark 151
van Deventer, Phillipa................151
van Druten (Bakkes), Anna133, 136, 138, 179, 331

Index

van Druten, Anna Bakkes52, 121, 138, 179, 309
van Drutten, Pete........................134
van Dyk (Bossert), Allison 331
van Eeden, Tanya........................52
van Gopel, Darlene 92
van Heerden (Marshall), Maureen 331
van Heerden, Kerrie + Mark.......331
van Heerden, Lynette 31
van Heerden, Rupert46, 48, 55, 56, 57, 58, 171, 245, 303, 312, 331
van Heerden, Rupert and Linda112, 162
van Helsdingen (Ward), Ann 332
van Helsdingen, Bev...................332
van Helsdingen, Kristen 332
van Huyssteen (van Heerden), Deanne 359
van Jaarsveldt (Thornton), Clare 118, 134, 149
van Kraayenburg (Reece), Barbara 333
van Niekerk (Knoetze), Connie...333
van Niekerk, Anne........................20
van Niekerk, Bev 332
van Niekerk, Brandon.....43, 56, 333
van Niekerk, Gail 15
van Niekerk, Glenda + Vicky-Lynne 334
van Niekerk, Pieter.......................15
van Niekerk, Rebecca.................216
van Niekerk, Rhona 270, 333
van Niekerk, Sybrand 333
van Rensberg, Cliff (Spook) 15
van Rooyen (Stals), Monica........334
van Rooyen, Brian 39, 334
van Rooyen, Des...........69, 108, 358
van Rooyen, Monica (Stals)........316
van Schalkwyk, George 334
van Schalkwyk, Matthys...............15
van Tonder, Andries, Ashleigh & Tracy 334
van Tonder, Gerry42, 77, 78, 85, 86, 171, 334, 339, 365
van Tonder, Jo............................334
van Vuuren, J 32
van Zyl, Pieter 334
Veale, Chantelle 214
Veldhuizen, Joyce.........................39
Venables, Anne 334
Venter, Bernie............................334
Venter, Ernie 108, 335, 361
Venter, Japie 108, 335
Venter, Melissa Stemmett 325
Verdelli, Coly Coly & Daniela......335
Verdelli, Vivienne 52, 335
Vermaak (Edwards), Caela 335
Vermaak, Daphne 39
Viljoen, Chris 15, 106, 329, 338
Viljoen, Derris.....................58, 335
Viljoen, Doodles11, 16, 17, 25, 63, *68*, 106, 234, 257, 262, 344, 358
Viljoen, E. 38
Viljoen, Fiona 335
Viljoen, Loma 275, 336
von Staden, Ann...........................15
Vorster (Donaldson), Susan 336
Vorster, Vera..............................274
Voster, Cheryll Enid....................336
Voster, Craig + Vaughan.............336
Voster, Vera 99
Voyce (Cornish), Sharon.......42, 336
Voyce, Allan 336
Voyce, Diane 100
Voyce, DJ..............................39, 336

W

Wade, Tim...........................127, 337
Wade-Pienaar, Tim...49, 50, 51, 337
Walker, Sharon 112, 199
Wallis 96
Ward, Carole8, 18, 50, 90, 91, 127, 130, 209, 312, 337
Ward, Dave 41, 321, 337

Index

Ward, Don 50, 54, 83, 339
Ward, Joe 48, 106, 127, 337, 339
Waring, Brenda 31
Waring, Brian 51, 340
Waring, Bruce 41, 51, 340
Waring, George Bruce 49, 54
Waters, Julie 44
Watkinson (Bossert), Janice 357
Watkinson (Wilson), Joe 340
Watkinson, Gail 225
Watkinson, Ron 108
Watson Harvey, Carey 246
Watson Robinson, Clare 127
Watson, Chunky 340
Watson, Colin 340
Watt, Darell 340
Wayland (Gilmore), Kathy 341
Wayne, Jody 241, 340
Weare, Dawn Lindsay 179
Weaver, Graham 358
Weber, Sheila 106, 189, 341
Weeden (Caldwell), Lizzee 341
Weeden (Parrat), Patti 341
Weideman, Lorraine 44
Weidemann (Holmes), Kathy 342
Weidemann, Albert 341
Weir, Shirley Jovner 342
Weir, Wendy-Lee 144, 207, 271, 342
Welch (Kent), Nolene 342
Wells (van Heerden), Lynette 360
Welsh, James 35, 172
Welsh, Jim 342
Wentzel (Bethell), Vivian 343
Wermuth, R 41
Wermuth, Robert 100
West, Amanda 176
Westgate, Cherryl 20
Weston .... *See* Bauwens
Weston, Christene 351
Westphal (Naude), Sandy 343
Wheeler Harley, Elmerie 127, 243
Wheeler, Syd 343
Wheeler, Wilhelmina 'Villie' 169
Whelehan, Jenny 343

Whewell, Wendy 48, *See* Weir, Wendy-Lee
Whincup (Ellaby), Irene 345
Whitcombe, Sharon 87
White, Blair 360
White, Chalky 48
White, Ellen 345
White, Jane 100
White, Neil 51, 94, 345
White, Tara Ann Duffy 345
Whiteman, John 282
Whitin, Lauren Ashley 224
Wickens, Reg 15, 69, 359
Wickham, Sussie 345
Widcombe, Sharon 87
Wiesner, Trevor 361
Wightman, Helen 110
Wightman, John 110, 130, 275, 336, 346
Wightman, Matt 88
Wilde, N 56
Wilke (Lipp), Stacey 346
Wilke, Gary + Ross J 346
Wilkes, G 37
Wilkes, M *38*
Wilkinson, Denise 15
Wilkinson, J 26
Willemsen, Neil 15
Williamson (Bowley), Geraldine . 349
Williamson (McGarvie), Eileen ... 349
Wilson (Doyle), Jenny 350
Wilson (Friedrichs), Carol 350
Wilson, Brian Peter 346
Wilson, Dave 350
Wilson, David 273
Wilson, Jonathan 172, 350
Wilson, Joyce 11
Wilson, Miss 11
Wilson, Nicky *244*
Wilson, Ray 350
Wilson, Richard 171, 346, 350
Windridge (Penberthy), Sheila ... 350
Windsor, Janet Evans 224, 237
Winsor (Evans), Janet 351

Index

Winter, Megan 15, 27, 99
Winter, Nan 15, 17, *28*, 99
Wiseman, Ruth 351
Wolfe (Riley), Ruth 134
Wood, Dawn 131, 187, 239, 351
Wood, Sharlene 140
Woodard (Pretorius), Lina 351
Woodfield, Malcolm 32, 123, 351
Woodfield, Murray 5, 76, 86, 100, 122, 195, 223, 270, 317, 321, 352
Woodhouse, Colin Frank 326, 352
Woolf (Burger), Marie 352
Woolf, Cheryll Enid .... *See* Voster
Wright (Bredenkamp), Cindy 352
Wright, Cindy 275
Wutete, S 100

Wyatt, Ray 15

Y

Yates, Alison (Hart) 43, 88, 92, 246, 353
Yeatman (Bradnick), Julie ... 171, 353
Yeatman, Julie Bradnick 120
Yefet (Coleman), Meryl 353
Young (Ashby), Lesley 353
Young, Patrick 99
Young, W *38*
Younghusband, Robin 353

Z

Zisengwe 101

NOTES

Past Pupils website - http://freewebs.com/thornhillhigh.

Prop Geldenhuys (email) - prop@peysoft.co.za

Book orders - (Lulu.com) - http://www.lulu.com/spotlight/Peysoftpublishing

Magazine - http://www.lulu.com/shop/preller-geldenhuys/thornhill-2015-magazine/paperback/product-22357025.html

www.ingramcontent.com/pod-product-compliance
Lightning Source LLC
Chambersburg PA
CBHW021912180426
43198CB00034B/150